Making Sense of Prostitution

Making Sense of Prostitution

Joanna Phoenix
Lecturer in Sociology
Department of Social and Policy Sciences
Bath University

palgrave

First published in hardcover 1999

First published in paperback 2001 by
PALGRAVE
Houndmills, Basingstoke, Hampshire RG21 6XS and
175 Fifth Avenue, New York, N.Y. 10010
Companies and representatives throughout the world

PALGRAVE is the new global academic imprint of
St. Martin's Press LLC Scholarly and Reference Division and
Palgrave Publishers Ltd (formerly Macmillan Press Ltd).

ISBN 0–333–74989–8 hardback (*outside North America*)
ISBN 0–312–22073–1 hardback (*in North America*)
ISBN 0–333–94599–9 paperback (*worldwide*)

This book is printed on paper suitable for recycling and made from fully managed and sustained forest sources.

A catalogue record for this book is available from the British Library.

The Library of Congress has cataloged the hardcover edition as follows:
Phoenix, Joanna, 1964–
    Making sense of prostitution / Joanna Phoenix.
        p. cm.
    Includes bibliographical references and index.
    ISBN 0–312–22073–1 (cloth)
        1. Prostitution—Great Britain. I. Title.
    HQ185.A5P46 1999
    306.74′0941—dc21
                                                    98—49903
                                                    CIP

10 9 8 7 6 5 4 3 2 1
10 09 08 07 06 05 04 03 02 01

Printed and bound in Great Britain by
Antony Rowe Ltd, Chippenham, Wiltshire

To my great cousin Evelyn Healey, my father Tony Healey and my mother Mina Healey

Contents

List of Tables

Acknowledgements

I owe a debt of gratitude to the many people who have provided support and encouragement throughout the production of this book. I should like to thank the Economic and Social Research Council for their studentship (award no. R00 4293 43272), which enabled me to undertake the PhD from which this book derives. I owe my thanks to the women who let me talk to them, who told me their stories and who went out of their way to welcome me. Unfortunately they must remain anonymous. My colleagues at Middlesex University and my friends in Bristol need a mention for being so willing to provide intellectual stimulation, light entertainment and much laughter. Kate Lyon listened patiently and always had helpful advice to give. No book is written in a vacuum, however, and there are a number of individuals whose help needs special acknowledgement. Sarah Oerton has read and reread virtually everything that I have written in connection with this project and provided insightful and incisive comments. Dee Cook's sheer good humour has been as invaluable as her suggestions on the draft manuscript. Pat Carlen, who provided me with inspirational supervision during my PhD, continuously reminds me why I became interested in research. Her support, encouragement and guidance have made a difference. The biggest debt I owe is to Sandy for her unending forbearance, bottomless cups of tea and love.

JOANNA PHOENIX

1 Introduction

This book is about women like Katrina, who at the age of eighteen was released from the secure psychiatric unit she had been placed in when she was 13 years old. She had no home of her own, no family or friends to support her, no job, no educational qualifications or marketable skills and no prospect of legitimate employment. That same year she began work as a prostitute and for the next two years she worked more or less full time. When asked about it, Katrina claimed that her entrance into and continuation in prostitution were the result of a consciously taken decision. Katrina asserted that, like most other women, she was simply trying to survive. Prostitution enabled her to earn enough money to support herself without recourse to crime and the possibility of imprisonment, to house herself, to avoid living on state welfare benefits or in poverty, and to provide herself with the financial basis to be independent and live life the way that she wanted. By her own account then, Katrina's involvement in prostitution provided her with a means of overcoming poverty, fashioning a better and more independent life for herself and securing economic and social stability.

Yet simultaneously interwoven throughout her account of prostitution as a survival strategy was a very different story. Katrina talked about how her life was very different from most other women's lives in that being involved in prostitution had resulted in persistent homelessness, about how she had been forced to work as a prostitute because of her involvement with various ponces and about how they had taken most if not all of her money, leaving her in penury and destitution. She described her fear of their violent reprisals should she not give them her money – reprisals that had actually resulted in her being hospitalised on three occasions. Katrina discussed how she had been subjected to repeated violence from punters and continual harassment from the police. In short, Katrina described her life in prostitution as a series of victimisations that had left her criminalised, in poverty, battered and abused, and above all else, trapped in prostitution with no means of resistance or escape.

Stories such as Katrina's are not new. Indeed nearly a century of research into prostitution has uncovered the same or similar stories. The data produced have prompted researchers to ask questions about how and why women become prostitutes, and about what type of problem prostitution is and what should be done about it. The answers have

almost always been concerned, to varying degrees, with trying to understand and apprehend the specific manner in which prostitutes are
either similar to or different from non-prostitute women.

These stories are intriguing for they are paradoxical. They are both
plausible and implausible. They are implausible because they are constituted by and within the profound contradiction of involvement in
prostitution as being both a means of securing material and social survival and a set of relationships that threaten that survival. Yet at the
same time, stories such as Katrina's are plausible in that the contradictions are rendered coherent and the stories come to be meaningful,
believable explanations both to the women telling them and to the lis-
teners hearing them. This is not to argue that prostitutes' stories are
somehow different from other people's stories by virtue of their paradoxical nature. All social actors are involved in the business of narrat-
ing stories about their lives that are both plausible and implausible. All
social actors experience contradictory material conditions. However,
what is to some extent unique about these prostitutes' stories is the
specific social circumstances that the narrators inhabit, the particular
contradictions they experience and the discursive strategies they use to
enable their stories to make sense.

Thus the general aim of this book is to make sense of women's contradictory meanings and experiences of involvement in prostitution.
This is achieved by theorising the manner in which the contradictions of
being involved in prostitution are accommodated by individuals so that
their continued involvement is made meaningful. This book provides
an explication of the conditions in which women are sustained within
prostitution. The specific aims are:

- to locate and analyse the ways in which prostitution is made sense
  of, within the law, academic discourse and prostitute women's own
  stories;
- to investigate the socio-structural influences conditioning women's
  engagement in prostitution;
- to investigate the meanings that prostitute women ascribe to their
  involvement in prostitution;
- to explain how it is possible for prostitute women to attribute
  apparently contradictory meanings to their involvement in prostitution.

But it would be a mistake to say that this book is only about women's
involvement in prostitution. The original questions guiding a research

project inevitably shift and change as the researcher becomes more knowledgeable about the research area, more interested in specific but tangential issues and begins to understand the complexity of the questions that s/he posed in the beginning. In some cases the final product bears only a passing resemblance to the original vision. This book is based upon a PhD thesis, which started as a set of questions about the circumstances in which prostitution is made possible; it has ended up as an ethnography of poor women who are also prostitutes. So although prostitution is clearly the subject of this book, it is also about much more than prostitution. It is about how some women who live in extraordinarily adverse economic conditions are able to understand their own lives and make sense of the choices they make in their struggle to overcome their poverty. It shows how the experiences women have within and outside their intimate relationships are shaped and structured by more fundamental economic relations between men and women – a dynamic seen most clearly when their intimate relationships turn violent. So whilst prostitution is the overall subject, this book also addresses how women negotiate their poverty and the violence they may experience at the hands of the men (partners, punters, police or ponces) with whom they are involved.

The main and general argument of this book is that involvement in prostitution is made possible for some women because, put simply, such involvement comes to 'make sense' because of the social and material conditions in which they live. In other words, one of the necessary preconditions sustaining women within prostitution is that the anomalies and contradictions of their lives are resolved and rendered coherent in a fashion that permits such involvement to be 'plausible' (that is, subjectively meaningful). This is most important given the two profound contradictions that become apparent in the stories the women tell. The first contradiction inheres in the question of difference and similarity. Thus whilst the law has constituted prostitutes as different from other women by virtue of the public nuisance it is assumed they cause, and by virtue of the supposed risk they present to public sexual health, and whilst academic literature has variously constituted prostitutes as either different from or similar to other women, prostitute women understand themselves as being, contradictorily, both the same as and different from other women. The second contradiction inheres in the mutually exclusive effects and representations of continued involvement in prostitution as both enabling and threatening material and social survival.

The specific argument I put forward is that engagement in prostitution comes to make sense via the construction of a specific 'prostitute identity' composed of three contingent and contradictory pairs of identifications: prostitutes as workers and as commodified bodies; prostitutes as businesswomen and as loving partners; and prostitutes as victims and as survivors. This contradictory identity is made possible by the symbolic landscape underpinning it, in which the meanings of 'men', 'money' and 'violence' are symbolically interconnected so that 'men' and 'money' and 'men' and 'risk' are conflated.

Thus the major theme developed in the course of this text is that women are sustained within prostitution because the paradoxes of their involvement (that is, being both like and unlike other women and experiencing and representing prostitution in opposed ways) are resolved by the discursive strategies that are employed to make sense of both the relationships they have with ponces, partners, the police and punters and of the material, social and ideological conditions they inhabit.

This book is divided into two parts. Part I clears the ground for the development of my argument by deconstructing and disclosing both the legal constitution of prostitutes and prostitution and the dominant explanations of women's involvement in prostitution. Chapter 2 examines how prostitutes and prostitution have been made sense of within the British legal framework. It explores the manner in which social policies constitute prostitutes as different from other women by virtue of the public nuisance they create and the public sexual health problem they pose. The effects of such constructions are detailed as both shaping and enabling specific forms of intervention. Chapter 3 is concerned with the theoretical enclosure of prostitution within (academic) discourses, which have variously constituted prostitutes as pathological individuals, socially dislocated women, members of a criminal subculture, economic entrepreneurs and victims of male violence. It argues that one of the primary questions framing previous work on prostitution is whether (and in what ways) prostitutes are like or unlike other (non-prostitute) women and traces the process of theoretical closure and reopening that has occurred.

Part II, which comprises two chapters, is an empirical study of the conditions in which women are sustained within prostitution. The overall aim of Part II is to analyse how the explanations offered by prostitute women for their engagement in prostitution can be made to make sense and become plausible. The two chapters are extremely long. I have chosen to not divide them because a predominant theme of both chapters is 'contradiction'. To divide the chapters would necessitate dividing the different aspects of the contradictions that are examined and the discursive strategies used by the women to accommodate such contradictions. To do so would mean running the risk of compartmentalising and thus 'flattening' the contradictions examined. Hence Chapter 4 examines the socio-structural influences conditioning the interviewees' engagement in prostitution. It offers a description of their struggle to survive (both economically and socially), the risks they encountered, the circumstances that constrained their lives, the context in which these struggles took place and how these struggles affected their perceived options and opportunities for the future. Concomitantly, Chapter 4 also provides a detailed description of the paradoxical stories that these women told. For within the socio-structural context described, involvement in prostitution was represented by the interviewees as both a way to secure their future economic and social survival and a threat to their survival. Chapter 5 brings forward the question of plausibility and charts the complexities and nuances of meanings that underpinned and sustained the interviewees' explanations. Particular attention is paid to the contradictory, diverse and multiple ways in which the interviewees were identified and located as prostitutes in relation to the people, practices and conditions surrounding them. Overall, Chapter 5 demonstrates how it is possible for the paradoxical narratives of involvement in prostitution to make sense within the social contexts in which prostitute women engage in prostitution.

An introductory note on definitions is helpful. Research into prostitution has a very long history, and even a cursory reading of the many sociological and criminological texts reveals two things. First, there is a call by researchers to 'recognise' that prostitution is not transhistorical or acultural and to contextualise any analysis within its specific setting (Scambler and Scambler, 1997). Second, and notwithstanding the increased attention to historical and cultural specificity (see especially Roberts, 1992; Scambler and Scambler, 1997; McKeganey and Barnard, 1996), prostitution is nonetheless treated as self-evidently conceptualised and defined. It is seen as nothing more and nothing less than selling sex. So, for instance, O'Neill (1997, p. 10) defines prostitution as 'the exchange of money for sex'. Similarly Hoigard and Finstad (1992, p. 8) define prostitution as: 'buying and selling sexual services for cash payment'.

In contrast this book uses four related concepts to frame the analysis: 'prostitutes', 'prostituting', 'prostitution' and 'prostitutionalisation'. Whilst the term prostitutes is commonly used to denote all individuals (male or female, heterosexual, lesbian or gay) who receive money, either directly or indirectly, for sexual service, in this book 'prostitutes' refers only to women who sell sex for money within the institution of prostitution. Similarly, although the term prostituting usually refers to the act of exchanging sexual services for economic rewards – which includes trading sex directly for money and for indirect economic benefits such as long-term financial security, short-term accommodation and so on – here 'prostituting' refers only to the direct exchange of sex for money within the institution of prostitution. 'Prostitution' is used to signify a social institution – or a set of relationships, discourses and practices that make prostituting possible and are culturally and historically located and specific. Finally, the term prostitutionalisation refers to the formal process of labeling an individual a prostitute and the consequences of involvement in prostitution, such as increased police surveillance, reduced economic opportunities and increased poverty.

METHODOLOGY

Describing and analysing the conditions in which sustained involvement in prostitution is made possible necessitated a method of investigation that provided information about (1) the structural influences operating on individual women and (2) the subjective, symbolic landscape within which their involvement in prostitution was made meaningful. To this end, data was collected through in-depth, semistructured, life-historical interviews. Access to the interviewees was gained via two gatekeepers: one worked for a sexual health outreach service (SHOS) whilst the other worked in a probation-run day drop-in centre for prostitute women and other women offenders[1]. This data was supplemented with three months of observation in one of the red light areas of MidCity[2] – many of the interviewees allowed me to spend time with them and I was able to observe their daily working routine, the mundanity of their involvement in prostitution and the benefits and risks of being a prostitute. Twenty-one prostitute women between the ages of 18 and 44 took part in the study. They worked primarily from the streets, although most of the women also worked from their own homes and in saunas or brothels. Since being engaged in prostitution these women had gained extensive experience of prostitution-related practices such as poncing, continuous arrest, prostitution-structured and prostitution-enforced poverty, violence and housing problems.

Throughout the data collection stage of the project I was acutely aware of the specific characteristics of the group of individuals who agreed to be interviewed. The means by which access is established ultimately determines the type of people the researcher will interview. In this case the interviewees were either in contact with the SHOS or the probation office, and both the SHOS and the probation office recognised that the women they saw as clients represented only a fraction of those who were involved in prostitution at that time in MidCity. The women who did agree to be interviewed were used to recounting their tales (such recounting being a key method by which the probation office and SHOS conducted their work). In addition they were women for whom prostitution had become a 'problem' inasmuch as they were either concerned for their health (and hence were willing to continue their contact with the SHOS) or had been ordered by the court to attend the day drop-in centre in exchange for deferment of their fines or as a punishment for prostitution-related offences. Consequently a question can be raised about the differences between the women who agreed to the interviewed and those who did not. Did their stories differ in any substantial way from those women not in contact with either the probation office or the SHOS? This book does not claim that the interviewees in any way represent the 'typical prostitute' – a woman who arguably does not even exist – and no generalisations are made based upon the specific experiences of these interviewees (and thus there is not a problem of generalisability). So for instance, simply because all but two of these women (19 white and one black)[3] had had black ponces, does not mean that all women involved in prostitution have ponces, or that all ponces are black. It only means that in the context of MidCity's jointly run initiative, and in the context of who was chosen (for whatever reason) or who agreed (again, for whatever reason) to be interviewed, at some point nearly all of these women had been ponced by black men.

Because the interviewees were to some degree a unique group of women – especially in terms of time, place and space – it is helpful to describe the context within which they lived and worked. They all lived and worked within two districts of MidCity (Greenvale and Birchfield). MidCity is a large English city with a diverse population of approximately one million inhabitants. It has a strong representation of the main minority ethnic groups (Table 1.1) and the two districts in question, Greenvale and Birchfield, also have a strong representation of the main minority ethnic groups relative to the rest of the city.

Table 1.1   Demographic comparison of the main minority ethnic groups in MidCity and England and Wales (per cent)

	MidCity	*England and Wales*
White	76	94
Black Caribbean, African, other	6	1.8
Indian, Pakistani, Bangladeshi	14	2.9

Source: 1991 Census information provided by 'MidCity' Council.

Whereas the population of MidCity as a whole includes approximately 20 per cent black and minority ethnic group members, Greenvale has 40–54.9 per cent and Birchfield has over 55 per cent. Birchfield has over three times the city average of Afro-Caribbean individuals compared with up to three times the city average in Greenvale (1991 Census information provided by 'MidCity' Council). Greenvale and Birchfield are perceived as 'inner city' areas, arguably because of the high proportion of minority ethnic groups and visible signs of urban decay and poverty, such as run-down or derelict properties, closed businesses, a lack of amenities such as shops and community centres, a high proportion of council or housing association and privately rented accommodation and so on.

All but one of the interviewees were white. Gail (aged 28) was the one exception and identified herself as of 'mixed parentage' with a white mother and an Afro-Caribbean father. Given the demographic features of Greenvale and Birchfield, it is not surprising that many of the interviewees had boyfriends, husbands or partners who were Afro-Caribbean.

The women had been involved in prostitution for between nine months and 26 years. The age at which they started ranged from 12 to 36, with an average starting age of 18 and a median starting age of 17. All but two of the interviewees had been ponced. All of them had endured physical or sexual attack, most often by ponces, but also by punters.

All but two of the women had been arrested for a prostitution-related offence at least once in their lives. None of them identified themselves as drug addicts but the gatekeepers had been specifically asked to facilitate access to women who were not drug dependent. Sixteen of the 21 had children.

These women's lives were the lives of 'ordinary' (albeit specifically located) women. Their involvement in prostitution was not the sole focus of their existence. All had taken at least one substantial break from prostitution (that is, more than six months and in most cases approximately one year). They were also mothers, lovers, friends, shoppers and so on, and were often embedded within their local community and took part in community activities. For instance they knew their neighbours, milkmen, rubbish men, schools, lollipop ladies, shop assistants and policemen. They seldom spent more than five or six hours per day 'working'; the rest of their time was spent socialising, taking care of domestic responsibilities and generally getting on with their lives. Indeed in most respects the 21 interviewees were a heterogeneous group of women from different places (although some of the women were local to MidCity, some had come from other English cities, and one was Irish and one German) struggling with a diverse range of circumstances and experiences and living in various living arrangements and household types.

Arguably, the only unifying features of these women's lives were: (1) their work as prostitutes; (2) the material, social and ideological world they inhabited; (3) the ways in which they made sense of their involvement in prostitution; and (4) what they had experienced as a consequence of their engagement in prostitution. In short, apart from their involvement in prostitution there was little common ground between them and little to distinguish them from any other group of women.

PROTOCOLS FOR THE ANALYSIS

Because one central element in what has loosely been called 'discourse analysis' has been concerned with how people learn to accommodate contradictions in their lives, and because even a preliminary analysis of the interview material suggested that contradiction characterised these women's involvement in prostitution, some of the protocols for the analysis were taken from the 'discourse analysis' perspective (see Foucault, 1972; Worrall, 1990). In particular there are three sets of interrelated notions that frame the analytical content of this book: theoretical closure, the suspension of 'autobiographical realism'; and a specific conception of 'identity'.

All theorising produces closure by tacitly drawing boundaries around what it is possible to say and how it is possible to say it. Yet in the process of constituting any social phenomenon as an object of knowledge (as in the case of academic explanation, legal constitution or, indeed, even personal accounts and explanations), spaces, gaps and openings occur that allow the posing of alternative questions and the pursuit of alternative explanations. In the process of elaboration those spaces, gaps and openings can be closed by the conceptual demarcations framing what is explicitly said. So for example, and as will be demonstrated in Chapter 3, differentiating between prostitutes and other women allows examination of the specific differences between these two groups of women but at the same time, foreclose the space to pose questions about their similarities.

It is one task of theory to reopen what has been closed, to construct different objects of knowledge and in so doing to pose different questions than have been posed before. Any particular explanation – be it academic, legal or personal – whilst producing closure, also hints at other possible understandings and indicates new questions, which in turn may provoke new and different understandings. Working within a discourse analysis perspective enables one to exploit the theoretical spaces, gaps and openings provided by previous studies, or existing within the legal construction of prostitution and women's own accounts. Thus the aim of this book is not to call into question the adequacy of the legal construction of prostitution or the accuracy of the personal accounts of the women interviewed, nor is it to refute previous explanations or challenge the validity of others' work on prostitution. Instead this book simply constitutes a new link in the chain of stories told about prostitution.

Framing the analytical project in such a fashion brings the conceptual demarcations that produce closure (and concomitantly can produce disclosure) into the analytical foreground. It permits an analysis not of what is said about prostitutes and prostitution, but how what is said is made possible. In short, it enables an analysis of the conditions in which it becomes possible to understand women's sustained involvement in prostitution in particular ways.

Whilst the adoption of such a perspective allows prostitution to be analysed in a slightly different way from the methods used in other projects (because it takes the conditions that enable the production of meaningful narratives as its object of analysis), it was nevertheless necessary to adopt a further analytical protocol when approaching the interview material. Specifically, in order to reveal the processes by which the contradictory and paradoxical tales of the prostitute women came to represent subjectively meaningful and believable stories explaining their continued engagement in prostitution, it was necessary to call into question and suspend the realism of their autobiographical narratives.

Traditional analyses of life historical interviews (which themselves are effectively autobiographical texts) assume (1) a (near) one-to-one correlation between the texts that are produced and life-as-lived, and (2) that the texts are indeed 'authored' by stable and unitary authors. Analysis framed by such assumptions treats autobiographical texts as though they are concerned with telling an unfolding and linearly progressing tale that captures what really happened (in this case) to prostitute women and as though they are produced by self-consistent individuals in touch with the unmediated social reality of their lives, assumptions that in any case are displaced in the 'discourse analysis' perspective.

In studies that are framed by a traditional conception of autobiographies, the task of the researcher is merely to distill from all the interview material those factors and processes which are recounted as leading to the interviewees' eventual and continued involvement in prostitution. And a principal methodological problem is 'knowing' and counteracting the extent to which the autobiographical narratives of prostitutes may or may not authentically, faithfully and immediately represent the lives led by the interviewees.

With the 'textual turn in sociology' (Hall, 1996), however, autobiographical narratives have been radically reconceived. More importantly, they have been reconceived in a manner that permits them to be opened, deconstructed and analysed in ways that bring into focus the accommodation of contradiction. Of particular relevance to this project are the critiques of the assumption that autobiographies are mirror representations of 'life as lived' and that autobiographical description is a clear process. So powerful have been these critiques that Roos (1994, p. 3) characterises them as producing a 'Fall from the Paradise of True Autobiographies', whereby every element of the common-sense conception of autobiographical narratives as texts written (or spoken) by authors about their lives is called into question.

In summary, the critiques amount to a reconception of autobiographies as problematic social products structured by the conventions of the genre (cf. Unsworth, 1995; Joannou, 1995; Jolly, 1995; Swindells, 1995). The implication, therefore, is that the analytical focus is *interpretation* rather than compilation and distillation. According to Roos (1994, p. 3):

> Upon leaving the Paradise of True Autobiographies, we have accepted the thesis that no text is innocent, independent of certain theoretical, conceptual and textual frames. Nothing we describe or see in the

world we 'just see'; it comes to us and through us always mediated by the current way of seeing things.

Thus autobiographical narratives are not understood as simple representational mirrors of an individual's life; rather they are understood as texts that have no essence behind the words (Denzin, 1989). There is 'no pure core of unmixed intentionality' (Scholes, 1989, p. 8) or central individual who authorises and gives meaning to their story that can be revealed through the reading or writing of an autobiography. There is only interpretation or new and different interpretations. Within the reconceived notion of autobiography, there is thus a framework that can be adopted that justifies and enables the researcher to move beyond a realist analysis of interview material.

Yet autobiographies are treated and produced by their narrators as though they are simple representational mirrors that relocate in the texts the 'real subjects' who can be found 'outside' in the 'real world'. Certainly the narratives related by the women interviewed for this project are just such realist productions.

The writings of Jacques Derrida go some way towards providing a justification for suspending the realism of autobiographical, life-historical interview material, regardless of how research subjects might understand them. Derrida's thesis of 'the fallacy of presence' – an illusion that simultaneously drives the effort to anchor the 'real subject' in the 'real world' yet permits that subject to be represented and relocated in a text – can be summarised by saying that no word or text actually represents the thing it is assumed to represent. Texts and words are not 'bounded units of meaning' (Denzin, 1989, p. 44) that convey their meanings discernibly and are distinguishable from other texts and words. Derrida (1972) suggests that the conception of texts as 'bounded units of meaning' is based upon the assumption that meaning is present and resides in the sign or referent. But, he argues, words and texts never operate as simple referents or without referring to something else:

> Whether in the order of spoken or written discourse, no element [that is, word] can function as a sign without referring to another element which itself is not simply present. This interweaving results in each 'element'... being constituted on the basis of the trace within it of the other elements of the chain or system. This interweaving... is the *text* produced only in the transformation of another text. Nothing, neither among the elements nor within the system, is anywhere ever

simply present or absent. There are only, everywhere, differences and traces of traces (Derrida 1972, p. 26).

Therefore words and texts only exist in transformations, traces and spaces, and meaning is created not from the centre, but at the margins (Scholes, 1989).

This argument goes beyond asserting that there are different superficial interpretations of a text, for example, being asked to go on the game by a boyfriend can be understood by the woman in question as either a request or a threat. Instead, if words and texts are unstable, if meaning exists at the margins through transformations and traces, and texts have no centres, then autobiographies cannot and will never be simple representations of 'life as lived'. Rather they are products whose very realism (that they represent 'life as lived') is an illusion.

When examining the interviewees' life histories it can be seen that the women narrators are not the centre, heart or essence of their texts. They are somewhere else. They are located within a set of personal experiences created by something or someone else. The centre is situated in the oppositional relationship between, for example, 'self' and very specific 'others' such as men, money, violence, protection and family. Hence the centre of the texts is found in the relationships between the woman (that is, self) and the man who put her on the game, the absent family, the present abusive partner, the anonymous others who have adversely influenced her economic, social or familial stability (such as social workers, probation officers, court officials and care assistants), the boyfriend, the punters, the police, and the money that has bought stability and the money that has held her in a relationship with her ponce. These oppositions give the narratives a specific sense of order and structure, and also help to produce distinctions as different relationships are emphasised. Thus even though the interviewees may have presented their stories as representational mirrors of their lives, as containing 'the truth' about what had happened to them and why they were involved in prostitution, calling into question the realism of their narratives provides the conditions in which they can be disclosed, as well as revealing the paradoxes contained therein and allowing an examination of the conditions in which plausibility is achieved.

One of the arguments of this book is that the contradictions of engagement in prostitution are accommodated (and thus plausibility is achieved) via the construction of a distinct identity (that is, a 'prostitute identity'). The term identity has been used in a number of different ways in the last few decades. For example it has been used to denote the 'essence' of a person, or a set of personal characteristics. It has been constructed to signify the central author (or self) who elaborates and gives meaning to their story, as in the identity that is created when individuals turn themselves into 'socially organised biographical objects' (Plummer, 1995, p. 34). This identity, so beloved of symbolic interactionism, is capable of self-consciously articulating its own subjectivity simply because it is the symbolic 'world maker' – that is, the central core of individuals who are able to create the 'meaning' of their lives in the stories they tell (ibid., p. 2). Common to this and other conceptions of 'identity' (such as those evident in some writings on political or cultural identities, for example lesbian or gay, feminist, black and so on) is that they rely on a notion of an essential self that is situated at the centre of awareness of an individual and has mastery over symbolic communication. However the notion of an essential, central and symbolically masterful self that is capable of being the 'true' author of its own narrative, which is itself a 'simple' mirror image of that self, is problematic (cf. Sampson 1989) and will therefore not be considered in this book.

To borrow from Barthes (1980), the 'prostitute identity' that is discussed in this book is not the 'prostitutes-who-are' (that is, the authors, essences, centres of awareness and so on), nor the 'prostitutes-who-were' (that is, the past selves that the 'prostitutes-who-are' reveal in their talk) nor even the 'prostitutes-who-narrate' (who in any case are unknowable) (cf. Joannou, 1995). The term 'identity' is not used here to denote the interviewees' 'selfhood', rather the term 'prostitute identity' is used to signify the portrayed self in the women's stories. It is the constellation of the different, diverse and multiple ways in which the women were represented in their stories. It is the personage constructed *within* the autobiographical narrative by and within the ways in which the respondents are positioned in their texts relative to others in a specific symbolic landscape (cf. Langenhove and Harre, 1993). The 'prostitute identity' discussed here is the space created in the demarcation and differentiation of the boundaries between self and other (cf. Habermas, 1987) that helps to organise the explicit accounts that individuals give of their lives. Without wanting to overstate the point, this 'prostitute identity' is the *mediated* identity that emerges in the women's discourses of their involvement in prostitution (cf. Weedon, 1987) and is neither 'authored' nor 'authorised' by the interviewees. By focusing on this prostitute identity it is possible to reveal the 'silent structure' of meaning in the interviewees' accounts. This is an important task, because it is this structure of meaning that conditions the ways in which the women have made subjective sense of their contradictory experiences of engagement in prostitution.

Part I
Prostitution Enclosed

2 Prostitutes, Prostitution and the Law

The legal contexts within which prostitute women work comprise, *inter alia*, the formal laws regarding prostitution and the publicly backed (and at times publicly funded) initiatives that frame particular forms of intervention into the lives of prostitute women. Within Britain's current legal framework, prostitution is conceived of as both a public nuisance problem and a public sexual health problem, and prostitutes themselves are constituted as different from other women. In combination these constructions permit very particular forms of intervention into the lives of prostitute women and thus help to structure the experiences they have of prostitution. This chapter examines the manner in which prostitution and prostitutes are made sense of within Britain's current legal framework.

Women working as prostitutes in Britain find themselves in an ambiguous legal position, for whilst the sale of sex is not an offence, many of the activities connected with it are. Indeed as Bresler (1988) notes, prostitutes are only criminalised when they attempt to work. Contemporary British law on prostitution has been framed by a negative regulationist approach. The law has not sought to abolish or legally repress prostitution by criminalising the sale of sexual services, as in the United States. Conversely the law in Britain has not been used to regulate prostitution by legalising it, as in the case of the licensed brothels in Amsterdam, Hamburg and Australia (see Perkins and Bennett, 1985). Rather British law addresses only those prostitution-related activities that it defines as injurious to the ordinary citizen or exploitative of prostitutes. It has attempted to 'maintain a more manageable form of prostitution divested of its disruptive and politically embarrassing characteristics' (Matthews, 1986, p. 188) by negatively sanctioning particular prostitution-related activities.

This approach was established by the Sexual Offences Act 1956, which deals with the various activities, relationships and behaviours that might aid, manage, exploit or encourage prostitutes. Specifically, the Sexual Offences Act criminalises the following:

- Causing or encouraging prostitution, which is also known as procuring women to become prostitutes (Section 22(1)).

- Living on the earnings of prostitution, which includes the gender-specific offences of poncing or 'men living on the earnings of prostitution' (Section 30(1)) and women exercising 'control, direction or influence over a prostitute's movements' (Section 31).
- Brothel keeping and associated activities such as landlords or tenants knowingly permitting their premises to be used as a brothel and keeping a disorderly house (Sections 33–6, and Disorderly Houses Act 1751, Section 8).

The Street Offences Act 1959 deals directly with prostitutes and prostitution and regulates the manner and means by which prostitutes and their clients can contact each other. It specifies the following offences:

- Loitering and soliciting by a 'common prostitute' in a street or public place for the purpose of prostitution (Section 1(1)).
- Solicitation by men for immoral purposes (Section 32).
- Persistent solicitation of women for the purposes of prostitution (Section 2(1)).

Since 1959 there have been two amendments to the legislation. First, the use of imprisonment as a punishment for women convicted of soliciting was abolished (Criminal Justice Act 1982). Second, 'persistent' kerb crawling was made an offence (Sexual Offences Act 1985).

In practice, then, the only way that prostitution can be practised without committing a criminal offence is as a one-to-one arrangement between two consenting adults in private. Moreover, whilst the law does not regulate the specific encounters or relationships between prostitutes and their clients, it does regulate other relationships that prostitutes have – particularly those which are judged to be exploitative of prostitutes. Hence living on immoral earnings and exercising control over prostitutes are offences.

Britain's current legal framework regarding prostitutes and prostitution was created by the *Report on Homosexual Offences and Prostitution* (Wolfenden Committee, 1957). This report explicitly argued that any attempt to abolish prostitution through the use of law was folly. The Wolfenden Committee claimed that prostitution has persisted across many different societies and throughout time despite the various legal efforts to eradicate it. They opined that its endurance could be explained in terms of the simple notion of supply and demand – as long as there are men who want to go to prostitutes, there will always be prostitution (ibid., pp. 79–80). Thus underpinning British law on prostitution is an acceptance of its existence, but an acceptance predicated on the notion that prostitutes and prostitution pose a specific public nuisance problem and are therefore subject to legal intervention.

THE 'PROBLEMS' OF PROSTITUTION: PUBLIC NUISANCE AND PRIVATE MORALITY

The understanding of prostitution as a problem of public nuisance has shaped and guided nearly a century of laws on prostitution in Britain. Central to the Wolfenden Report was the assumption that the proper function of the law is 'to preserve public order and decency, to protect the citizen from what is offensive ... and to provide sufficient safeguards against exploitation and corruption of others' (Wolfenden Committee, 1957, pp. 9–10). Combined with this assumption, the report also differentiated between matters of criminal law and private morality, arguing that regardless of the fact that certain forms of sexual behaviour are regarded by many individuals as 'wrong', 'sinful' or 'objectionable', it is not within the ambit of the criminal law to intervene into the private sexual lives of individuals. This differentiation was not new to Wolfenden. Indeed in 1927 the Street Offences Committee argued that the law should not adjudicate over or intervene in issues of 'private morals or ethical sanctions', and that the proper focus of the law should be actions by individuals that injuriously affect the rights of others. Directly drawing on the arguments contained in the *Street Offences Committee Report* (1928), the Wolfenden Committee asserted that the focus of legislation on prostitution should not be concerned with the sale or purchase of sexual favours but rather the related activities of prostitutes and others connected with them that cause 'affront' to ordinary members of society. In short Wolfenden recommended that prostitution should be seen as a matter of private morality, except when it creates a public nuisance.

Throughout the report the Wolfenden Committee stressed that prostitution causes a problem of public nuisance because the visibility of prostitutes insults 'public decency' (Wolfenden Committee, 1957, p. 81). The committee was strident in its assertion that this was the case because 'those ordinary citizens who live in these areas ... cannot, in going about their daily business, avoid the sight of a state of affairs which seems to them to be an affront to public order and decency' (ibid., p. 82). Such was the strength of the Committee's conviction

about the offensive nature of the visibility of prostitutes that when recommending the removal of the then legal necessity of proving annoyance before proceeding against a prostitute they remarked as follows:

> In our view both loitering and importuning for the purpose of prostitution are so self-evidently public nuisances that the law ought to deal with them as it deals with other self-evident public nuisances, without calling on individual citizens to establish the fact that they were annoyed (ibid., p. 87).

In other words, underlying the British legislation on prostitution is the assumption that the mere presence of prostitutes in public places is enough to cause a public nuisance.

The report's articulation of the type and manner of public nuisance caused by prostitution was fairly unsophisticated in that it relied on the ill-specified and yet self-evidently conceptualised notion of 'an affront to public decency'. However, since then there have been several attempts to specify the exact nature of the nuisance caused by prostitution. For example Sion (1977, pp. 15–16) asserts that the problem of prostitution inheres in the way that prostitution creates an environment where property values and businesses in red light areas decline through the 'bad reputation' of that area; where 'innocent and decent men' are accosted; where road traffic is disrupted by kerb crawlers; where fear of molestation is increased by the presence of men on the streets late at night; where other women may be corrupted because they 'may imitate prostitutes in times of financial distress'; and where young children are 'continuously exposed to the manifestation of prostitution. Similarly the *Criminal Law Revision Committee's Seventeenth Report* (1985) added to this list of nuisances the nuisance of neighbourhoods acquiring a 'reputation for vice' if off-street prostitution in the form of brothels were legalised (CLRC, 1985, p. 14). In more recent works it has been argued that prostitution causes a public nuisance because it creates an atmosphere that increases both the fear of crime experienced by individuals, particularly women, in communities where prostitution occurs (Matthews 1993), and neighbourhood decline, in that once certain 'incivilities' (including activities such as soliciting and kerb crawling) become regular features of a neighbourhood, a dynamic is put in place that both attracts more crime and criminal activities and undermines the stability of the community (see Wilson and Kelling, 1982; Skogan, 1990). More practically, it has also been argued that one of the more significant public nuisance problems that prostitution poses in a society of car drivers is the sheer increase in the volume of traffic, with all the attendant problems of noise, congestion and pollution (Matthews, 1993).

The conceptualisation of prostitution as causing a public nuisance was resurrected in the 1980s in the campaign to criminalise kerb crawlers. Matthews (1986) and Edwards (1987) have described the role of local community groups, tenants' associations and feminists in the early 1980s in bringing attention to the problem of public nuisance by the clients of prostitutes. The problem, it was claimed, was that non-prostitute women in the streets and public spaces of red light areas were being sexually harassed and 'kerb crawled' by punters. Hence for those groups and individuals fighting the campaign to criminalise kerb crawling, prostitution was a public nuisance in that it was adversely affecting the safety of all (other, 'innocent') women. Calls for action culminated in the Criminal Law Revision Committee's (1984) recommendation that the law on men who solicit prostitutes be tightened in such a manner that they would be criminalised for their actions.

The Sexual Offences Act 1985 did just that by introducing the offence of 'persistent kerb crawling'. Matthews (1986, p. 192) interpreted the introduction of the Sexual Offences Act 1985 as signalling a shift in the approach to the 'problem' of prostitution:

> Although the Criminal Law Revision Committee maintain a formal commitment to Wolfenden's style of regulationism, there is clearly a marked shift in approach towards a more overt and more systematic 'enforcement of morals', together with a broader shift to the Right, and a gradual erosion of that brand of liberalism which once underpinned Wolfenden's approach.

Whilst such an amendment may have signalled a shift in the constitution of prostitution in terms of private morality, in the 1990s the construction of the problem of prostitution as one of public nuisance was given renewed vigour by various vigilante groups who sought to remove street prostitution from their neighbourhoods and communities. One such campaign was the Streetwatch and Care Association in Birmingham. In the spring of 1994 a campaign was launched with the explicit purpose of ridding Balsall Heath of its street-working prostitutes. The campaign was directed at embarrassing both prostitutes and punters through the highly visible presence of protesters on the streets and the use of placards to notify the punters that the registration numbers of their cars were being recorded. As Raja Ahmin, spokesman for the Association, asserted:

None of the girls live in the area, none of the girls think anything about throwing used condoms in people's gardens or what we might think about having to see prostitution all the time. As far as we're concerned Balsall Heath is for the Balsall Heathers – we want a safe community and that means getting rid of prostitution (Newstalk, BBC Radio 5, 3 June 1996).

By the end of the summer of 1994, most of Britain's major cities had at least one such campaign. These campaigns added a new complexity to the construction of prostitution as a problem, in that whilst clearly drawing on more diffuse notions of public nuisance, they also drew a direct causal link between the existence of prostitution in particular neighbourhoods, a lack of personal safety and crime.

One of the interesting features of British law on prostitution is that it has been reliant on the notion of prostitutes being different from other women. Clearly this is the case, if only because within the law there is a category of offenders known as 'common prostitutes', who are distinct and different from both non-prostitute women and other offenders. An examination of the legal definitions of 'prostitution' and 'common prostitute' illuminates the manner and way in which the law underscores an assumed difference between prostitutes and women not involved in prostitution.

'Prostitution' has never been defined in statute, thus the meaning of the term arises from common law, which stipulates that sexual intercourse is not a necessary component of prostitution (Rook and Ward 1997, p. 262), rather prostitution merely entails 'that a woman offers her body commonly for lewdness for payment in return' (Darling J. [1918] K. B., 635 and 637). Subsequent case law established that, indeed, no actual physical contact between a man and a woman is necessary for prostitution to occur (Webb [1964], 1, Q. B., 357): all that needs to happen is for a woman to be paid for an 'indecent act' (or sexual service). Thus, as prostitution has been defined in law, there is a conflation of the activity of selling sex and a group of individuals. Such a conflation is further noted in the legal category 'common prostitute'. As stated earlier, it is an offence for a common prostitute to loiter or solicit for the purpose of prostitution. The meaning of 'common prostitute' is very clear. A common prostitute is a woman who 'is prepared for reward to engage in acts of lewdness with all and sundry, or with anyone who may hire her for that purpose' (Morris-Lowe [1985], 1 All E. R., 402). Without wishing to overstate the point, as constituted in British law, prostitution (as the activity of selling sex) is defined in terms of a category of persons (that is, 'common prostitutes'), which is in turn defined in terms of the activity of selling sex.

It is in an examination of the reasons for retaining the category of offenders called 'common prostitutes' that the clear distinction the law draws between prostitutes and non-prostitute women is most visible. In the Wolfenden Report there is a discussion of whether or not to retain the category of common prostitute. The committee acknowledged that there were several objections to retaining the category, especially in terms of (1) the fact that the term is not defined within statute law; (2) the legal anomaly created by defining an offence in terms of the persons committing it, which is unprecedented in relation to other offences; and (3) the presumption of guilt that precedes women into court who have in the past had this label attached to them. However the committee argued that it was important to retain the category in order for the law to provide a 'safeguard from wrongful arrest which ... [it] affords women who are not "common prostitutes"' (Wolfenden Committee, 1957, p. 88). Whilst they explored the possibility of redefining the offence with no reference to a category of persons, the committee asserted that such a legal move would leave the police unable to distinguish between non-prostitute women and prostitute women:

> We have in mind the possibility that any woman might, from ignorance or indiscretion, put herself in a position in which she might be said to be loitering, and by conduct which was quite innocent give rise to a suspicion in the mind of an observant policeman, that she was loitering for the purposes of prostitution. She might, for example, be waiting for a friend who had been unexpectedly delayed, and from anxiety over the growing delay enquire the time of a number of male passers-by.... [A] policeman might quite legitimately reach the *prima facie* conclusion that she was loitering for the purposes of prostitution and arrest her accordingly (ibid., p. 89).

In other words, because some women might engage in what appears to be the same behaviour as prostitutes, the Wolfenden Committee felt that it was necessary to formalise within the law the distinction between 'innocent' women and 'common prostitutes' in order to protect the former from wrongful arrest. Therefore at the heart of British law on prostitution is a notion of the difference between prostitutes and 'innocent' women, which inheres not in their behaviour and activities (for a single act of 'lewdness' does not confer on a woman the legal label 'common prostitute'), but rather in the manner in which prostitutes are 'indiscriminate' in that they offer sexual services to 'all and sundry'. Prostitutes are not the same as other women because they operate with a fundamentally different set of sexual values. The very visibility of such women thus causes the public nuisance that is the problem of prostitution. According to the Wolfenden Committee, 'the simple fact is that prostitutes do parade themselves more habitually and openly than their prospective customers, and do by their continual presence affront the sense of decency of the ordinary citizen' (ibid., p. 87).

Interestingly, at the same time as constructing prostitutes as a group of morally different and sexually indiscriminate women, the committee also constructed them as different from other women by virtue of some type of pathology that they possessed. When discussing a proposed structure of penalties for prostitution-related offences, the committee recommended that young prostitutes should be remanded at an early stage in their career in order to enable a full social report to be submitted. The point of such a penalty would not be punishment *per se*, but rather to enable Social Services to investigate the psychiatric or medical problems that had led to the young women's involvement in prostitution. This was an unusual recommendation because at that time the courts were empowered only to levy a fine on prostitution-related offences. Thus remanding in custody for up to three weeks an offender convicted for the first or second time of a prostitution-related offence created a certain discrepancy in punishments. The committee, however, felt that this discrepancy was justifiable in terms of the 'benefits' that would accrue from full medical and social reports on the young women (ibid., p. 94).

The understanding of prostitutes as different from non-prostitute women also occurs later in the report in relation to 'living on the earnings of prostitution'. Here the committee was adamant that the relationship between prostitutes and ponces is not as exploitative as it first appears. According to the committee, the relationship between a prostitute and her ponce is usually instigated by the woman, and 'seems to stem from a need on the part of the prostitute for some element of stability in the background of her life' (ibid., p. 99). In other words, prostitutes' lives are so unstable that they have need of what has been thought of as an exploitative relationship. They are unlike other women because behaviour such as taking or demanding a woman's earnings has a fundamentally different meaning for prostitute women.

One result of the legal constitution of the problem of prostitution as one of public nuisance is the generation of a set of laws and policing strategies that focus not on prostitution, *per se*, but on particular forms of prostitution and prostitution-related activities. Hence, the police aim to reduce or end street prostitution but tolerate the growth of less visible forms of prostitution such as sauna work, brothel work and home work, which are seen as causing less public nuisance. For example 'zones of tolerance' have been created where particular forms of prostitution are permitted, as in the case of Birmingham City Council's recent considerations (O'Neill, 1997; cf. Matthews, 1986; Smart, 1995). Indeed the Street Offences Act 1959 facilitated the targeting of street prostitution by:

- removing the need to produce evidence to prove 'annoyance' in order to proceed with a loitering or soliciting charge (Wolfenden Committee, 1957, pp. 86–7);
- increasing the police's discretionary powers with regard to cautioning (Matthews, 1986);
- creating the legal category 'common prostitute' (a category conferred on a woman after two cautions for loitering or soliciting), who can be proceeded against on the evidence of two police officers (Matthews, 1986; English Collective of Prostitutes, 1997).

Matthews (1986, p. 189) has asserted that a regulation system was thus introduced that was capable of much 'deeper intervention' than had hitherto been possible by employing more punitive measures against a smaller (and more containable) prostitute population.

But it has also been argued that the 'streamlining' of the regulation of street prostitution has made street workers a special and unique category of offenders. As noted above, current legislation constructs the offence around the offender herself, rather than around specified forms of behaviour, and hence 'women with one or more previous conviction(s) find themselves under scrutiny and their mere presence on the streets often leads to further arrest and prosecution' (Edwards, 1997, p. 61).

Moreover, by permitting subsequent convictions to be based on the label 'common prostitute' and the evidence of two police officers, the Street Offences Act 1959 created an exceptional and discriminatory situation in which the principle of 'innocent until proven guilty beyond reasonable doubt' was turned upside down through a procedural system in which prostitute women could be tried not on the evidence against them, but on their previous records and the 'cautions which stamp and condemn' them (English Collective of Prostitutes, 1997, p. 85).

A second effect of the construction of the problem of prostitution as one of public nuisance is the comparative underenforcement of provisions designed to protect prostitute women from exploitation (Matthews, 1986; Edwards, 1997). For focusing legal and police attention on the public nuisance caused by prostitution creates a situation in which attention is deflected away from less public and less visible prostitution-related activities. Indeed Matthews (1986, p. 208) reports that in 1978, whilst there were thousands of convictions for soliciting-type offences, only fourteen people were tried for procuring and only eleven of those fourteen were eventually convicted. Edwards (1997) explains the failure to police the legal proscriptions against the exploitation of prostitutes as resulting from the manifest inequality of treatment that the law itself gives to prostitute women. Matthews (1986) and Smart (1995) comment that the existing legal provisions are woefully inadequate in that they fail to differentiate between individuals who share monies with prostitute women and individuals who extort, exploit, control and/or intimidate prostitute women, whilst also requiring the women themselves, to bring charges and give evidence against the individuals who exploit them. Whatever the case may be, there is little doubt that current legislation and the failure to implement the Criminal Law Revision Committee's proposals to tighten up the provisions against procuring, living off immoral earnings and brothel keeping (CLRC, 1985) mean that prostitute women receive only a modicum of protection from the exploitative, coercive and violent actions of those individuals who would take advantage of them.

THE 'PROBLEMS' OF PROSTITUTION: PUBLIC SEXUAL HEALTH

The construction of prostitution as a problem of public sexual health is not unique to the late twentieth century (see Mahood, 1990a, 1990b; Walkowitz, 1980; McHugh, 1980; Bell, 1994). Mahood (1990a, p. 20) notes that in 1497 Aberdeen Council passed an Act that declared that all prostitutes should be branded so that the general public could identify them as possible carriers of syphilis.[1] In the nineteenth century the Contagious Diseases Acts 1884, 1866 and 1869 legally formalised the construction of prostitution as a public sexual health problem. In the century that has passed since then the association of prostitution with sexually transmitted diseases has never totally disappeared, and with the arrival of the world-wide AIDS/HIV pandemic it began to be deployed in a new and slightly different way. Similar to the construction of prostitution as a problem of public nuisance wherein prostitute women are understood as different from other women (by virtue of their different values and morals), in the construction of prostitution as a public sexual health problem there is also an understanding of prostitutes as different from non-prostitute women, but here the difference is located in prostitutes' bodies and their lifestyles. This section describes the encoding of prostitutes as sexually unclean and diseased others (both in the nineteenth century and today) and the particular forms of intervention that such a construction has enabled.

Spongberg (1997), in an examination of nineteenth-century British medical discourses on women's bodies in general and venereal disease in particular, demonstrates how venereal disease was feminised and how medical literature on syphilis and gonorrhoea influenced the construction of prostitutes as different from other women because they were contaminated individuals. One of her central arguments is that in the nineteenth century there was a considerable shift in the medical discourse on venereal disease from inscribing femininity as generally diseased to inscribing prostitutes' bodies as the primary site of venereal disease. Spongberg asserts that the dominant medical discourse on male and female bodies until the late eighteenth century was a Galenic model of sexual similarity, whereby women's sexual organs were simply the inverse of men's, that is, vaginas were seen as interior penises, labia were seen as the foreskin, the uterus was seen as the scrotum and so on (ibid., p. 3). But in the nineteenth century the Galenic model of sexual similarity gave way to a model of sexual difference, in which the male body represented the standard of health and the female body became an aberration, and, thus it was that 'femininity' generally became akin to 'diseased' (ibid., pp. 5, 27–34).

In a detailed discussion of nineteenth-century medical literature, Spongberg demonstrates how the association between venereal disease and women was once again transformed. Earlier notions that any and all women could transmit venereal disease gave way as prostitutes became progressively pathologised, until in the late nineteenth century prostitutes, unlike other women, were represented as *necessarily* diseased (ibid., pp. 13, 35–60):

> Prostitutes were made to appear not merely as fallen women, but something less than women. This of course created a gulf between the upright woman and the fallen woman. The prostitute's body became not only the representative sexualised female body, but a site of abnormal indulgence. The proverbial sterility of prostitutes was seen as a key to their pathology. In contrast the body of the virtuous

woman came to be desexualised, her sexual characteristics co-opted
as maternal characteristics. In this way the body of the prostitute
came to be synonymous with venereal disease. Prostitutes were not
merely agents of transmission but somehow inherently diseased, if
not the disease itself (ibid., p. 45).

That prostitutes and venereal disease were symbolically fused together
is evident in the language used during the 1850s when the terms 'social
disease' and 'social evil' were deployed interchangeably to describe
both venereal disease and prostitution.

The construction of prostitutes as different from other women
because they were seen as the primary site of venereal disease (and by
implication a public sexual health problem) enabled the deployment of
a particular type of intervention into the lives of prostitute women
through the Contagious Diseases Acts of 1864, 1866 and 1869 (see
Mahood, 1990a; Roberts, 1992; Walkowitz, 1980). The first of these
Acts set up a 'police morals squad' (Roberts, 1992, p. 248), which was
empowered to stop any woman suspected of being a common prostitute. The woman was then ordered by a magistrate to undergo a medical
inspection, and if she refused she was confined in a Lock Hospital
where she was forcibly examined and, if found to be infected, detained
for up to three months. Originally these measures applied only to a
number of garrison towns, but the 1866 and 1869 Acts expanded the
scope of the legislation: a larger number of towns were encompassed by
the Acts, police powers were extended and a system of registration of
prostitutes and fortnightly medical inspections were introduced. Many
contemporary commentators have noted that underlying the Contagious Diseases Acts was a struggle for, and over, the extension of state
regulation and control over its populace and the policing of working-
class sexuality (McHugh, 1980; Walkowitz, 1980).

But the Contagious Diseases Acts were resisted by campaigners
seeking their repeal and by individual women who were subjected to
compulsory medical interventions (Walkowitz, 1980; Bell 1994).
Throughout the 1870s and 1880s opposition to these Acts grew, until
they were suspended in 1883 and finally repealed in 1886. This, however,
did not mark the end of the construction of prostitution as a problem of
sexual health, because as Bland (1985) has demonstrated, during the
First World War the Defence of the Realm Act 1918 (which effectively
reintroduced the procedures set up by the Contagious Diseases Acts)
was underpinned firstly by the image of the prostitute body as wholly
different from that of other women because it was unclean and infectious,

and secondly by government claims that venereal disease had incapacitated 30–40 per cent of the men of some military units. Hence compulsory medical intervention into prostitute women's lives was reintroduced as a means to 'protect' soldiers.

The end of the Second World War saw the successful introduction and widespread use of penicillin to treat venereal diseases, in particular syphilis and gonorrhoea, and with this the construction of prostitutes once again shifted. They were no longer represented as different because they were a threat to public sexual health, but rather because they were seen as being a threat to themselves. Consequently the image of prostitutes as diseased 'others' disappeared from the medical discourse on venereal disease until the emergence of HIV/AIDS (see Spongberg, 1997, pp. 180–2).

With the onset of the HIV/AIDS pandemic the image of the prostitute as a threat to public sexual health resurfaced. In the 1980s and early 1990s popular discourse revived the notion of prostitutes as reservoirs of sexual disease by scapegoating them as transmitters of the HIV/AIDS virus. Drawing on the older construction of prostitutes as sexually contaminated, strategic use was made of the 'junkie whore' stereotype, that is, a drug-dependent woman who trades in sex to fund her habit (Roberts, 1992, pp. 335–7). Various calls were made to restrict or segregate prostitute women (see English Collective of Prostitutes, 1997). Such was the climate of hostility towards prostitutes on the ground that they were contaminated with the HIV/AIDS virus that in the late 1980s and early 1990s several commentators accused the media of conducting and fuelling a witch hunt against prostitute women (O'Neill, 1997; Roberts, 1992; English Collective of Prostitutes, 1997). In 1992 the *Sunday Express* reported that the King's Cross police alleged that 'of the 50 regulars who work the streets around the station ... three out of four have the virus' (*Sunday Express*, 29 April 1992). But the allegation was found to be completely unsubstantiated, and was in fact based on the opinion of the arresting police officers as to whether individual prostitutes might be infected (English Collective of Prostitutes, 1997).

During the 1990s there has been a notable sophistication in the symbolic conflation of the threat to public sexual health through HIV/AIDS and prostitution. Whilst prostitutes continue to be constructed as purveyors of sexual ill-health, attention is focused not on individual prostitute women but on their lifestyle and behaviours that are represented as being high risk (that is, increase an individual's chance of contracting HIV/AIDS). Therefore prostitutes have been constituted as unlike other women because they are assumed to act as a 'bridge' over which HIV/AIDS can spread to the general populace. Within the last decade there has been a plethora of HIV/AIDS-related research into prostitute women in terms of promiscuity in their personal lives, whether or not they use condoms in their work as prostitutes and in their personal relationships, their drug use and so on. Such research has sought to quantify the actual extent of the HIV-related risk behaviours in which prostitute women are thought to engage (Green *et al.*, 1993; Kinnell, 1989; McKeganey and Barnard, 1996). After a detailed ethnographic study of drug and condom use amongst street-working prostitutes, McKeganey and Barnard (1996, p. 87) asserted the following:

> Perhaps the first point to make here is that we see no benefit whatsoever in responding to the assumed threat of HIV transmission associated with prostitution by increasing the social control of prostitutes. In addition to being ineffective in eradicating prostitution, such measures are likely to increase HIV-related risk behaviour by forcing prostitutes into increasingly covert styles of working and out of contact with helping agencies.

In a similar vein, Ward and Day (1997, p. 141) claim that:

> Prostitute women who inject drugs and share equipment are clearly at increased risk of HIV infection in the same way as other drug injectors. Prostitutes who do not inject may also be at increased risk because of their sexual contacts – either with clients or non-paying partners.

The point I am making here is that rather than pathologising prostitutes' *bodies* (as happened in the earlier invocation of prostitution as a problem of public sexual health), in late-twentieth-century Britain it is prostitutes' *behaviour* that has been increasingly scrutinised as different and threatening at the same time as pathologised. The construction of prostitution as a threat to public sexual health has been rejuvenated by the depiction of prostitutes as engaged in high-risk behaviour and as being the 'bridge' for HIV/AIDS transmission into the wider population. So within the context of the world-wide AIDS pandemic, prostitutes in Britain have been represented as being unlike other women because they pose a threat to heterosexual society 'symbolised in the "innocent victims" – the clients' wives, girlfriends and children' (McKeganey and Barnard, 1996, p. 58).

The importance of the recasting of the threat to public sexual health that prostitutes are said to pose in terms of high-risk behaviour cannot be underestimated for it has created new types of intervention into prostitutes' lives. These are aimed at educating high-risk groups about their high-risk behaviours and supporting those individuals in their attempt to alter such behaviours. In practice this has meant the growth of multi-agency 'outreach' projects whose aims include the dissemination of information and the provision of practical support for prostitute women, that is the provision of sexual health information and condoms, the establishment of sexual health clinics specifically for prostitute women and so on. By 1997 most of the major British cities had at least one such project, including the SAFE Project in Birmingham, the Praed Street Project in London, the Health Shop and POW! (Prostitute Outreach Workers) projects in Nottingham, the Sheffield AIDS Education Project, the Cardiff Outreach Project, the Wandsworth Female Sex Workers Project, the Women's Health in Prostitution Project (WHIP) in Leicester, Manchester Action on Street Health (MASH) and the SCOT-PEP and Centenary Project in Edinburgh. In most cases the projects are funded by the district health authorities (see Ashford, 1995).

Whilst the 'outreach' projects can be broadly (and somewhat super-ficially) categorised as 'welfarist' in their approach in that they seek to provide support for the well-being of prostitute women, underpinning them is the revival of the construction of prostitutes as sexually contaminated, as noted above. Overs asserts that such projects have at their base the perceived threat that prostitution poses to the general population:

> The funds are not directed at sex workers for their own sake, but because they are viewed as people particularly likely to infect others.... It is important not to misunderstand the nature of this benevolence – it has nothing to do with women's health.... There has been no change in policies or motivation, but rather these are pragmatic moves to protect the clients (Overs, 1994, p. 114).

Thus whilst the sexual health projects may appear to be benign in that they provide women with both sexual health information and medical support, as Cohen (1996) has argued, interventions that appear to be welfare based (rather than 'punitive') and less formal often permit greater, more inclusive and less accountable intrusion into the lives of individuals.

CONCLUSION

Prostitution is seen as constituting two particular problems: a problem of public nuisance and a problem of public sexual health. Hence British prostitutes are constructed as the objects of both criminal justice (through arrest, conviction and the imposition of fines) and sexual and public health intervention (educating them in terms of their high-risk behaviour). The conditions that make these interventions possible are structured and underpinned by the fact that Britain's current legal framework constitutes prostitute women as unlike other women by virtue of their supposedly different sexual values and morals and by the assumed threat that prostitutes' bodies and lifestyle pose to the general populace.

Chapter 2 carries forward the theme of prostitutes' difference (and similarity) by examining the manner in which prostitution is treated in academic discourse and the way that prostitutes are constituted as either unlike or like non-prostitute women.

3 Ways of Talking about Prostitutes and Prostitution

This chapter examines the academic discourse on prostitutes and prostitution with a view to understanding how it is that various explanations make the type of sense about women's involvement in prostitution that they do, and as a means of setting the scene for the empirical investigation that follows in Part II. It deconstructs existing explanations in order to reveal the conceptual demarcations drawn and not drawn that form the basis upon which particular types of question can be asked about prostitutes and specific answers can be given.

As Foucault has argued, discourse is characterised by a patterned dispersion. In other words it is the 'gaps, intertwined with one another, [the] interplays of differences, distances, substitutions and transformations' that define a discourse (Foucault 1972, p. 37). In this respect, research on prostitutes forms a chain of interlinked ideas, notions and arguments, constituted within the gaps and spaces created by other research on prostitutes and prostitution. This is not to argue that the academic discourse on prostitutes has followed a linear progression from ideas and explanations that only partially contained the truth to increasingly sophisticated explanations that will eventually lead us to enlightenment and a 'true' understanding of women's involvement in prostitution. Rather it is simply to assert that the discourses examined in this chapter are interlinked, and both open new points that allows new questions to be asked and answered, and close the theoretical space to pursue different analyses.

Bedevilling the academic discourse on prostitutes and prostitution has been a central and fundamental question: in what ways are prostitute women like or unlike other women? To date there have been four ways in which the question of difference (or similarity) has been addressed. As will be demonstrated in the course of this chapter, prostitutes have been constituted as though they are:

1. essentially biologically and/or psychologically different, and hence neither the same as nor similar to non-prostitute women (Lombroso and Ferrero, 1895; S. and E. Glueck, 1934);
2. different from non-prostitute women – a difference inherent in the unique social subculture and milieu that prostitutes inhabit (Wilkinson, 1955) or the poverty that prostitutes experience (Benjamin and Masters, 1964; Finnegan, 1979; McLeod, 1982) – and yet the same as non-prostitute women – a similarity structured by the relationship between mainstream normal society and the subculture within which prostitutes exist (Wilkinson, 1955);
3. the same as non-prostitute women, because prostitution is like any other job (McLeod, 1982);
4. in some respects different from non-prostitute women – for example in terms of the social consequences of engagement in prostitution – but in other respects similar to non-prostitute women – for example in terms of being 'typical' women a society structured by particular sets of economic or gender relations (McLeod, 1982; Hoigard and Finstad, 1992).

Each of the above constructions of prostitutes is constituted within the spaces created by other theories, and thus the questions that can be asked about women's involvement in prostitution and the explanations that can be provided have become increasingly intricate and detailed. For example, conceiving of prostitutes as different from other women because they inhabit a criminal subculture constitutes a gap that makes questions and explanations about the *specificity* of the different social processes experienced by prostitute women somewhat more complex. It is the body of sociological and criminological literature on prostitutes, moreover, that provides the basis for this book's assumption that prostitutes are indeed both different from and the same as non-prostitute women. Indeed the women discussed later in this book were interviewed with the purpose of exploring how they made sense of the contradiction that has been the focal point of academic work on prostitution, that is, their being both different from and similar to other women.

This chapter organises the discourse on prostitutes and prostitution in terms of 'ideal types' of explanation (see Weber, 1949). The literature is organised into four dominant explanatory models: the pathological model, the social dislocation and criminal subculture model, the economic position and poverty model and the gender and male violence model.

THE PATHOLOGICAL EXPLANATORY MODEL

In the ideal-type pathological explanatory model, the questions 'what causes a woman to become a prostitute?' and 'what does it mean to be a prostitute?' are fused together in such a way that the cause of a woman's involvement in prostitution is coterminous with what being a prostitute means. In other words, the logic of such explanations is that some type of individual abnormality or pathology causes women to become prostitutes, and that being a prostitute means to be a woman possessed of an individual pathology. The pathological explanatory model transforms women involved in prostitution into 'prostitutes' who are utterly separate and distinct from 'ordinary women'.[1]

Perhaps the most explicit and well-known version of this explanation is that put forward by Lombroso and Ferrero in *The Female Offender* (1895). In this study Lombroso and Ferrero adopted the methodology and framework for analysis that Lombroso had already developed when examining male criminals. Specifically, *The Female Offender* was part of Lombroso's aim to devise 'a new strategic method of proceeding against crime, based upon a study of its aetiology and nature'. Lombroso was one of a group of social thinkers who employed positivist thinking (a form of thinking where categories of individuals such as criminals or prostitutes are assumed to be identifiable by inherent characteristics rather than the specific activities in which they engage) and inductive methods (the accumulation of evidence to confirm a theory), meticulously carried out and recorded, in the search for the 'natural' and 'organic' causes of criminality. He had modified his atavistic theory of crime, which stressed that criminality was a result of 'regressive' evolution, to a theory of degeneracy as *one* of the causes of criminality. Moreover by 1895 Lombroso had begun to claim that certain social factors were of great importance in determining criminality. He considered that education, or the lack thereof, was not a significant factor in an individual's criminality whereas density of population, immigration and poverty were (Lombroso, 1968, pp. 146–50).

In *The Female Offender* Lombroso and Ferrero studied 'normal women', the females of various animal species and prostitutes, and argued that prostitution is the feminine equivalent of criminality in men. They asserted that in the lower species, females are superior in intelligence, strength and longevity, whereas in the higher species (such as humans) males surpass them. For Lombroso and Ferrero the differences that exist between males and females result from the development and

evolutionary changes males undergo as a result of struggling for possession of females. At the same time, females in general have a tendency
towards perpetuation rather than development because their maternal
functions produce a 'retardation' of evolution. So, for instance, preg-
nancy and motherhood neutralise a woman's moral and physical inferi-
ority, and aid the development of 'lofty sentiments, complete altruism
and far-sighted intelligence' (Lombroso and Ferrero, (1895).

Lombroso and Ferrero examined the weight, height, brain size, nerv-
ous system, hair, senses, physiogamy and intellectual and moral characteristics of so-called normal women and concluded that these features
vary less among women than among 'normal' men. They also claimed
that there are fewer cases of monstrosity, degeneracy, epilepsy and
insanity among 'normal' women than 'normal' men (each of these being
a cause of criminal behaviour in men). However, although they asserted
that women commit fewer crimes than men and that women who do
commit crimes possess fewer 'degenerative' qualities than men, after a
similar examination of prostitutes they claimed that prostitutes exhibit
more degenerative qualities and a greater number of criminal characteristics than ordinary female offenders, and certainly more than 'normal'
women. Hence they argued that prostitution is the feminine equivalent
of criminality in men:

> We have seen, and shall see more and more, how the physical and
> moral characteristics of the delinquent belong equally to the prosti-
> tute, and how great the sympathy is between the two classes. Both
> phenomena spring from idleness, misery and especially alcoholism.
> Both are connected likewise, with certain organic and hereditary tend-
> encies. (Lombroso, 1968, p. 186)

They concluded by claiming that 'Prostitution largely takes the place of
crime for women, thus explaining why women seem less criminal than
men, and also giving a probable reason why women's criminality is
greatest in old age, when prostitution no longer offers a profession'
(ibid., p. 192).

In summary, Lombroso and Ferrero explained women's involvement
in prostitution by claiming that prostitutes are individual women possessed of a pathological nature resulting from evolutionary degeneracy
and the influence of various social factors, such as population density
and poverty.

The pathological explanatory model was further developed by S. and
E. Glueck in their study *Five Hundred Delinquent Women* (1934). They

argued that prostitutes are poor women who are also psychologically pathological:

> They were born and bred in households in which poverty or near-poverty and its attendant evils and miseries were a common lot. Their fathers were inefficient, irregular workers who ... could hardly support their abnormally large families.... And the homes of many of the families were unattractive, crowded and set in unwholesome neighbourhoods, where children could hardly be happy or develop healthily (S. and E. Glueck, 1934, p. 299).

According to the Gluecks, prostitutes' psychological pathology derives from their economic and family backgrounds, and that 'more serious than the physical milieu in which these girls were raised was the unfortunate psychologic atmosphere of their homes' (ibid., p. 299). In the summary of their empirical findings they asserted that prostitutes come from 'broken homes', that their parents are 'of low mentality', that the moral standards in their homes are 'low'; that conflict abounds, and that disciplinary practices are 'unintelligent'. This 'unfortunate psychologic atmosphere' created women 'burdened with feeblemindedness, psychopathic personality and marked instability [who] find it difficult to survive by legitimate means' (ibid.) Such 'instability' results in 'illicit sexual indulgence' (ibid., p. 300). The Gluecks used as evidence of their argument the observation that over half of their sample engaged in some form of prostitution.

But as stated above, the Gluecks did not dismiss economic factors in their explanation of why women engage in prostitution. Indeed a little later in their text they gave the same weight to economic factors as they did to psychological factors: 'In the long run, a fundamental attack upon the problems of antisociality depends ... on the raising of the status of the economically underprivileged ... it is clearly the profit-making motive that is involved in its [that is, prostitution's] promotion (ibid., p. 309).

In their final analysis the Gluecks asserted that psychological problems and economic status factors alone compel women to enter prostitution because possession of a psychological abnormality reduces women's 'inhibitions' and 'constraints', so that when such women experience poverty it is likely that they will engage in prostitution.

Thirty years later Benjamin and Masters (1964) presented a slightly different construction of prostitutes as individually abnormal women. They constructed two categories of prostitute: 'voluntary prostitutes' and 'compulsive prostitutes'. Voluntary prostitutes are women who 'may be said to have voluntarily entered into the life on a more or less rational basis and mainly as a result of free choice' because of the women's need to provide for themselves and any dependents they may have. Compulsive prostitutes are women who 'engage in prostitution mainly because they are compelled to do so by their own psycho-neurotic needs' (ibid., p. 91), which result from a deep trauma in early life. Hence Benjamin and Masters discuss the *psychopathology* of the economic exchange between compulsive prostitutes and punters. They comment that such an exchange has profound symbolic and neurotic meaning and fulfils the masochistic, self-degrading needs of the women that emanate from the abuse and trauma they suffered early in their childhoods (ibid., pp. 280–2). The authors stress that the categories voluntary prostitutes and compulsive prostitutes are ideal types and that most prostitutes are located along a continuum between these two extremes.

In summary, Benjamin and Masters deploy a dual explanation for women's engagement in prostitution. Compulsive prostitutes possess an individual psychological abnormality that predisposes them to involvement in prostitution, whilst voluntary prostitutes engage in prostitution because of the poverty they have experienced and the social environment in which they grew up.

Discussion

The pathological explanatory model is one of the less complex links in the chain of explanations for women's engagement in prostitution, but one which has some useful theoretical openings and spaces. Indeed contained within the pathological explanations are many of the elements of a more sophisticated and contemporary understanding of prostitution.[2]

Underpinning the texts by Lombroso and Ferrero (1895), S. and E. Glueck (1934) and Benjamin and Masters (1964) is a simple binary differentiation between prostitutes and non-prostitute women, so that, by definition, to be a prostitute is not to be an ordinary woman. This differentiation is framed by the conceptual conflation in all three texts of the act of selling sex (that is, prostituting) and prostitutes, whereby the selling of sex is transposed into a visible behaviourial manifestation of a particular category of individuals (prostitutes) who are pathological. As a result prostituting and, by extension, prostitutes, are denuded of their sociality. The theoretical space is ultimately closed to questions and explanations that are any more intricate than 'what is inherently wrong with prostitutes that they are not like other, ordinary, non-prostitute women?' Hence Lombroso and Ferrero quantified the physical characteristics of degeneracy, and the Gluecks and Benjamin and Masters proposed different types of psychological pathology as primary causes of women's engagement in prostitution. Moreover the conceptual conflation of prostitutes and the act of selling sex closed the space for all of them to ask questions about the social context within which prostitute women operate. Benjamin and Masters constructed prostitution as merely the various activities of prostitutes. Lombroso and Ferrero and the Gluecks referred to prostitution as specific instances of criminal behaviour.

To be fair, all three studies were framed by a more general assumption that human behaviour is essentially constrained and free will is illusory (see Matza, 1969, p. 6). At the time when Lombroso and Ferrero produced their text (1895), positivism and the doctrine of determinism were directly challenging the dominance of strict legalism and judicial orthodoxy, which depicted criminality as a result of individual hedonism (Beccaria, 1996). By the time the Gluecks (1934) and Benjamin and Masters (1964) produced their texts, positivism had reached its height. Hence it is unsurprising that within these texts there is a conceptual differentiation between prostitutes and 'ordinary' women. Moreover, because the doctrine of determinism also privileges individual pathology it is unsurprising that there is a denial of the sociality of prostitutes, prostituting and prostitution in these texts.

As stated above, contained in the pathological explanations are many of the elements of a complex and contemporary understanding of women's involvement in prostitution. Specifically, each text hints at other possible constructions, questions and explanations that have been picked up and developed by other authors and have often led to the construction of very different objects of knowledge and innovative theoretical explanations of women's engagement in prostitution.

Firstly, none of the pathological explanations examined here deny that social factors influence women's decision to engage in prostitution. Importantly, all three texts cite poverty as a crucial factor in this respect. Lombroso and Ferrero explicitly asserted that age accounts for an increase in female criminality later in life when prostitution can no longer provide women with the money to survive, an assertion that arises from the authors' implicit assumption that women engage in prostitution for money. Similarly the Gluecks' gave equal explanatory weight to economic underprivilege as they did to psychological pathology. They represented prostitutes as different from other women because they are both psychologically abnormal women and poor women, and traced their respondents' 'problems' back to the economically deprived conditions in which they were raised. Benjamin and Masters went even further in their explanation by invoking a notion of 'process' and 'agency', claiming that poor women make a rational economic choice in becoming prostitutes.

The understanding of prostitutes as poor women did not displace the conceptual differentiation between prostitutes and other women. Instead, one of the questions informing the three analyses was: why do all poor women not become prostitutes? This question opened the theoretical space for questions about the *social* differences between prostitutes and other women, which in turn created the conditions for an increasingly intricate body of knowledge about prostitutes. But as a result of the problematic essentialism (that is, 'a form of analysis in which social phenomena are understood not in terms of the specific conditions of their existence, but in terms of some presumed essence or interest' – Carrington 1993, p. xiv) that shaped the work of Lombroso and Ferrero and the Gluecks their explanations did not manage to break out of the construction of prostitutes as different and distinct from other (normal) women, because in these texts prostitutes are primarily abnormal women. In each theory both prostitutes and normal woman are ascribed biologically fixed and immutable characteristics ('essences') such as the social role of motherhood (Lombroso and Ferrero, 1895) and sexual chastity (S. and E. Glueck, 1934). Hence prostitutes' failure to conform to prescribed behaviours, according to the logic of these two explanations, must be evidence of their difference and their pathology. Benjamin and Masters were prevented from pursuing further analysis by their assertion that voluntary prostitutes are merely analytical ideals. And so, even when the hard determinism in Lombroso and Ferrero's and the Gluecks' explanations was not adopted, Benjamin and Masters could only ask questions and produce an analysis of prostitution that elaborated the specific determinants conditioning the differences between prostitutes and other women.

In summary, pathological explanations of women's involvement in prostitution are of limited usefulness because the theoretical space created within such explanations forecloses the possibility of pursuing an analysis of prostitutes as similar to other women and as social actors located within specific contexts. Nevertheless such explanations do hint at other constructions and theoretical possibilities, particularly questions about the *social* difference between prostitutes and other women.

Such questions have been picked up and explored within the social dis-location and criminal subculture explanations, which are discussed in the next section.

THE SOCIAL DISLOCATION AND CRIMINAL SUBCULTURE EXPLANATORY MODEL[3]

The social dislocation and criminal subculture explanatory model focuses on women's relationship to, and position in, the wider society to explain their engagement in prostitution. Questions are asked about the extent to which women are segregated, or cut off, from legitimate or accept-able social relationships and institutions, and attention is focused on the degree to which they may have 'fallen through' what are perceived as normal, constraining institutions and relationships such as the family or work. In addressing what it means to be a prostitute, integration and engagement in illicit and often illegal relationships and institutions is stressed so that the degree of involvement in, for example, a criminal subculture, can be highlighted. In its ideal type, the social dislocation and criminal subculture explanatory narrative posits a 'hard' social determinism, whereby involvement in prostitution is seen as the result of subtle and complex social forces. Most importantly, the individual is conceptualised as 'committed to an ethical code which make his [*sic*] misdeeds mandatory' (Matza, 1969, p. 18). Thus, for example, prosti-tute women are seen as belonging to and committed to a normative sys-tem that makes their engagement in prostitution virtually inevitable.

In the early 1950s the British Social Biology Council commissioned research into 'the individual and general problems of prostitution' (Wilkinson, 1955, p. xi). The result was Wilkinson's *Women of the Streets* (1955), which attempted to incorporate the perspective of pros-titutes. Underpinning Wilkinson's analysis is the assumption that in some respects prostitutes are different from non-prostitute women but in other respects they are the same. They are women who are both within and without normal society. This can be seen in Wilkinson's construc-tion of prostitutes as (1) social satellites and (2) members of an outcast, deviant subculture.

Wilkinson summarised the backgrounds of the women she inter-viewed as follows:[4]

After an early life in which, one after another, the social institutions fail her, a girl drifts to London, where she finds eventually that she means even less than she did at home in her own town. She may work and eventually find herself mixing with people who belong to a society which both suggests and sanctions prostitution. She is in a city where the value of the individual is at its lowest, and she has no ties of affection with her family (Wilkinson, 1955, p. 107).

According to Wilkinson, after arriving in London in their late teens or early twenties, and after working in legitimate jobs for some time, there is a pause in the future prostitute women's lives that she describes as being in a 'drifting, disorganised state'. Eventually they 'start working in milk bars and cafes, which are often the last stages before prostitution'. In these locations, and during their drifting state, women may hear of prostitution through friends, or may even work with women who are prostitutes, and 'eventually accept the suggestion of some friend that they should go out with her' (ibid.)

So for Wilkinson the process of entering prostitution can be divided into three consecutive stages. First, at some point in the woman's life the various social institutions within which she is located 'fail' her. Second, the woman is dislocated from 'normal' society, which occasions a 'drifting and disorganised' state. Third, whilst drifting the woman is introduced to prostitution. Wilkinson stresses that this 'is a slow process and the girl is used to the idea by the time she accepts it' (ibid., p. 108).

Wilkinson's narrative is a long description of the various social processes that women who become prostitutes go through and the environments they inhabit, and how those processes and environments 'guide' and 'channel' them into prostitution. By examining those processes the reader can uncover Wilkinson's construction of prostitutes as social satellites. She characterises the 'pre-prostitute', disorganised, drifting stage as one in which the woman stands in a position of 'irrelation' to normal society. She is not hooked into the ordinary institutions of everyday life such as family and motherhood. She experiences social rootlessness insofar as she has 'slipped through and round situations in which others would have been stable' (ibid., p. 107).

The concept of social rootlessness is premised on Wilkinson's assumption that all members of society are forever searching for and developing ways of belonging to or of being anchored into society: 'We are all held into a pattern of reasonably predictable behaviour from our earliest years. . . . Our bondage is not unwelcome, and we seek to reinforce it by self-imposed discipline, membership of groups and organisations, so that we shall never "not belong"'. Furthermore, 'This belonging to groups, from the family outwards, is a socially conditioned state, for it seems that fundamentally we each exist in personal isolation which we are at pains to destroy' (ibid.).

Hence Wilkinson constitutes prostitutes as social satellites – women who are extruded, disengaged and disconnected from society. They are not located within the restraining and constraining relationships and institutions that lock non-prostitute women into 'legitimate' society and into regular and accepted actions and ways of behaving. Women who become prostitutes live outside mainstream society. In this respect Wilkinson constructs prostitutes as different from non-prostitute women by virtue of their previous lack of social embeddedness and their social disorganisation.

Wilkinson asserts that the disorganised drifting and disconnection from society experienced by prostitutes is an outward manifestation of a 'disorganised personality'; a personality that is 'unable to benefit from the social organisation of life' (ibid., p. 108). Whilst she does not argue that engagement in prostitution has a psychopathological basis, she does state in many places that prostitutes do have psychopathological problems – for example she describes the prostitute and punter relationship as fulfilling a woman's pathological 'need to debase the male or father figure' (ibid., p. 85). She suggests that the 'disorganised personality' of prostitutes is a result of the 'social deficiencies' they may have experienced in their early years, or of sudden occurrences such as the birth of an illegitimate child or a marriage breakdown that may have 'dislodged' them later in life:

> The situation may be summed up as one where recurrent failures within social institutions, which she anticipated would remain constant have produced in a girl feelings of unimportance and apathy, render her vulnerable to people and opportunities promising some compensation (ibid., p. 245).

And thus 'It seemed to me that the personality which must result from the processes causing this state of social irrelation in a woman would be sufficient to account for her accepting the suggestion of the situation and becoming a prostitute' (ibid., p. 108).

To recapitulate, women who become prostitutes experience a state of drifting and disconnection from society; a social rootlessness that is consequent on various social deficiencies, so that involvement in prostitution offers them 'compensation'. Hence there is no one 'cause' of prostitution in Wilkinson's analysis. She claims there are three possible contributory factors: (1) experiences that cause a breakdown in the woman's relation to society, (2) 'immediate' or precipitating causes of engagement in prostitution such as the need for money (although she also claims that a breakdown in a woman's social life and the need for money will only lead to prostitution if the woman has 'a particular personality and is in a particular situation' – ibid., p. 84) and (3) the personality of the individual. However,

> There is a danger in this over-simplification of factors which are no more than phases of a dialectical process, and the analysis of these factors is submitted in the belief that any factor alone is insignificant and none can be isolated with the comment: 'This is the cause'. The cause is past experience, plus present situation, plus personal interpretation of them both (ibid., p. 243).

Thus Wilkinson feels able to explain why some women with similar experiences (of social deficiencies) do not engage in prostitution while others do. She does not contend that involvement in prostitution is simply the result of this factor or that, but rather the result of a complex interplay between past and present environments and the woman's personality, attitudes and motivations.

Wilkinson's representation of what being a prostitute means facilitates an examination of her construction of prostitutes as members of a social outcast group. Once a woman engages in prostitution a process of stabilisation occurs. The woman finds a sense of embeddedness and belonging that was previously unachievable:

> Once a girl has become a professional prostitute, one perceives the phenomenon of *stabilisation*. . . . She becomes a *member of that society* of which she has been on the fringe in her state of instability. . . . Local, geographically *cohesive groups* may form in this society, but transcending this is the fact that the woman's status is now defined, she *belongs* to the group of prostitutes and is able to talk about 'us'. (ibid., pp. 108–9, emphasis added).

The social state of drifting and the psychological sense of lack of belonging are resolved, but their resolution has only been made possible by joining a 'restraining' and 'constraining' social group that 'has its own class structure with varying standards of behaviour', and whose 'basic unit is often the family, consisting of the prostitute, the ponce and his, her or their children . . . [a] spontaneous gathering together of people who find that they like to live together in a certain way' (ibid., p. 110).

In short, prostitutes stop drifting and become prostitutes because they become embedded in a new (and deviant) subculture.

Wilkinson's explanation represents a normalisation argument. The implication of her analysis is that in joining the 'prostitute society', women impose on themselves a 'discipline and social membership' (ibid., p. 107). Prostitutes become 'normal', if deviant, members of society in that they are hooked into specific and deviant social institutions and structures. Therefore, for Wilkinson prostitutes are the same as non-prostitute women in that they are 'normal social actors' embedded in distinct social networks, but different from other women in that the social networks to which prostitutes belong are criminal and deviant.

Having argued that 'prostitute society' is a subculture, Wilkinson presents this as an outcast social grouping in two senses. First, the members of the prostitution subculture have rejected 'normal' society and its values, beliefs and norms. Wilkinson often refers to women involved in prostitution as having renounced the standards of behaviour in normal society and chosen a different way of life. For example, 'She [the prostitute] has openly renounced standards acceptable to ordinary society, she has acquired a profession where she is needed ... and most important of all, where she finds herself in the company of people who are like herself in personality and outlook (ibid., pp. 108–9). Indeed Wilkinson argues that the ponce–prostitute relationship is a freely chosen, significant and almost necessary relationship in a society of people that are 'participat[ing] in a new sort of social life' (ibid., p. 111).

The second sense in which Wilkinson presents prostitutes as outcasts is that there is a difference between prostitutes and the social group to which they belong and 'normal society'. Throughout her narrative she asserts that behaviour that is unacceptable to 'normal' members of society (for example violence by ponces) is acceptable to prostitutes:

> The stories of the violence with which the ponce treats the prostitute are not all exaggerated, but the interpretations of its significance are often quite wrong. We are dealing with a class of people whose behaviour standards are utterly different from our own.... A beating-up is of far less significance to the girl herself than others who hear about it imagine (ibid., p. 122).

The implication of this is that prostitutes are different from other women because fundamentally similar events, relationships and circumstances take on different meanings when experienced by prostitutes. Thus in Wilkinson's view, physical violence by a boyfriend, which would be understood as violent abuse by 'ordinary' women, is simply not significant or even particularly out of the ordinary for prostitutes. This is a very important conceptual idea and is examined in greater detail in the discussion that follows.

Other examples of Wilkinson's construction of prostitutes as outcasts who are different from other individuals are her descriptions of the banality with which criminality and 'anti-sociality' are treated in 'prostitute society', the 'disinclination [of prostitutes] to apply themselves to work or to personal organisation', and the way in which prostitutes treat each other with 'kindness, generosity and hospitality' but also display 'intolerance, lack of loyalty and even deliberate betrayal' (ibid., pp. 130–1).

Having discussed Wilkinson's representation of prostitutes as different from other women by virtue of their social rootlessness prior to their involvement in prostitution and their subcultural location afterwards, it is necessary to note that, contradictorily, she also presents them as being the same as other women. As noted above, the assumption that all individuals are 'forever searching for ways of belonging' permitted her to invoke a normalising argument whereby prostitutes are normal social actors embedded in deviant social networks.

But, prostitutes are also depicted as the same as other women because they inhabit a subculture that exists in tandem with 'normal society'. For Wilkinson the prostitute subculture is not different (in the sense of radically distinct and separate) from normal society, but merely a refraction from normal society. This conceptualisation of the subcultural position of prostitutes is not unique to Wilkinson. Many of the explanations of deviance that have highlighted the subcultural position of individuals have represented deviant subcultures as existing either *in opposition to* mainstream culture, whereby the values and norms that guide individuals' behaviour and actions are a reaction against mainstream culture, or *in tandem with* mainstream culture, whereby the subcultural norms and values are a distorted mirror-image of mainstream norms and values (see Muncie *et al.*, 1996, pp. 33–7). But in both conceptions the subculture is not distinct or separate from mainstream culture; rather the subculture exists in a close relationship with mainstream society as both reacting and refracting subcultures rely utterly on mainstream society for their existence.

In constructing prostitute society as a refraction from mainstream culture, Wilkinson represents prostitutes as women guided by fundamentally similar norms and values as those which guide other women, although these norms and values are expressed in different ways.

Hence Wilkinson asserts that prostitutes, like non-prostitute women, enmesh themselves in familial relationships. For prostitutes, however, these 'familial' relationships only '*mirror* normal love relationships' (ibid., p. 110, emphasis added) because while they are basically the same they are also a distortion of them in that they are characterised by 'intense emotion' and 'violence' (ibid., p. 112). Moreover prostitutes, like other women, form friendships and allegiances, but again these friendships are only refracted expressions of 'ordinary' friendships because prostitutes often steal from one another, and they 'are unable to sustain the same attitude towards, or relationship with, people for long' (ibid., p. 133).

Discussion

The social dislocation and criminal subculture explanatory model provides a more complex explanation of women's involvement in prostitution, and some of the possibilities inherent in the pathological explanations are picked up and developed.

Underlying Wilkinson's (1955) text is the assumption that in some respects prostitutes are different from non-prostitute women but in other respects, they are the same. For Wilkinson the difference between prostitutes and other women does not reside primarily or even necessarily in prostitutes' pathology, and the similarity between prostitutes and other women is invoked by the notion of a refracted, deviant subculture.

Wilkinson's assumption that the difference between prostitutes and other women is inherently social is underpinned by the demarcation line she draws between prostitutes as a group of individuals and prostitution as a social location. She makes frequent reference to 'the prostitution society' and the 'prostitution counter-culture'. Moreover she provides a detailed description of the variety of activities, locations and relationships encompassed by the term prostitution. The assumption that there is social difference between prostitutes and other women and Wilkinson's differentiation between prostitutes and prostitution allow questions other than those that framed the explanations offered by Lombroso and Ferrero (1895), S. and E. Glueck (1934) and Benjamin and Masters (1964). Namely, instead of asking 'what is the abnormality that causes prostitutes to be different from other women?' Wilkinson was able to investigate the social conditions that lead some women (prostitutes) to become different from other women (non-prostitute women). Hence she developed the notions of 'rootlessness', 'drifting disorganisation' and ultimately, 'belongingness' to a deviant subculture.

Although Wilkinson pursues a more intricate (and more sociological) set of questions about women's engagement in prostitution, she is nevertheless reluctant to shed all notions of pathology. The invocation of the notion of psychological pathology in what is otherwise a sociological analysis of prostitution, was partly influenced by Wilkinson's totalising inscription of 'difference', which resulted in her failure to provide a fully social analysis of prostitution. As demonstrated above, Wilkinson constructed prostitutes as social outcasts. Clearly at one level this cannot be doubted, for prostitute women are perceived to be outside normal society because they engage in socially unacceptable and illegal activities that make them subject to criminal process. However, Wilkinson's construction implies much more than this. Her prostitutes stand both within and without society. They operate with values that are a refraction from mainstream 'normal' societal values, and hence their relationships are mirror-images of 'normal relationships' (Wilkinson, 1955, p. 112). Although this conception of difference structures a concomitant conception of similarity between prostitutes and other women, ultimately prostitutes are presented as totally different from other women in *all* aspects of their lives. This construction of difference is combined in Wilkinson's text with the removal of the demarcation line she drew earlier between prostitutes and prostitution: prostitute women became synonymous with their subcultural location.

A difficult question that arose for Wilkinson was, why don't all women who undergo the process of 'dislocation' and enmesh themselves within deviant subcultures engage in prostitution? Wilkinson argues that the social process of 'rootlessness' only leads to prostitution if women have a 'particular personality', that is, a 'disorganised personality' (ibid., pp. 84–5). Thus a notion of psychological pathology is introduced into Wilkinson's otherwise social explanation (in any case the linking of criminality with psychological pathology is a dominant theme in studies that examined deviant behaviour at the time that Wilkinson was writing – see Muncie *et al.*, 1996).

One of the more important consequences of Wilkinson's conception of the difference between prostitutes and other women is that little theoretical space is left for others to pursue more elaborate and complex questions about the similarities between prostitutes and other women. Nevertheless her analysis does offer some potentially promising theoretical gaps. Of particular importance is her assumption that the differences that exist between prostitutes and other women are primarily social. This line is maintained throughout her analysis, for failure to do so would have prevented an examination of the unique and socially specific conditions of existence for prostitutes. As noted above, this assumption provokes questions about the specificity of the social processes experienced by prostitute women, which in turn provokes an examination of the specific sets of practices and relationships in which prostitutes are located. Thus an analysis that places prostitute women in their culturally and historically specific social context is enabled.

A second promising theoretical space is opened up by the demarcation line that Wilkinson draws between different types of prostitute, although the full potential of this is not fully explored in her text because it is not seen as an object of further analysis. Wilkinson makes repeated reference to 'professional prostitutes' and 'isolated prostitutes' – the difference being whether or not the women are located in particular sets of activities and relationships. By differentiating between types of prostitute a theoretical space is created for more complex questions, for such a differentiation permits an analysis not only of women's engagement in prostitution as a social institution, but also of different types of prostitutions, such as 'bread and butter trade', 'high-class work' and 'drug-related work'.

This book focuses only on one of these types of prostitution – 'bread and butter' prostitution – but it is framed by the assumption that the specific conditions of existence for involvement in prostitution that are outlined in Chapters 4 and 5 below only apply to those women interviewed and only to the specific type of prostitution they are engaged in.

The third promising theoretical space is opened by the line Wilkinson draws between prostitutes and prostitution (although as noted above, the differentiation between prostitutes and prostitution was eventually removed by Wilkinson). Wilkinson addresses separately the social conditions that influence women's involvement in prostitution and their personal interpretations of those conditions, although she acknowledges her inability to develop this part of her analysis. For example she made the following comment about her chosen method of case history: 'it does not show the way the women themselves saw the experiences, and it is this, not the objective reality of the situation, which influences their behaviour (ibid., p. 245).

The space that was opened by Wilkinson at this point is very important for it provokes the broad question of how prostitutes themselves can make sense of their engagement in prostitution, and it creates a theoretical gap in which the examination of that 'sense' can be constructed as being fundamentally interlinked with but not reducible to either the social processes experienced by the women or the sets of relationships, practices and activities that they engage in as prostitutes. Moreover it opens a space to examine women's identity as prostitutes, which is the subject of Chapter 5.

In a related fashion, Wilkinson's assertion that prostitutes see violence differently from other women raises an interesting set of questions that are also examined in Chapter 5. To recapitulate, Wilkinson claims that prostitutes are often beaten by their ponces, but the way in which they understand such events is not the same as the way in which ordinary members of society understand them: for prostitutes the experience of physical abuse is banal, ordinary and to some extent expected (ibid., p. 122). This argument allows an examination of (1) the social effects of engagement in very specific prostitution-related relationships, (2) the meanings that individual prostitute women ascribe to their experience of victimisation and (3) the conditions in which those meanings are made possible.

A final promising theoretical gap is opened by Wilkinson's conception of prostitutes as women existing, contradictorily, both within and without mainstream society. This provokes a very complex set of questions. First, what contradictions do prostitute women experience as a result of their engagement in prostitution? Second, how do prostitute women negotiate their contradictory experiences? Third, how do prostitute women make sense of the contradictions they experience?

The link in the chain of ideas about women's involvement in prostitution that social dislocation and criminal subculture explanations explored (as exemplified by Wilkinson) was a complex development in the story of prostitutes as told by academics. In addition to pursuing a more social analysis, the social dislocation and criminal subculture explanations questioned (1) the specific social conditions in which involvement in prostitution becomes possible, and (2) the different ways in which prostitutes make sense of their lives in prostitution. The economic position and poverty explanatory model picked up and explored the first of these two questions and it is that development which is outlined in the following section.

THE ECONOMIC POSITION AND POVERTY EXPLANATORY MODEL

The third major explanatory model of prostitutes and prostitution develops the type of social analysis that was seen in the social dislocation and criminal subculture model, but instead of privileging prostitutes' subcultural location, the specific *economic* conditions shaping women's engagement in prostitution are brought to the analytical foreground. In the model's ideal type, women are seen as inhabiting a social environment that offers few opportunities to earn an independent income. Engagement in prostitution is consequently seen as an economic decision because prostitution is assumed to be an economic activity. The economic position and poverty explanation rests on a 'soft' determinism emphasising the social processes that make prostitution a viable way of earning a living. Thus the question of what it means to be a prostitute is addressed by representing prostitutes as economic agents. And of course the economic position and poverty explanatory narrative has become so dominant in contemporary British and American analyses of prostitution that most writers assert that women engage in prostitution because of the constraints of the traditional labour market (see Scambler *et al.*, 1990; Romenesko and Miller, 1989; Taylor, 1991; Campbell, 1991; Roberts, 1992). It is a narrative that is taken to be self-evident. Economic explanations usually take one of two forms: either women are compelled and/or channelled into prostitution because there is no other way of earning money (see Finnegan, 1979); or they choose to engage in prostitution because the money that can be earned through prostitution is much greater than that to be had from the other economic options open to them (see Overall, 1992). In the texts that draw on this narrative, the main area of debate concerns the degree of choice a woman exercises in becoming a prostitute (see Jenkins and Swirsky, 1997).

The economic position and poverty explanatory model fundamentally shifted the chain of ideas on prostitution by developing the idea that prostitutes are similar to other poor women, which was hinted at in the pathological explanations. As a result these explanations have added a degree of sophistication both to the existing analysis of women's involvement in prostitution and to the questions that can now be asked.

Women Working (McLeod, 1982) was one of the first studies both to assume that prostitutes and other women are the same and to analyse what women gain from prostitution. McLeod argues that prostitutes are poor women grappling with the constraints imposed upon them in a 'capitalist society' in terms of the specific difficulties they encounter in their attempt to secure an adequate income (ibid., pp. 1–2). According to McLeod, 'Women's generally disadvantaged social position in the context of a capitalist society is central to their experience as prostitutes.... Women's entry into prostitution is characterised by an

act of resistance to the experience of relative poverty or the threat of it'
(ibid., p. 25).

McLeod argues that women's poverty is generated by (1) a labour
market that is structured on the notion of male breadwinning and
female dependency, which results in the exclusion of women from
effective economic participation, and (2) the segregation of domestic
and child care responsibilities from the labour market (ibid., pp. 14,
18). She contends that women with few marketable skills and little
training are especially disadvantaged by such a system. For McLeod,
women's poverty is created by a social and economic structure in which
they have limited access to means of supporting themselves and any
dependents they may have, independently of men. Therefore some
women, of necessity, need to find alternative means of earning a living.

McLeod asserts that prostitution has a 'pull' factor in terms of hold-
ing certain attractions for many poor women. Of particular importance
is the opportunity it presents to combine child care and domestic responsibilities with full-time work. Engagement in prostitution is attractive to many poor women because, in McLeod's view, prostitutes are
free to choose their work hours, can work from home, and can move in
and out of work as they desire. Moreover it provides women with com-
paratively higher incomes than could be obtained from legitimate work
(ibid., pp. 26–8). Hence for McLeod, involvement in prostitution is a
rational economic act, resisting women's relative poverty: 'Recruitment
to the ranks of prostitute is not appropriately characterised as only con-
cerning a small group of highly deviant women. It is secured by women's
relative power [to men] still being such that for large numbers, sex is
their most saleable commodity' (ibid., p. 1).

In this part of her analysis McLeod constructs prostitutes as 'economic entrepreneurs' – as workers who are the same as other women
and not different by virtue of being pathological, criminal or socially
dislocated individuals who are part of a deviant subculture. Prostituting
is a chosen economic activity. Prostitutes are women workers whose
choice of employment is conditioned by 'capitalist relations of power'
and who resist those relations by achieving a degree of economic independence. In this respect McLeod is attempting to capture the underlying influences structuring and channelling ordinary but poor women in
a certain direction (towards involvement in prostitution) while acknow-
ledging that women do have choices.

McLeod's analysis moves towards the separation of the material
conditions that make prostitution a viable way of earning a living from
individual motives and reasons for engaging in prostitution. Female

poverty – resulting from a 'capitalist economic structure' with deeply embedded 'sexist assumptions' (that is, the gender division of labour) – contextualises individual women's choices.

The rest of McLeod's text discusses how involvement in prostitution is the same as involvement in any other form of 'women's work', with the exception that it has different social consequences for the individuals involved. McLeod asserts that many features of a prostitute's life that seemingly distinguish her from other women, are in fact experiences that *all* women share. Indeed the sale of sex is not the sole preserve of prostitutes:

> Women working as prostitutes also point out quite often that married women can be in the situation of being prostitutes which demonstrates that women who are prostitutes appreciate the poverty of many women within marriage which results in their bartering sex for goods because they lack any other substantial income of their own (ibid., p. 28).

Similarly, McLeod argues that violence, either from ponces or punters, is primarily to do with women's position in society and the pervasiveness of 'male to female' violence in general, rather than being unique to prostitution (ibid., pp. 44–51). Emotional detachment during sexual encounters is explained as 'part of women's sexual repertoire in a day to day way' (ibid., p. 38). In order to demonstrate McLeod's construction of prostitutes as the same as other women, it is helpful to quote her at some length:

> prostitutes may manipulate their situation to a degree, but they are ensnared in general economic processes and pressures. Distinctive amongst these are *the disadvantages they share with other women.* Prostitution offers a way out of women's particularly low wages and the difficulty of combining domestic and child care responsibilities with securing an adequate income. But overall hangs the power of male domination. With seemingly few exceptions, prostitutes can work a lifetime but have little to show for it and often live in fear – *like their sisters engaged in other forms of domestic and waged labour –* because of the influence of the ideology of love, the endemic nature of male:female violence and the superior capital and organisational endowment of men (ibid., p. 58, emphasis added).

Hence in McLeod's view, being a prostitute means being the same as other women in two senses. First, many of the experiences prostitutes have (for example violence) are experienced by all women in contemporary society. Second, prostitutes' working experiences are like the experiences of all working women. There is nothing particularly distinctive about prostitutes themselves, their backgrounds or their working experiences in comparison with other working women in a society structured by capitalist relations and sexism.

In apparent contradiction, McLeod also depicts prostitutes as somehow different from other women. She makes frequent reference to 'women who are prostitutes' and 'women who are in the position or situation of being prostitutes'. The difference between prostitutes and other women inheres, according to McLeod, not in the individual women, their activities or subcultural location, but rather in a process of legal scapegoating that confers on prostitutes a criminal status (ibid., p. 40). This criminal status conditions an extraordinary vulnerability that leaves prostitutes (or more specifically, certain groups of prostitute women, such as street workers) open to legal harassment and discrimination and generates the need for protection by ponces: 'The control of prostitutes by ponces [occurs because of] their position as women – *exacerbated by their criminal status* (ibid., p. 44, emphasis added). Furthermore, 'the situation of prostitutes also provides a specific example of the way in which the law can discriminate against certain groups as bearing sole responsibility for various forms of "social blight"' (ibid., p. 2).

It should be noted that McLeod does not portray prostitutes as formally deviant (that is, engaged in law-breaking behaviour), although she acknowledges that prostitutes can be deviant. For her, prostitutes' criminality is unlike other forms of criminality in that it results from being scapegoated by the state in its attempt to protect public morality (ibid., p. 23).

The apparent contradiction between constructing prostitutes as both the same as and different from other women is resolved by McLeod's explanation of the legal discrimination experienced by prostitutes. She contends that the law and its enforcement enshrine sexist attitudes and are 'shaped by sexist assumptions regarding women's sexuality' (ibid., pp. 2, 91–119). She asserts that the 'scapegoating stigma ... defines prostitutes as responsible for prostitution', and (tautologically) the stigma itself is derived from a sexist ideology that affects all women (ibid., pp. 47, 116, 140, 146). Thus in the process of analysing the difference between prostitutes and other women, McLeod erases the apparent contradiction that arose earlier. For her, prostitutes are different from other women only inasmuch as they are more vulnerable to state-sanctioned oppressive practices that affect all women. In short, any differences there may be between prostitutes and other women are not differences in the specific conditions of existence within which prostitutes and other women are situated, but differences in degrees of vulnerability to male domination and legal stigmatisation.

Hence, and in summary, McLeod constitutes prostitutes as 'economic entrepreneurs' – as women struggling to earn a living. Women engage in prostitution to make money and resist the poverty imposed upon them in contemporary society.

Discussion

The economic position and poverty explanatory model in general, and McLeod's (1982) text in particular, have fundamentally shifted and added an additional level of complexity to the types of question that can be asked about prostitutes and prostitution and the types of answer that can be provided. McLeod begins her analysis with a quote from a woman called Sally: 'You want to get across that we are *ordinary* women' (ibid., p. 1). Rather than differentiating between prostitutes and non-prostitute women, McLeod insists that not only are prostitutes the same as other women, but that prostitution is the same as any other form of economic activity.

McLeod's proposition that prostitution is like any other form of women's work was certainly an innovative one in the early 1980s, for it displaced the construction of prostitution as an abnormal activity and replaced it with the construction of prostitutes as workers. McLeod combined this with a differentiation between the activity of selling sex and prostitution as a social institution, which enabled her to raise questions about how women's involvement in prostitution is structured by the same (or similar) social, material and ideological processes as those structuring and conditioning all women's economic participation. Consequently it provided her with the theoretical opening to ask: what is it about being involved in prostitution that is different from other 'women's work'?

However within McLeod's text the theoretical space is closed to an exploration of the differences between prostitutes and other women because of her emphasis on the similarities between prostitutes, other workers and other women workers. Firstly, McLeod's analysis rests on the assumption that prostitution is the same as all other economic activities in which women engage, except in terms of legal scapegoating. McLeod deploys a unitary, naturalised and common sense conception of 'work' as any form of paid labour, which limits the analysis to recognising only the dissimilar *effects* that involvement in prostitution has on prostitutes in comparison with legitimate workers. This closes the analysis to questions about the differences between the unique practices, activities and relationships of prostitution and ordinary, everyday work. Moreover, because McLeod explains these effects in terms of the 'oppressive regulation' of gender infractions enforced by the state, she has not separated the effects of being legally scapegoated as a prostitute from the effects of being identified as a 'bad woman' (that is, one who breaches sexist prescriptions about appropriate behaviour for women). Instead the consequences of being outside prescribed ideological modes of living are blended together as further examples of the oppressive regulation of women's sexuality in a society structured by capitalism.

Secondly, McLeod's analysis employs essentialism with regard to men and women. She depicts men and women as single categories corresponding to fixed, stable (and indeed pregiven) meanings, and as possessing invariable, immutable attributes (or 'essences'). However, unlike the 'essences' in the narratives by Lombroso and Ferrero (1895), S. and E. Glueck (1934) and Benjamin and Masters (1964), her 'essences' are not fixed in individuals' biological or psychological make-up, but rather in their shared social position and location. McLeod's 'essences' are the shared interests that she understands as the objective (and universal) effects upon the individual of being situated within a pregiven social structure. This makes it possible for her to explain the conditions of existence of prostitutes as epiphenomenal to the 'universal oppression of women' (that is, sexism), which similarly structures the experiences of all women. She therefore writes as though all men are afforded power over all the women with whom they come into contact – prostitutes or not. The construction of men as 'all-powerful' is notable in McLeod's discussion of prostitutes' ability to control their working environment. Although she accepts that prostitutes can exercise control over what they do or do not do when interacting with clients, she argues that men have 'cornered the market'. Prostitutes are controlled by 'men's spending power as clients', by men as ponces and by men as managers (ibid., pp. 42, 44–52).

The difficulty that arises from this essentialism is that it prohibits questions and theorising about (1) the differences between prostitutes and other women, (2) the differences between groups of prostitutes (for example black prostitutes, 'high-class call girls' and so on), and (3) how and under what conditions prostitutes can gain control over their own work and lives. But, in fairness, these questions were not part of her object of inquiry.

Whilst McLeod's text opens up the theoretical space to examine the objective social, economic and ideological effects of being formally and officially named a prostitute (constituted within her separation of the label 'prostitute' from individual prostitutes), her explanation can recognise only prostitutionalised women. For in her narrative prostitutes are defined in relation to the label 'prostitute'. Prostitutes are only ever women 'caught' within the scapegoating, stigmatising and criminalising processes that McLeod outlines, so prostitutes who are not processed within the criminal justice system because they engage in prostitution in a way that is not traditionally policed are occluded. Notwithstanding this, the circularity of her argument is not unique to her. It is a problem of labelling theory in general wherein the causes of a social act (prostituting) and the effects of that act (stigmatisation) are explained in terms of a social category (prostitutes).

A final problem with McLeod's analysis inheres in her construction of prostitutes as 'economic entrepreneurs'. There can be no doubt after nearly a century of empirical research that prostitute women are poor women. But McLeod presents prostitutes as 'economic entrepreneurs' because their very existence, and in particular their ability to earn an adequate income, continuously confronts and resists a social structure based on women's economic dependency and sexual passivity. To underpin this set of contentions it was necessary to separate the individual motives for selling sex and the material conditions in which engagement in prostitution becomes a viable option, but to depict this as an act of resistance *per se* required interpreting and transposing the individual reasons women gave for their involvement in prostitution into a political agenda set by the researcher. Thus the construction of prostitutes as 'economic entrepreneurs' translated the economic motives of prostitutes into politically subversive acts.

These difficulties with McLeod's text do not detract from the fundamental contribution it has made to the body of explanations for prostitutes and prostitution. Of particular importance is the demarcation between the activity of selling sex and prostitution – for example McLeod asserts that 'prostitution exists in tandem with marriage' and argues that it is necessary to examine '*entry* into prostitution' (ibid., pp. 25, 28). She, also draws parallels between prostitution and 'work', which provokes questions about prostitute women's engagement in a wide range of relationships, activities and practices, rather than just the narrower 'selling of sex', which was the primary focus of her analysis.

Secondly, in presenting prostitution as a form of paid labour McLeod lays the groundwork for an economic analysis of women's involvement in prostitution. Highlighting the economics of prostitution is important because it permits researchers to recognise both the poverty of prostitutes and the similarities between prostitutes and poor women. Thus McLeod both complicates and adds sophistication to the earlier construction of prostitutes as primarily different from other women. Moreover she opens a theoretical gap for two questions: what are the differences between other poor women and prostitutes, and what are the culturally and historically specific economic conditions for continued involvement in prostitution? These questions are explored in detail in Chapter 4.

Thirdly, and as alluded to in the above discussion on some of the difficulties with her analysis, McLeod's text introduced a much more acute notion of *effect* and *consequence* than had been seen in previous work on prostitution. Her assumption that prostitutes and other poor and working women are the same opens a very important theoretical gap. To wit, if prostitutes and other women are the same, are *all* women prostitutes? What are the differences? The differences, according to McLeod, inhere in the consequences of engagement in prostitution. Although the space to examine those consequences is ultimately closed in her text by the manner in which 'sameness' is constructed, the issue of 'effect' remains open to examination in a way that does not translate those consequences into epiphenomenal manifestations of an overarching social system.

Finally, McLeod very successfully demonstrates the necessity to differentiate between involvement in prostitution and inclusion in a specific social category – that is, prostitutes. Notwithstanding the difficulties in her analysis in terms of deploying labelling theory, separating prostitutes as individuals involved in prostitution from prostitutes as individuals named as thus in official processes prompts questions about the wider range of consequences of being named a prostitute. In particular it makes it possible to examine not just the social, material, ideological processes structuring the formal labelling of an individual as a prostitute, but also the conditions in which individuals can think of themselves as both prostitutes and not prostitutes.

In summary, the economic position and poverty explanatory model has opened the way for more sophisticated explanations of prostitutes and prostitution by highlighting the similarities between non-prostitute women and prostitutes. In particular it raises questions about (1) a wider and more fully contextual range of processes structuring women's engagement not in the activity of selling sex, but in the social institution of prostitution as a unique constellation of relationships and practices;

(2) the social conditions structuring the differences between prostitutes and other women; (3) a wider range of effects and consequences of engagement in prostitution; and (4) the conditions in which it is possible to be named a prostitute (either by formal agencies or the individual).

THE GENDER AND MALE VIOLENCE EXPLANATORY MODEL

The fourth major explanatory narrative of prostitutes and prostitution is the gender and male violence model. This model presupposes that there are differences between prostitutes and other women, and that such differences are the result of the effect that prostitution has on prostitutes. It is an explanatory model that allows increasingly intricate questions to be asked about prostitution in relation to the transaction that takes place, that is, the sale of sex.

In its ideal type, the gender and male violence model explains prostitution as a manifestation and result of men's control over women's sexuality. Women become prostitutes because of prior victimisation by men. For example they may have been sexually abused as children, introduced to prostitution by an abusive, controlling man and so on. In fact, however, only a few texts (for example Dworkin, 1979; Barry, 1979, 1995; MacKinnon, 1987) assert that the existence of prostitutes and prostitution is reducible to women's victimisation. Most, including Hoigard's and Finstad's (1992) analysis, which is discussed below, assert that prostitution is also linked to women's poverty. The gender and male violence model explores women's involvement in prostitution in terms of financial and physical coercion. For example it could be argued that women are forced into prostitution through violence. Prostitutes are represented as 'casualties' of a male-dominated system, in that they are women with few if any resources to resist the social forces that sexually commodify all women.

Hoigard and Finstad's *Backstreets: Prostitution, Money and Love* (1992) is a good example of the gender and male violence explanatory model. It is an interesting study, full of rich ethnographic detail (the data were collected in Oslo), and it examines the lives of prostitutes and prostitution in relation to their routine, everyday existence, specifically in terms of the 'similarities and differences in the encounter that takes place between participants in prostitution and other encounters between men and women' (Hoigard and Finstad, 1992, p. 9).

Thus Hoigard and Finstad begin their analysis with the assumption that there are differences *and* similarities between prostitutes and other women and that such differences and similarities are constituted by, and within, the specificity of women's engagement in prostitution. They construct prostitutes as 'social wreckage' and 'victims', and prostitution as 'violence against women' and 'corrupted sexuality'. To demonstrate this, the following section investigates Hoigard and Finstad's answers to the following questions. Who are likely to become prostitutes? How do women become prostitutes? What is it to be a prostitute?

On the assumption that there are sociological differences between prostitutes and other women, Hoigard and Finstad assert that, in general, the social background of prostitutes is relatively unambiguous. Prostitutes come from the working class, have irregular home lives and find it difficult to adjust to school or work (ibid., p. 15). They further assert that prostitutes have extensive experience of institutions such as 'orphanages, women's homes, reform schools, child and adolescent psychiatric institutions, alcohol and drug rehabilitation clinics and prison' (ibid., p. 16). The institutional backgrounds of prostitutes are important because

> institutions are ... important training grounds for prostitutes. ... In institutions, young people in trouble are stowed together like surplus wreckage. They often run away together without money. What could be more natural than that they exchange knowledge about ways to survive? (ibid.).

The authors stress that these social backgrounds do not 'cause' women to become prostitutes, rather they are backgrounds of women who *could* become prostitutes. In an examination of how women with such backgrounds become prostitutes, they argue that

> The road to prostitution is a process in which the women's experiences cause a breakdown in their respect for themselves, for other women and also for men. Such individual experiences are seldom sufficient reason for prostitution. It is only when the experiences are translated and incorporated into the collective experience which girls share with other youths that prostitution becomes a viable option (ibid., p. 17).

They also highlight the importance of learning 'what it is to be a woman or a man', which occurs within the collective experience outlined above. Most importantly, they assert that 'an essential and necessary self-transformation [must occur] before [a woman] begins to prosti-tute herself', and that this self-transformation is learning that 'a woman's body is her most important asset' (ibid., p. 18). They argue that, 'In addition to the well-known factors of social class, economics and the degree of involvement in normal society, the degree to which a woman adopts this female image as an image of herself is crucial' (ibid., p. 19).

When these biographies and self-images as sexual commodities are 'translated and incorporated into the collective experience', a subcul-ture of sharing often arises whereby 'prostitution is an act of solidarity and abstention is sponging'. At this point Hoigard and Finstad contest the stereotype of the 'sleazy pimp' who lures or threatens unwitting young girls into prostitution (ibid., p. 20).

Thus Hoigard and Finstad present prostitutes as 'social wreckage' who, rejected by society, eventually find 'belongingness' in a group where prostitution is not only 'normal' and 'acceptable', but also signi-fies solidarity. Clearly drawing on the type of analysis to be found in Wilkinson's (1955) text, Hoigard and Finstad invert the social disloca-tion and criminal subculture explanatory model by claiming that prosti-tutes are rejected by, rather than reject, society. Furthermore it is prostitutes' shared experience, as women rejected by society, that binds them together.

Hoigard and Finstad further claim that women engage in prostitu-tion solely for money: 'Money is *the* reason for prostitution. We know of no woman who prostitutes herself for any reason other than money' (ibid., p. 40). This statement is important. The authors emphasise that women's *reasons* for becoming prostitutes are distinct from the *pro-cess* of becoming prostitutes (that is, shared biographies, learnt atti-tudes towards their own bodies and belonging to a subculture). In so doing they distinguish between the individual motivations a woman might have for entering prostitution and the social conditions that make prostitution a viable way of earning a living for some women. This distinction is theoretically helpful because it allows further ques-tions to be asked about the specificity of engagement in prostitution. And it demonstrates that Hoigard and Finstad see prostitution as primarily an economic activity rather than an 'abnormal' or even devi-ant one.

In other places in their text Hoigard and Finstad constitute prosti-tutes as 'victims of male domination' and 'victims of violence against women'. To deconstruct and reconstruct these two portrayals it is useful to examine the authors' understanding of prostitution itself. They assert that prostitution is 'generated' in a social system in which sexuality is a commodity for exchange and where women's sexuality is seen 'as something that is surrendered, traded, or not traded'. Within such a system, women 'have to create access to the benefits of society via men's use of women's sexuality' (ibid., pp. 186, 187). For women who are not prostitutes, the link 'between sexuality and money is now in the process of loosening.... For steadily growing numbers of women, sexuality is no longer *primarily* a means of being supported' (ibid., p. 185, emphasis added). But prostitutes are different because sexuality *is* their primary means of support.

The construction of prostitutes as 'victims of male domination' is noticeable in Hoigard and Finstad's discussion of sexuality as a commodity: 'The fact that women's sexuality is (also) a means of exchange and a marketable commodity is part of men's oppression of women' (ibid., p. 187). In this instance, prostitutes are 'victims' of the system. Prostitutes constitute an oppressed group and their victimisation is at a social level. For Hoigard and Finstad, prostitutes are different from other women because they bear the brunt of male domination.

Hoigard and Finstad also represent prostitutes as 'victims of violence against women' in relation to the effects of engagement in prostitution. In a section entitled 'Prostitution as Violence Against Women', the authors catalogue the shattering personal effects of prostitution. These include the complete destruction of the prostitutes' personal love lives, the destruction of their self-respect and self-image, and a burden of guilt, shame and self-disgust. They assert that these personal effects are so overwhelming, enduring and devastating that 'it makes it reasonable ... to say that customers practice gross violence against prostitutes' (ibid., pp. 114, 115).

They further claim that prostitutes are victims of violence against women in a more traditional sense – that is, physical assaults by punters and ponces (ibid., p. 116). Hence, as prostitution is both an act of male domination and a form of violence against women, for Hoigard and Finstad prostitutes are both individual victims of male domination and 'symbolic victims of violence against women'. Their construction of prostitution as violence against women is premised on a view of sexuality in general as 'unfolding', 'characterised by personal satisfaction occurring simultaneously with satisfaction of someone else'. Without overstating the point, they use the image of 'unfolding' sexuality normatively in that they imply that it is a 'preferred' expression of sexuality. They also claim that 'one cannot engage in such behaviour with impunity.... When calculation, money and long-term objectives creep into personal relationships, it usually ends badly' (ibid., p. 187). The act of prostituting, thus becomes violence because it confronts and contravenes sexuality as 'unfolding' by being sexuality as 'calculation'.

Underpinning Hoigard and Finstad's analysis of how and why women engage in prostitution is the assumption that prostitutes are the same as other women in some respects but different in other respects. Prostitutes are understood to be 'normal as women', 'normal women' and 'not normal women'. Each of these will be dealt with in turn.

For Hoigard and Finstad, prostitutes are 'normal as women' in that they do not possess specific abnormalities that cause them to be prostitutes. Furthermore they are normal women because the use of sexuality as a means of obtaining something is not atypical of all women in a social system that is based on women's subordinated sexuality.

However, at the same time, and seemingly contradictorily, Hoigard and Finstad also depict prostitutes as 'not normal women' (or different from other women) in two senses. First, they argue that prostitutes' pre-prostitution histories are not statistically typical. Prostitutes have a set of life experiences that are different from most women's life experiences, and these life experiences have resulted in their being 'social wreckage'.

Second, Hoigard and Finstad construct prostitutes as 'not normal women' because the experiences they have *after* becoming prostitutes are dissimilar from those of most women. They assert that whilst the life experiences and effects of engagement in prostitution do not warrant a conceptual line to be drawn between prostitutes and other women, the marked dissimilarities between them need to be highlighted. In other words, whilst there are connections between the role of prostitutes and women's role in society, there are also striking differences between the experiences of the women in those roles. 'The similarities are there. But they can easily be exaggerated. Prostitutes' experiences and destitution are so overwhelming that important qualitative differences become apparent' (ibid., p. 117). Furthermore, 'The manner in which the prostitute relates to her sexuality as a commodity for trade does not differ from how other women relate to their sexuality because it is atypical: it differs because it is overwhelming and dominating' (ibid., p. 186).

Thus for Hoigard and Finstad the 'difference' that makes prostitutes 'not normal women' is the way in which involvement in prostitution has an all-encompassing effect on the individual woman.

Discussion

The gender and male violence explanatory model, exemplified by Hoigard and Finstad's (1992) text, provides the last and arguably the most complex link in the chain of explanations of prostitutes and prosti-tution. Of vital importance is their presupposition of differences be-tween prostitutes and other women, as this opens the space for them (and the reader) to recognise the specificity of involvement in prostitu-tion *per se*. Before examining some of the promising theoretical av-enues that are opened by Hoigard and Finstad's text, a few of the problems with their analysis will be outlined.

The most striking problem with Hoigard and Finstad's analysis is that which has haunted most studies that seek to make sense of women's involvement in prostitution; namely the question of 'differences' and 'similarities' between prostitutes and other women. Although Hoigard and Finstad explicitly state at the beginning of their text that their prim-ary aim is to construct an explanation of prostitution that recognises both the similarities and the differences between prostitutes and other women, the theoretical space to do so is ultimately closed during the course of the text. Hoigard and Finstad fail fully to distinguish prostitu-tion from views and images of women's sexuality more generally. This failure is most clear in their attempt to 'use' prostitution and prostitutes as a magnifying glass, 'illuminating normality' (ibid., p. 9). Their expli-cation of prostitution as a social phenomenon rests on the assumption that prostitution is possible because society views women's sexuality as being subordinate to men's (ibid., p. 186). Prostitution, according to the logic of such an argument, is nothing more and nothing less than a spe-cific manifestation of the sexual commodification of all women and their subordinated sexuality.

Ironically for Hoigard and Finstad, the consequence of removing the distinction between prostitution and sexuality is that the sameness of prostitutes and other women is made absolute. For if the economic sub-ordination and sexual commodification of *all* women is the underlying cause of involvement in prostitution, then all women are prostitutes.

The second area of difficulty is Hoigard and Finstad's construction of prostitutes as 'victims', a construction that is framed by the manner in which they conceptualise the difference between prostitutes and other women. They never explicitly define the word prostitute and they also use the term 'prostituted women'. As noted above, the line that Hoigard and Finstad draw between prostitutes and other women is based on the particular effects of repeatedly using sexuality in a 'calcu-lating' fashion. Hence they remark that all women use sexuality as a means of exchange at some point in their lives, but prostitutes do it so often that it has 'extreme consequences for them' (ibid., p. 117). They go on to argue that using sexuality as a means of obtaining something involves all women in a set of 'defense mechanisms' and 'survival techniques'. Moreover, commodifying one's sexuality has very specific effects on individuals. Thus in this instance prostitutes are not women prostituting or involved in prostitution *per se*; they are women who suffer the 'overwhelming' and 'devastating' consequences of turning themselves into sexual commodities on a regular basis. Hoigard and Finstad therefore conflate prostitutes with the effects of being involved in prostitution. Hence their use of the term 'prostituted women'.

The conflation of prostitutes with the effects of involvement in prostitution is, as noted in the earlier discussion of McLeod's (1982) text, a problem that arises when attempting to explain one side of a behavioural transaction by the other – that is, trying to explain the effects of engagement in prostitution in terms of being a prostitute and *vice versa*. In Hoigard and Finstad's text this has resulted in prostitutes being defined only as 'victims' of men:

> In our prostitution research, we have confirmed and elaborated some impressions we had at the outset – like our impression of the women's total social destitution.... But the idea that prostitution constitutes a gross form of violence was not even a vague impression (Hoigard and Finstad, 1992, p. 116).

By making prostitutes' experience as victims of the violence of men the defining characteristic of prostitutes, Hoigard and Finstad close the theoretical space for a discussion of non-victimised prostitutes or prostitutes who do not see themselves as victims.

Notwithstanding the above mentioned problems, Hoigard and Finstad's analysis offers some very promising theoretical avenues of pursuit, for example in relation to the conditions that structure the sense prostitutes make of their engagement in prostitution. Much of their text focuses on the personal accounts and stories of individual prostitutes (see pp. 40–124, where they detail what their respondents said about being engaged in and leaving prostitution). And yet they never ask questions about how individual prostitutes can tell the stories they do about engagement in prostitution. Their text begs the question of why individual prostitutes recount the stories they do and how these stories can be made meaningful.

Secondly, Hoigard and Finstad blur the conceptual boundary between the 'personal' and 'objective' effects of involvement in prostitution. Throughout their study there are references to the criminalisation, poverty, housing difficulties, lost futures, social rejection, bitter self-hatred, repeated suicide attempts, drug and alcohol addiction and 'split' sense of self that prostitutes experience. Such a blurring of the boundaries between the various effects of engagement in prostitution invites a new set of questions to be asked in which the personal and social effects of engagement in prostitution can be separated from one another.

Thirdly, Hoigard and Finstad's portrayal of prostitutes as 'symbolic victims of violence against women', and their suggestion that 'prostitution is a matter of violence' (ibid., p. 175) provokes questions about the specific conditions that structure the ways in which prostitutes make sense of their status as 'victims':

> The women's reactions to prostitution have many similarities with the reactions of women who are survivors of incest and rape. The feelings that are burned out of the body, self-disgust, guilt, the sense of being a split personality are also central descriptions of these women. Information about such types of emotional reactions to these forms of sexual assaults has attained the status of established facts. This is not true for prostitution research. This is *new* knowledge (ibid., p. 115).

Such statements lead one to ask about the conditions that make it possible for prostitutes to understand their experience of being victimised, and whether, and in what ways, the forms of violence that prostitutes experience differ from or are the same as the violence that other women experience.

In summary, gender and male violence explanations (such as that by Hoigard and Finstad) provide an important link in the chain of explanations of prostitutes and prostitution. The analysis provides an understanding of prostitution that increases our knowledge about what structures women's involvement in prostitution and what it means to be a prostitute. Moreover, such explanations provide the basis from which to examine in greater detail the specific differences and similarities between prostitutes and other women, and in so doing raise questions about how prostitutes can accommodate the specific contradictory experiences they have.

CONCLUSION

This chapter has outlined and analysed various ways in which academic discourse has made sense of women's engagement in prostitution. It has shown the differing, often contradictory manner in which academic explanatory narratives construct prostitutes and what engagement in prostitution has come to mean. What this chapter has not done is to provide a detailed recital of the empirical data the various selected narratives have used in the construction of their stories. For a start, much of this data resonates with the empirical data used in the project discussed in Part II of this book. But more importantly, the objective of this chapter has not been to demonstrate that the empirical findings of previous studies are somehow invalid, inaccurate, distorted or biased. Rather the main purpose has been to identify the process of theoretical closure and reopening that has occurred within the literature on prostitution in order to set the scene for the empirical investigation that follows.

I have argued that one question has been a constant theme in the sociological and criminological narratives of prostitutes and prostitution: are prostitutes different from or the same as other women? However none of the texts examined have managed completely to displace the 'either/or' analysis that such a question structures. Notwithstanding this, and as has been demonstrated, with each theoretical model the questions that can be asked and the answers that can be given become increasingly intricate, so that exploiting the theoretical spaces opened by the specific texts outlined above enables the exploration of a new line of enquiry: how prostitute women can live within the fullness of the contradiction of being both different from and the same as other women. It is to this question that Part II is directed.

Part II
Prostitution Disclosed

4 Risk, Poverty, Poncing and the Contradictions of Involvement in Prostitution

Being a woman in contemporary British society is to be actively engaged in the business of 'risk' – of negotiating and calculating insecurities, uncertainties, costs, potential harms and benefits. As modernity fractures the old social structures, as the welfare state (ostensibly) provides for 'basic survival' and as the rhetoric (and practice) of equality between men and women gains popular support, women are allegedly freed from a life (structured by early industrialisation) of confinement to the home, dependency on male relatives and restricted employment opportunities. Now, equality in education, legislation that prohibits sexual discrimination in the workplace, birth control technologies that permit 'planned parenthood' and break the link between sexuality and reproduction, and equal access to financial institutions and financial support (such as being able to have bank accounts and claim welfare benefits without the permission or mediation of men) mean that women have choices. Women are able to choose whether or not to marry, to have children, to work after marriage, to divorce and so on.

Choices bring with them risks and uncertainties. For despite the rhetoric of equality between men and women, social relations of inequality continue to structure women's poverty and economic dependency on men (see Beck, 1992; MacDowell and Pringle, 1992; Barrett and McIntosh, 1982; Pahl, 1989; Scott, 1984; Lister, 1992; Millar, 1997). Various forms of social differentiation (such as age, ethnicity, sexual preference and disability) combine with the material realities of individual women's class locations to enable some women to avert the risk of poverty whilst simultaneously circumscribing other women's ability to avoid poverty.

The lives of the women who were interviewed for this project were marked by 'riskiness'. Their lives were largely unremarkable, mundane and ordinary. They struggled to live on social security benefits, were dependent on men who 'let them down', left them or from whom they were desperate to escape. They fought to raise their children and negotiated the difficulties of unemployment, housing problems, violence and criminal records. These women were like many other working-class women in that they faced up to their risks and made choices in their struggle to survive. Some of these choices were commonplace, such as claiming social security benefits, whereas others were more extraordinary, such as engaging in prostitution.

This chapter explores the risks that structured the interviewees' lives. But it does not examine those risks in order to determine which particular one (or ones) brought about the women's involvement in prostitution. Rather it focuses on the risks in order to (1) facilitate an understanding of the contradictory material realities of engagement in prostitution, and (2) explore in close detail the paradoxical and seemingly incoherent explanations offered by the interviewees for their involvement in prostitution. Of course the outstanding paradox is that prostitution both enabled and threatened the interviewees' social and material survival. There exists a fundamental discontinuity between the effects of engagement in prostitution that the women recalled and the stories they told about this engagement. But in their recollections, narratives and explanations the women indicated that, as they could see no alternative to their current lifestyle, they had to live with the contradictions.

In this chapter it is argued that the lives of the 21 interviewees were marked by riskiness prior to, during and after their involvement in prostitution. Struggling to ensure their economic and material survival, the women were caught between the risks and benefits of living life independently (where the greatest risk was poverty), dependency on the state (which left them vulnerable to the regulatory practices of welfare benefits) and dependency on a particular man or a particular family (which left the women exposed to increased risk of violence and exploitation). Moreover, in the women's attempts to negotiate those risks and benefits, they recalled economic and material circumstances that gradually but relentlessly funnelled away their options and opportunities for traditional and conventional lives (such as marriage or legitimate employment) towards less than conventional ways of living (such as crime and prostitution).

The economic, social and ideological circumstances that the prostitute women recalled, the specific risks they encountered and the strategies they used to limit their risks structure and constitute the contradictions and paradoxes of their stories. For against the backdrop of diminishing options and opportunities, involvement in prostitution came to signify both an opening of opportunities and a closing of opportunities. Within the context of lives shattered by the effects of poverty, violent and brutal relationships, homelessness and destitution, social censure and ostracisation, involvement in prostitution signified a way forward and a strategy by which the women could improve their options and opportunities for material and social survival. At the same time, in the context of the hassle of street life, the risks of violence, ponce-instigated destitution and homelessness, the difficulties of being arrested, fined and potentially imprisoned and so on, involvement in prostitution represented a closing down of future options and opportunities and a strategy for survival that backfired and trapped the women.

Hence, by analysing the context that structured these women's lives, the coherence of their narratives is called into question and the seamless connections that are drawn in those narratives between poverty and striving for independence, violence and the realities of powerlessness and involvement in prostitution are prised apart. An examination of the risks encountered by the interviewees suggests that the paradoxes and contradictions of their involvement in prostitution are repressed in the women's efforts to render a plausible account of their lives. The contradictions are never openly acknowledged or discussed in their narratives; instead they are accommodated.

This chapter therefore describes some of the women's struggles to survive, the risks they encountered, the circumstances that constrained their lives, the context within which these struggles took place and the manner in which the struggles affected their perceived options and opportunities for the future. It examines the poverty the respondents experienced both prior to and during their engagement in prostitution, their negotiations (and rejections) of 'family' and the ambiguities they felt about their dependency on men. In so doing the chapter highlights the implausibility and 'incoherence' of the women's narratives of entering into, returning to and continuing with prostitution.

POSSIBILITIES FOR THE FUTURE: PROSTITUTION AS A WAY FORWARD

The construction of prostitution as a gendered survival strategy is predicated upon prostitute women's understanding of their lives as characterised by limited possibilities, opportunities and options for legitimately securing material and social stability. In other words, prostitution becomes a way forward into the future when it is placed in a specific chronological context, that is, in relation to what came before in the women's lives. So, in relation to various aspects of the interviewees' lives in which other options and opportunities were fading away, prostitution signified a means by which to achieve a better social and material future. In the context of the poverty that marked the lives of all the interviewees – the state-enforced destitution brought about by living on social security benefits, the social censure that structured their experience of single parenthood, the community ostracisation that resulted from having children of mixed parentage, the ever present possibility of being victims of homelessness or a housing crisis and the respondents' rejection of being dependent on men – involvement in prostitution was seen as an opportunity for future survival. Similarly, the immediacy of the cash exchange between prostitutes and punters, the informal organisation of the institution of prostitution and the myth that money from prostitution is 'easy money' were all deployed in the interviewees' portrayal of prostitution as an easily accessible, unlocked door behind which lay new, wider social networks, friends and, most importantly, economic stability.

This section analyses (1) the economic, social and ideological conditions structuring the types of risk the 21 interviewees faced in their lives outside prostitution, (2) their limited ability to avoid or evade those risks and (3) what the women said about prostitution. It is suggested that engagement in prostitution was seen by the interviewees as a way of halting or reversing the economic and social deterioration of their lives.

Poverty

All the interviewees had experienced poverty, which was often cited by them as the precipitating cause of their engagement in prostitution. For some time, lack of educational qualifications, few marketable skills, unemployment, low pay, living on social security benefits, lone motherhood and housing difficulties have been used as signifiers of poverty (Daly, 1989; Fiorenza and Carr, 1987; Room, 1989; Lister, 1992). Both separately and combined, these circumstances reduce the opportunity to participate fully in social life (see Room, 1995). They act as barriers to the exercise of citizenship, regardless of whether citizenship is conceived in strictly legalistic/civil terms or in broader terms of social citizenship (Lister, 1990). In other words, poverty acts as a constraining force in an individual's life. But because poverty conjoins with differentiation, both in its causes and its effects, it affected the lives of the 21 interviewees in specific ways.

'No One Would Employ Me': Legitimate Work and Poverty

It is often thought that having paid employment is one of the primary ways of avoiding poverty. But it has been demonstrated that jobs that are low paid, have little status or security and/or are organised on a casual, part-time or flexible basis are a cause of rather than a guard against poverty (see Glendinning and Millar, 1987, 1992; Millar, 1997). Although recent economic restructuring has meant that all workers have become subject to poorer working conditions (especially unskilled and semi-skilled young people), the majority of people working in casual, part-time, flexible, low-paid and insecure jobs in late-twentieth-century Britain are women (Lonsdale, 1992, p. 92), a situation that has resulted from mainstream economic practices, sexual differentiation and the complex (but unrecognised) interplay between the so-called 'public' sphere of paid employment and the 'private' sphere of unpaid domestic work, wherein notions of gendered responsibilities and work are constructed and constituted (see Davidoff and Hall, 1987). The interviewees' experiences of legitimate work accord with the experiences of women in paid employment more generally.

As the interviewees possessed few if any educational qualifications (Table 4.1), no real vocational training and few marketable skills, their ability to obtain legitimate work was extremely limited. This is reflected in the paid employment that they had undertaken. All but one of those who had worked legitimately at some point in their lives had been employed in either the unskilled service sector (such as waitressing) or the unskilled retail sector (such as shop assistant work) (Table 4.2).

The one exception was Sophie, who had worked as a legal executive secretary – a job that had been relatively stable, secure and well paid. The others, however, had worked in jobs that were poorly paid and typically without a formal contract (that is, they had worked as part-timers or casual workers), and consequently they had had little security, stability or prospect of occupational mobility, promotion or training. Most importantly, these jobs had offered no protection or guard against poverty.

Another pattern of economic activity, specific to women, has been identified by Martin and Roberts (1984) in their study of economic participation over the course of women's lives. Martin and Roberts show that the rates of women's economic participation and the types of work they undertake (full-time, part-time, casual or flexible) relate to whether or not the women are mothers, regardless of their marital status or the ways in which their domestic responsibilities are divided (Martin and Roberts, 1984, pp. 114–15). Martin and Roberts conclude that women's

Table 4.1   Educational qualifications of the interviewees

Interviewee (age)	Educational qualifications
Andrea (27)	None
Anna (36)	None
Barbara (24)	None
Christina (23)	4 'O' Levels, 2 'A' Levels
Diane (37)	None
Fiona (41)	School Leaving Certificate
Gail (28)	None
Georgie (35)	None
Helena (35)	None
Ingrid (44)	None
Janet (37)	None
Jasmine (30)	None
Katrina (20)	3 GCSEs
Lois (21)	None
Margie (32)	None
Michelle (33)	None
Olivia (28)	1 RSA (typing)
Patsy (42)	None
Ruthie (25)	None
Sammy (18)	None
Sophie (28)	8 'O' Levels, 2 'A' Levels

rates of economic participation over their lifetime are 'M'-shaped, in that rates of work dramatically decrease upon the birth of the first child and only begin to pick up when the youngest child is of school age (ibid., pp. 116–34). This pattern characterised the work experiences of the women interviewees in this study. Those with the most extensive experience of legitimate employment had left around the time their first child was born. Olivia (aged 28), who had worked as a waitress for two years, left because she had become pregnant. Similarly, Helena (aged 35) and Jasmine (aged 30), who had worked, respectively, as a clothing machinist and a care assistant, had left just before the delivery date of their first child. This 'career break' had had two important consequences. First, by removing themselves from paid employment the women had been left with few options for economic survival beyond dependency on their boyfriends/husbands or social security benefits. Second, employment breaks have been shown adversely to affect women's employment prospects and occupational mobility when returning to paid employment (ibid., p. 151). Hence, after divorcing their husbands both Fiona (aged 41) and Helena (aged 35) had found it impossible to

Table 4.2   Interviewees' experience of legitimate employment

Name (age)	Type of employment
Andrea (27)	None
Anna (36)	None
Barbara (24)	None
Christina (23)	Unskilled retail trade worker
Diane (37)	Press operator, hot iron operator
Fiona (41)	Unskilled retail trade worker
Gail (28)	Hairdresser, bar work, strawberry picking, seasonal retail trade worker
Georgie (35)	Bar work, nightclub work, casino work, stripping
Helena (35)	Sewing machinist, retail trade worker
Ingrid (44)	Waitressing, bar work
Janet (37)	Tailoring assistant, summer jobs
Jasmine (30)	Care assistant
Katrina (20)	YTS only
Lois (21)	None
Margie (32)	Jewellery engraving
Michelle (33)	None
Olivia (28)	Waitressing
Patsy (42)	None
Ruthie (25)	Promotion work, telephone sales
Sammy (18)	None
Sophie (28)	Legal secretary

obtain jobs (full- or part-time) as machinists. Instead, both had taken on casual cleaning jobs (which were much lower paid). So in terms of a life-time perspective, and in terms of a static 'snapshot' of the women's legitimate work histories, their economic participation had done little to protect them from poverty, and arguably had even caused their poverty.

Of course not all the interviewees had been equally affected by low-paid, disadvantaged jobs. Thirteen women had excluded themselves from paid employment altogether, seven of whom had never had legitimate employment. Instead they had relied on social security benefits, male partners or prostitution to secure a living. All 13 had perceived that they had no prospect of securing paid employment, either because they had no educational qualifications, and thus had nothing to offer employers, or because they thought that no one would employ them. But far more important for many of these respondents was the fact that they viewed their criminal records as automatic bars to legitimate work:

I'd like a job, but I don't know how I'm gonna get one with my record – or even how to go about it now! (Olivia, aged 28).

No one wants to give a sex offender a job (Andrea, aged 27).

Andrea said that as far as she was concerned soliciting and loitering for the purposes of prostitution were sexual offences and would be perceived as such by employers. Both Anna (aged 36) and Katrina (aged 20) had similarly excluded themselves from the search for legitimate employment; in their case, because their criminal records included manslaughter, and like Andrea they anticipated that potential employers would refuse to give them jobs.

Understanding their criminal records as blocking all prospect of legitimate employment was particularly relevant given that all but two of them had been convicted of a prostitution-related offence. In the informal conversations that took place in the probation-run drop-in centre, it was clear that the women were generally confused about the implications of having such criminal records, particularly in terms of whether or not the convictions were ever 'spent' or whether or not they were classified as 'sexual offences'. The women also believed that potential employers would see them as 'tarts', 'slags' and unreliable workers because their offences were prostitution-related.

Many of the other women had had such bad experiences with job training schemes that they had chosen to opt out of legitimate employment:

> I got a YTS and I was going to work from nine to five just to get some qualifications to sort my life out. But if you're on a YTS, they treat you like dogs man! And there's never anything at the end anyway (Katrina, aged 20).

> I got a job as a trainee tailor. You didn't get much money – it was just for the training, like – and you didn't get much of that. I left and haven't had a job since and I don't want one now (Janet, aged 37).

Thus it was not just a case of whether or not the women had children to look after, rather it was a lack of confidence in their own abilities or their perception of themselves as unemployable that created the conditions in which these women had removed themselves from the labour market. The experience of dead-end, badly paid jobs, 'training' jobs and the possession of criminal records had all contributed to the women's view of legitimate work as a closed option.

Removing themselves from the formal labour market or failing to maintain a regular working history had had profound consequences for the individuals involved. Whereas for some men it might have meant *temporary* dependence on parents/relatives or the state, for the working-class women in this study it had meant taking one or more of three options, each of which had its own specific risks and consequences. They could have become dependent on state welfare benefits, or dependent on particular men, or provided themselves with an income in ways that are typically illegal and/or criminogenic.

Within such a context, the interviewees saw prostitution in terms of juxtaposing their very limited and restricted legitimate work opportunities with the attraction of earning money by engaging in prostitution, where the 'wages' were perceived to be much higher than those to be had in legitimate work, where there were no interview and recruitment procedures, where the employment conditions were effectively self-regulated and wages were paid immediately, and earnings were curtailed only by the physical limitations of the individual woman. In short, in comparison with earning money through legitimate employment, involvement in prostitution was seen as a very attractive option. The following quotes demonstrate this:

I've done a bit of waitressing. . . . But I thought, 'F∗∗k me! I ain't sitting here all week for this. I could make that in half an hour [on the beat]' (Ingrid, aged 44).

When I was 16, I was a press operator – as in hot iron – it lasted about a month. But I'd already done a bit of hustling like, so . . . that money was no good, it was easier on the beat, so I'd gone back to it (Diane, aged 37).

This old friend of mine used to come into the card shop and see me, like, and I ended up going with her again [that is, back to the beat]. It was the money. I was getting fifty pounds a week working in that card shop. I could earn that working the street for an hour! (Christine, aged 23).

So in terms of recruitment procedures, comparative earnings, regulations and so on, involvement in prostitution was constituted as an opening of options. Because of the perceived difficulty of obtaining and sustaining legitimate employment, the women were able to represent involvement in prostitution as a strategy that offered the prospect of economic stability.

Living on Social Security

From its inception the welfare state, and in particular its social security system, has been structured by a particular construction of 'the family' (Cook, 1987). The dominant belief structuring social security provision is that most individuals are located within families (as either a bread-winner, housewife or dependent) and that families share their resources equitably. Indeed the very reason for the introduction of social security provision was to fill the gap in men's ability to provide for their families (Land, 1982). At its inception half a century ago, the benefit system was divided between non-means-tested (but contributory) benefits, which were designed with the 'lifetime breadwinner' in mind, and means-tested benefits, which were to act as a 'safety net'.

Although the exact nature and level of social security benefits has altered considerably in the intervening years, the position of women claimants has not. Firstly, women rarely qualify for non-means-tested benefits and thus are typically in receipt of what was Supplementary Benefit and is now Income Support (Pascall, 1986). The restructuring of benefits in the 1980s and 1990s has had particular and deleterious effects on women. The tightening up of individuals' rights to non-contributory means-tested benefits in the 1980s especially disadvantaged already impoverished women (Lister, 1992). The general transfer of responsibility for social security provision that has taken place through-out the 1980s and 1990s, whereby individuals have been encouraged to provide for themselves by taking out private insurance and thus provid-ing their own safety net, has made women particularly vulnerable because the type of work that most women undertake does not bring in enough money to pay for such provision (Lister, 1992; Millar, 1997). Secondly, women (particularly working-class women and single mothers) are often constituted as posing a 'threat' to the system. As the structure of the benefit system articulates with ideological constructions of 'woman-hood', 'motherhood' and 'wifehood', women are always and already constituted as potentially fraudulent claimants (that is, 'scroungers') – especially under the rules of cohabitation, whereby cohabitation is treated as evidence of an economic relationship (Pascall, 1986; Cook, 1987, 1989). The question of cohabitation received particular emphasis in the 1980s and early 1990s with the shift from non-means-tested bene-fits to means-tested benefits, as with means-tested benefits the resources and income of the family unit are aggregated, regardless of the distribu-tion of resources within that unit (Lister, 1992). And the constructing of single women as potentially fraudulent claimants has enabled the DSS to police women claimants more stringently and regularly than male claimants (Campbell, 1984). For women claimants there is the ever present threat that if their lives are found wanting, if they form new relationships with men or if they take in male lodgers their benefits may be summarily withdrawn (Pascall, 1986; Lister, 1992). When this is coupled with pay-out levels that prohibit a standard of living above that of bare subsistence, social *security* for some women is more often mythical than real (see Spicker, 1993, for a discussion of whether social security can ever really be provided through a benefit system). Thus the alternative options for women who wish to avoid the regulatory practices and penury of living on the dole are limited to financial dependency on men, finding legitimate employment or supplementing their paltry income with crime. Of course for working-class women the choices are further circumscribed by the types of employment open to them or the working-class men they may be dependent on (Cook, 1987).

These difficulties were voiced by most of the women in this study. All of them had lived on social security benefits (ranging from a minimum of one year to a maximum of twenty years). For several women the inability to live on benefits and/or the difficulties arising from leaving abusive, violent male partners and seeking aid through the benefit system were understood as being precipitative causes of their involvement in prostitution. For example Gail (aged 28) recounted that before she had become involved in prostitution, she and her four children had left her violent boyfriend. She said she had just woken up one day and contacted a social worker. The neighbourhood housing officer had helped her get a new flat and social security had agreed to pay for the removal van to move her, and thus one night she had 'done a runner'. However Gail had needed bedding, beds and a cooker in the new flat and had 'applied for a loan or grant or whatever from social security [but] they'd refused it all'. Gail had been unable to pay for a baby-minder in order to get a legitimate job and had been told by a casual acquaintance that she could 'get sorted' by becoming involved in prostitution.

Gail's example illustrates the risks women encounter and the struggle they have to survive when they refuse to remain dependent on violent men. Gail had been unable to find legitimate employment and was thus dependent on the benefit system. She recalled that all her benefits had stopped after a year. The flat she was living in had been raided by the police in order to arrest her ponce, who was living with her. When social security was informed of this they had stopped Gail's benefits on the ground that she was cohabiting. Gail noted the irony of this event. Social security officers had correctly assumed that there was a financial relationship between her and her ponce, but they got the nature of that relationship wrong. Gail was not living off her ponce – he was living off her.

Similarly Jasmine (aged 30) commented that when she and her two kids had left her mentally ill and occasionally violent boyfriend, she had had no option but to 'sign on'. However within the first three months:

> I had problems with my electricity. I'd had no money and I wasn't due to be paid and I had no electric and I was living on sixty pounds a week with two kids. I was trying to feed and clothe them, feed and clothe myself, electric, gas, water rates. You know, all these bills and I was in over my head. I was panicking. I thought I've got to do it [become involved in prostitution]. I've got no choice! In the end I had NO CHOICE.

Several other women recounted the same or similar tales. Lois (aged 21) said she desperately wanted to leave prostitution but found it difficult to do so because living on benefits was impossible. Ruthie (aged 25) commented that after leaving prostitution (due to the birth of her daughter) she had had to return two months later because '[I] couldn't live off social security – FULL STOP. I was used to a nice lifestyle and I wasn't gonna go back to Carly's dad!'

Gail's, Jasmine's, Lois' and Ruthie's tales vividly demonstrate the extent to which these women's lives were circumscribed by the ideologies of single womanhood and 'ideal families' in the practices of social security provision. Refusing to be dependent on particular men and unable to find legitimate employment, claiming benefits may at first sight have appeared to be the best option for these women, but it was a risky option with a high cost. It resulted in the closure of future options and opportunities as the realities of subsistence level pay-outs, the regulatory practices of the DSS and mainstream economic practices that ensure an extremely limited range of employment opportunities conjoined. Hence for the interviewees signing on had at first been an enabling act, but it had proved to be a costly one.

Within this context, the interviewees discussed their engagement in prostitution as though it was nothing more and nothing less than a means of earning money without the 'hassle of signing on'. They simultaneously talked about the restrictions and constraints of claiming social security benefits and the informal organisation of the institution of prostitution, where there are no structures, procedures or officials regulating income in the form of tax or bureaucratic regulations about levels of income earned or hours worked. Involvement in prostitution was viewed as a particularly effective strategy for earning a reasonable amount of money compared with subsistence-level benefit pay-outs. The women told of the differences in earnings and 'freedom' between the dole and engagement in prostitution, and described prostitution as a way of 'sorting out' their poverty and fashioning better lives.

Single Parenthood, Poverty and Community Ostracisation

Given the degree to which single parenthood can affect and constrain working-class women's lives, it is surprising that only a few of the single-mother interviewees commented on their status as single mothers. Thirteen of the 21 women were single mothers, 12 of the 13 were white women and eight of the 13 had children of 'mixed parentage'. All the single mothers were working class and all had struggled to survive on inadequate welfare benefits. Apart from discussing the practical diffi-culties of surviving on benefits or combining childcare with legitimate employment, single motherhood, in itself, was not particularly men-tioned. Indeed it was more often used as a descriptive label to signify the degree of poverty the women had experienced and the difficulties they had had in finding, obtaining or sustaining legitimate employment. Georgie (aged 35) recounted:

> When I took this house – it was a right dive – and me being a single parent, not being able to get a job, because in MidCity there are no jobs and things are hard. To me, I had no choice but to go back to it [that is, prostitution] just to try to keep my head above water. Because I found myself for the first time, just totally in debt. I was a single parent and no matter what improvement I tried to do, things just didn't seem to get any better.

Arguably, recent discussions on the 'underclass' (Murray, 1990) from all sides of the political spectrum have both disabled and enabled 'single motherhood' as a legitimate speaking position. The vilification of young, working-class, single mothers as immoral and degenerate and as causing 'incivility' (Dennis and Erdos, 1992), crime, economic inactivity among able-bodied adults and eventual community destruction (Murray, 1990) effectively silences any socially validated position from which to speak as specifically *single mothers*. In response to the theses of Murray and others, it has been asserted that exclusion and poverty are at the heart of the underclass. Within such responses, single motherhood has been constituted as a social status that is likely to produce exclusion and result in the impoverishment of those individuals so situated. This response creates a validated and not a socially condemned position from which to speak – that is, single mothers can speak as *poor* women with children (see Oerton and Atkinson, 1997).

However the respondents did discuss their status as single mothers when they talked about their mixed parentage children. They recollected episodes in which their children had been discriminated against or called names, and how their lives had been circumscribed by other people's understanding of them as 'dangerous' and 'threatening' because their children were of mixed parentage. For example Janet (aged 37) explained why she only put pictures of her two white children on display and no pictures of her mixed parentage child:

> I have two pictures of me white kids in the bedroom and I find that when they [the punters] see them, they come back more . . . . I think that they think if you go with a black man, they feel insecure. They think that once you're with a black man that that black man has you working for him. See, if they seen my halfcast baby there, I don't think they'd come back as quick.

Similarly Michelle (aged 33) was very aware of the assumption that she was 'beyond the pale', 'dangerous' and potentially criminal because she had mixed parentage children. When she had told her family, at the age of sixteen, that her forthcoming baby was going to be of mixed parentage, her family had 'wanted me to get the child adopted or move out'. She had left and 'found it real hard to manage with all the stigma around me, you know, being a single mother at that age and having a baby that wasn't white'. Her family had 'cut her off' when they discovered that she was going a have a second mixed percentage child. When this child had died of cot death the police had kept 'coming round, saying that because her father was a black man they were gonna have me under investigation for murder, like'. According to Michelle, this was because, in the words of the police, she was 'a tart who f∗∗ked black men'. Thus Michelle's status as unmarried, as a single mother and as a woman transgressing the norms of 'white womanhood' were condensed into the police's description of her.

One of the risks of having children of mixed parentage is social isolation, not just from white communities as a result of being labelled as 'dangerous' and 'threatening' (or at least in breach of white womanhood), but also from black communities. Lois (aged 21) talked about the difficulties she had had when her black neighbours would not accept her or her child and had continually complained to the local housing office about them. Whilst the housing office had not evicted her, they had moved her to a flat in a different estate. Ingrid (aged 44) said that she had had problems with her black neighbours for the same reason (that is they had not accepted her or her child because her child was of mixed parentage).

These stories were by no means unusual. The interviewees' lives as single mothers had contributed to their construction of their future prospects as closed. In practice, their single motherhood had increased their poverty by making it difficult for them to sustain legitimate work. It had denied them valid positions from which to speak, and for those whose children were of mixed parentage it had led to ostracisation by their families, affected their lives in prostitution, in the sense that punters perceived them as 'not safe' because they had been involved with black men, and adversely affected the 'help' they received (or did not receive) from formal and informal agencies.

With respect to the ostracisation suffered by these women, prostitution offered a 'new' community. The women spoke of the ever-increasing number of friends they had made while working as prostitutes and how deep these friendships were. Many commented that this had resulted from two things: the shared experience of 'being on the game', which had provided the women with an immediate common bond; and the strengthening of this bond because so many of the white women working in prostitution in MidCity had relationships and children with black men (arguably a result of the demographics of MidCity – see Chapter 1) and this gave them a sense of 'sameness'. Georgie (aged 35) demonstrated this when she talked about the friends she had made during her time in prostitution:

> You form close friendships...coz you find you can confide in each other and things like that – you know? And it feels as if you have to. I suppose when I was younger [that is, not on the game] I used to look and think I was something different – what with me kid being half-caste and everything. People looked down on me. And a lot of the girls who work feel the same. So we had to build up friendships with each other, knowing what we all know about what each other's doing. You build up tight friendships.

Two others discussed how involvement in prostitution had increased their circle of friends, widened their social networks and given them a sense of community:

Before I started working I didn't have friends. The only friends I really had were the ones from cleaning which I worked with and I didn't know them very long. But since working [as a prostitute] I've got loads of friends.... The one thing we have got is a good friendship – if one of us gets in trouble, we all help each other out. We take our kids out during the day and all that.... I've got more of a life now than what I did before (Helena, aged 35).

We used to make each other laugh. Um, I mean we used to go out for the night [her and her boyfriend]. It was quite funny and the girls would be stood there on the corner and um, we would stop the car and have a little natter and sometimes never get to where we was going. If I was passing through or whatever, I used to stop and have a natter like. We all get on quite well. It's good having friends (Fiona, aged 41).

Several other interviewees described the 'blues' as the focal point of socialising for prostitutes in MidCity. 'Blues' are unlicensed, illicit and often criminogenic clubs in derelict and squatted houses in Greenvale and Birchfield. They are generally run by Afro-Caribbean men for Afro-Caribbean men and (usually) white women.

The feeling that involvement in prostitution had provided the interviewees with a community was vividly demonstrated in the vignettes related by various women about leaving local authority care or running away from home, school or a violent partner. These women did not speak of prostitution as an individual answer, solution or course of action, but rather as a 'normal' part of the activities of the group of people that they had been or were involved with. Thus a number commented on the closeness they felt with their friends and the sense that they and their friends were 'in it altogether'. Ingrid (aged 44) and her friend had absconded together, shoplifted together, went 'on the pull together' and entered prostitution together. Similarly Diane (aged 37) and her friend had done (and still did) everything together, including absconding and prostituting. In both instances the friend had 'introduced' them to prostitution and from there they had expanded their network of friends and shared experiences. Hence, through the notion of 'community', involvement in prostitution had come to represent an opening of social options against the backdrop of life in local authority care and community ostracisation (from both white and black communities because their children were of mixed parentage).

Housing Problems, Homelessness and 'Doing a Runner'

Studies of women's housing have demonstrated that women's access to housing is mediated by, and primarily secured within, their relationships with particular men because of (1) the ways in which the ideologies and practices of sexual differentiation locate men and women differently in terms of economic practices, social security provision and so on, and (2) the ways in which housing provision, policies and practices are structured by and constituted within a dominant ideology of 'familialism' (Watson and Austerberry, 1986; Coleman and Watson, 1987; Pascall, 1986; Sexty, 1990).

Women's housing experiences are most clearly understood in relation to their experiences as women, in terms of both the provision of housing and the chance of achieving (or otherwise) housing security via their relationships with men. The housing experiences of the interviewees were no different from those of most working-class women with few financial resources at their disposal. Any security they may have attained was risky and had come at a cost.

Women's housing *insecurity* is also mediated by and through their relationships with particular men – especially when these relationships break down or simply become intolerable (Watson and Austerberry, 1983). The main causes of women's homelessness in general are physical abuse and marital breakdown (Watson and Austerberry, 1983; Dibbin 1991). By removing themselves from the 'family', women place themselves at risk of losing what little access they have to housing security. Women in such a situation often find themselves weighing up the risks of staying in violent, intolerable or abusive relationships against the risks of going. Although the interviewees' experiences of housing insecurity accorded with the housing experiences of women more generally, the primary cause of their housing insecurity was violence and abuse rather than relationship breakdowns.

The housing difficulties experienced by the interviewees were profound. It would be difficult to overstate the extent to which housing problems had contributed to the circumscription of future opportunities and options for the women, or to overemphasise the connection between housing difficulties and the women's engagement in prostitution (Table 4.3). Housing difficulties were identified by three women as being the principal cause of their involvement in prostitution, whilst three other women saw them as incidental to their initial involvement in prostitution (cf. Carlen, 1996). Eighteen of the 21 women had experienced some type of housing difficulty at some stage in their lives: for

Table 4.3   Reasons for the housing difficulties experienced by the interviewees

Name (age)	Reason
Andrea (27)	(1) Did a runner (absconded from local authority care, ran away from ponces and violent partners). (2) Prostitution-related housing difficulty (evicted due to neighbours' complaints).
Anna (36)	(1) Did a runner (ran away from home before 18 years old, ran away from ponce and violent partner). (2) Economic difficulties precipitating housing crisis (relationship broke down, which precipitated homelessness). (3) Prostitution-related housing difficulty (tied housing, evicted due to neighbours' complaints).
Barbara (24)	(1) Prostitution-related housing difficulty (tied housing, 'on the move'). (2) Did a runner (ran away from parents' home and local authority care). (3) Economic difficulties precipitating housing crisis (sleeping rough and kipping at friends' houses).
Christina (23)	(1) Did a runner (ran away from parents' home, violent partner and ponce). (2) Prostitution-related housing difficulty (tied housing).
Diane (37)	(1) Did a runner (absconded from local authority care, ran away from violent partner and ponce).
Fiona (41)	(1) Economic difficulties precipitating housing crisis (marriage broke down, causing potential homelessness through an inability financially to sustain accommodation).
Gail (28)	(1) Did a runner (ran away from violent partner/ponce). (2) Prostitution-related housing difficulty (tied housing).
Georgie (35)	(1) Did a runner (ran away from violent partner and ponce).
Helena (35)	(1) Economic difficulties precipitating housing crisis (divorce led to potential homelessness through an inability to afford accommodation).
Ingrid (44)	(1) Did a runner (absconded from local authority care and ran away from violent partners and ponces). (2) Prostitution-related housing difficulty (prostitution-related eviction).
Janet (37)	(1) Did a runner (ran away from father's home). (2) Prostitution-related housing difficulty (tied housing, 'on the move').
Katrina (20)	(1) Prostitution-related housing difficulty (tied housing, 'on the move'). (2) Did a runner (ran away from foster family).

Lois (21)	(1) Did a runner (ran away from parents', sister's and foster carers' homes, ran away from ponces and violent partners).
	(2) Prostitution-related housing difficulty (tied housing).
Margie (32)	(1) Did a runner (ran away from violent partner/ponce).
	(2) Economic difficulties precipitating housing crisis (rent arrears and possible eviction).
Michelle (33)	(1) Prostitution-related housing difficulty (tied housing, 'on the move').
	(2) Did a runner (ran away from violent partner/ponce).
Olivia (28)	(1) Prostitution-related housing difficulty ('on the move').
Ruthie (25)	(1) Did a runner (ran away from violent partners/ponces).
	(2) Prostitution-related housing difficulty ('on the move').
Sammy (18)	(1) Did a runner (absconded from local authority care).
	(2) Prostitution-related housing difficulty (tied housing).

most of these women, this had meant continual (or recurring) housing problems. Thus 12 of the women commented that they had never had secure accommodation of their own at any point in their lives. The types of housing problem the 18 women had experienced ranged from at times having no housing whatsoever to having only 'casual' or 'temporary' housing (such as 'kipping at a mate's'), to having been unable to maintain the housing that had been acquired because of their inability to pay the rent and bills. Prostitution had come to be seen as a way of obtaining the financial means to secure accommodation. Interestingly, even though seven of the 18 women talked about times when they had had no accommodation and had consequently 'slept rough', none of the women defined themselves as having been homeless at any point in their lives. Arguably, this attests to the concealed nature of women's homelessness (Watson and Austerberry, 1983) and that homelessness is routine for women who leave (or abscond from) local authority care.

In terms of turning to prostitution as a solution to housing problems, the reasons for doing so can be divided into two types: (1) the need to escape from a brutal relationship ('doing a runner') and (2) economic crises. In both cases the accommodation had been tied to the respondents' relationships with their families and/or particular men, and when these relationships had broken down or become untenable a housing crisis had ensued. Such events enabled 18 of the 21 interviewees to construct narratives of funnelling and foreclosing futures. In this context, involvement in prostitution was talked about as a strategy whereby the women could sort out their housing problems, successfully negotiate the risk of leaving brutal men and obtain an independent income to secure their own housing (if only temporarily). Hence these 18 women described prostitution as a way of obtaining the funds to buy housing security.

'Doing a Runner'

Fifteen of the 18 women who had had housing problems recalled times in their lives when they had had to leave their accommodation. Typical were stories of 'doing a runner' when a relationship had become untenable, usually because of violence and abuse (see also Dibbin, 1991). For the younger interviewees, abuse within the family or foster family, dislike of being in local authority care and/or not wanting to be under the control of or dependent on their families had also caused them to 'do a runner'.

The act of 'doing a runner' was recalled as having significance only inasmuch as it had affected the interviewees' choice of future actions and the risky situations that had followed (that is, potential homelessness and destitution). In other words, the significance of doing a runner inhered in what happened afterwards. In the following extracts the younger interviewees highlight some of the ways in which 'doing a runner' had set in place a series of events that had eventually led to their involvement in prostitution. Lois (aged 21) spoke of the time immediately preceding her first step into prostitution:

> When Dad had a heart attack, I was given the choice of living with me aunt and uncle or being adopted . . . I chose me aunt and uncle's. But I went there and I suffered sexual abuse and was getting beaten up by my 16-year-old cousin. So I finally ended up running away. . . . I done a runner but me Dad picked me up. Then he packed me off to my mother's, but I done a runner from there and went to my sister's. . . . I lived with her for a while but I couldn't take her boyfriend – he raped me – so I done a runner again. . . . [JP: Where did you go?] I just slept here and there and everywhere. I just found different mates to stop off with. . . . I finally went to my other sister's.

Lois later explained that she had been 'put on the game' by the boyfriend of the sister she had gone to live with. The following extracts recount very similar stories:

> But I did, basically, live, from when I was twelve, on my own. You know? [JP: Really?] Yup. I'd run away from home. My dad was very, very strict. At the time you think, 'You're just being wicked to me. My

big sister can do everything and I can't'. Me friends were allowed out and I wasn't. So I ran away – I'd got nowhere to stay, so I stayed with this prostitute I knew (Andrea, 27).

I got put into a remand home – for being out of me parent's control. Then approved school. Well, that didn't work because I was locked up! So, I just run away with another couple of girls.... Well, it wasn't long after that I started working. I'd abscond, find a chap, take off, go down the beat and then I'd be picked up by the cops and taken back. I'd abscond again (Ingrid, 44).

I was put into care when I was thirteen – beyond parental control .... I was in an assessment centre for three years! So I started running off and I'd be on the run for three or four months. I would live with a prostitute – she was an older woman – but I wasn't doing it. I was like, just there looking after her kids. Run off about twelve times – the last time I run off with a girl who'd already hustled and that's when I started (Diane, 37).

These extracts demonstrate two points. First, when the women had done a runner they had 'drifted' inasmuch as they had sorted out their accommodation 'as they went along'. In doing a runner the women had become homeless, but a form of homelessness that was concealed in that it was non-institutionalised (see Watson and Austerberry, 1983). Second, doing a runner was seen by the interviewees as a route into prostitution. In most cases they talked about being 'introduced' to prostitution as a result of the people they had encountered in their struggle to survive their homelessness (cf. Carlen, 1996).

For the older women, doing a runner had usually been to escape from violence and abuse by their boyfriends/partners (cf. Dibbin, 1991; Sexty, 1990). In common with the younger women, it had resulted in homelessness. The older respondents cited it as a cause of their entrance into, return to or continuation in prostitution. After leaving their accommodation the older respondents had often found themselves living with friends, sleeping rough, moving into B&B accommodation and so on. Caught in a situation of weighing up the risk of staying with partners who had already demonstrated their violence and in all probability would be violent again against the risks accompanying the uncertainties of doing a runner, the women had often perceived the risk of staying as greater. But in doing a runner the women had found themselves with the extra financial burden of paying for accommodation for themselves and their dependents, and/or seeking help from anonymous agencies.

> I was with him and working and he used to beat me up and he would be with other women and then he'd come back.... He was an alcoholic and I started seeing the doctor for depression and he told me I had to get out of me situation. That it was no good.... So one day I just waited for him to go out and I just went, me and the baby. I went to a hostel. Give up me house that I'd lived in for seven years. And went into a hostel. They rehoused me, *but right next door to his family*! I had him back in the end (Diane 37).

Diane explained that after this episode, she had managed to get an exchange to a town some fifty miles away (Hightown) and threw her boyfriend out. But he found out where she had moved to. She said:

> I got beat up [by the boyfriend].... Anyway, I got this friend who I had for years, and I came back and she, um, I was stopping at her house with her – he burgled me house while I was gone.... I was stopping at me friend Beth's and like she was looking after the baby while I worked. I wasn't bothering with anybody, I was just on me own and one day Freddy spotted me – he dragged me along the street and beat me up and raped me. I went back to me friend's and I thought, 'Well, I'm going to have to go into a hostel and get rehoused *again*'. I just gave up my house in Hightown and just had the removal people come and buy all the stuff. I hardly got anything for it – but I got away from Freddy (Diane, 37).

Andrea's, Lois' and Georgie's experiences also demonstrate the high cost of doing a runner from a violent partner:

> I've moved more times than I can count. For domestic violence mainly. I've had, it must be at least fifty places. Before I got this place – well I used to leave everything full of everything. I'd just pack my bags and leave, you know, a few clothes for me and a few clothes for the baby (Andrea, 27).

> Well, I pulled a fast one on him [her violent ponce]. It was just one way of proving to him that he didn't have the full control over me that he thought he did. So like, he was moving and we were meant to go with him.... I put all my stuff separate and when we got to the flat, I went upstairs and I said 'Bye, see ya, I've had enough!' And I went downstairs, got in the taxi and took all my stuff to a girl's house and I stopped there for about a month. I didn't work at first, but then she

started saying that she wants rent, fifty pounds a week. Well, I weren't on the social, I had nothing, I couldn't go and sign on because he'd be by the social, knowing where I was, so I couldn't do that – so the only way I could get her fifty pounds a week was the streets and I still had to move myself to somewhere else (Lois, 21).

I took a liking to him, you know [laughter] but he was violent. Oh yea, very violent. [JP: How did you cope with that?] Um, I used to have this habit of just running away from home a lot. Like, I'd build up a house, get all my furniture in there and then he'd probably give me a beating. I'd be black and blue from head to foot and whatever and I'd run away. Sometimes I came back and he'd have sold my furniture, or done this or that or the other. In the end, it was like, I started having an affair with this guy. I just went to him. I lived with him and stopped working for a while (Georgie, 35).

These extracts illustrate the extra financial burden and the uncertainty of housing or economic survival that result from doing a runner. Most of the women talked about 'running off', 'just leaving' and so on, leaving all their material possessions behind, except what they had needed at that moment. Some women had gone into hostels, others had stayed with friends or new boyfriends/ponces. Thus it was that, in the context of the real and tangible material consequences of doing a runner, the interviewees constructed tales of circumscribed futures.

Economic Difficulties Precipitating Housing Crises
In addition to housing difficulties caused by flight from physical violence and abuse, four of the interviewees spoke of housing problems that had resulted from economic difficulties. Fiona (aged 41) recounted that she had left her husband and moved into a house with her new boyfriend and her mother, but they had not been able to meet the rent. They faced possible eviction, and consequently Fiona had felt that the only option she had was to engage in prostitution. Margie (aged 32) said that after doing a runner from her boyfriend/ponce and going to live with her mother, she had stopped working. However when she had gone back to her flat a few months later she had found that she had accrued four months of rent arrears and that the council was going to evict her. She had gone back to prostitution to earn the money to pay off the rent arrears.

Anna (aged 36) talked about when her boyfriend had left her and her three children, plunging them into immediate financial crisis. Anna said that she had been unable to pay the rent on her privately rented flat and was threatened with eviction. She had returned to prostitution in order to avoid eviction. Helena (aged 35) commented that after her divorce she had had no income and had only avoided homelessness by living with her ex-husband and his new wife.

Rejecting and Embracing Dependency

Dependency was a theme that continuously cropped up in the interviewees' narratives. It was invoked by the women to explain their involvement in prostitution and, as has been suggested, it was a structuring principle of the women's material circumstances. Many of those who had grown up in local authority care had rejected the dependency that is structured by the care system – a rejection that had provided them with the motivation to run away. Similarly, for those women who attributed their involvement in prostitution to the need to 'sort out' pressing problems, multiple debts and so on, being dependent on particular men or their own families was an option they had rejected. In this instance dependency was seen as creating the problems that generate 'unsortedness' (dependence on men who were abusive, who did not provide economically and who exploited the women). The rejection of dependence on particular men (for whatever reason) had often precipitated immediate financial crises in the interviewees' lives. And as described in the preceding sections, the interviewees' material and social security had been mediated through a relationship of dependence on their families or on particular men. Thus the circumscription of the women's options and the risks characterising their lives had been caused, in part, by the economically dependent relationships they had had with their male partners and family members, and by the women's rejection of such dependency.

Many of the interviewees saw their families or their childhood in terms of unwanted and forced dependency that had included various forms of abuse, neglect and/or restrictions that were perceived to be unduly harsh. And in many cases, their childhood had been marked by devastating violence. Twelve of the women recalled being battered or sexually abused by their carers. Some of the women talked openly about the abuse they had suffered, how this had shaped their understanding of relationships with men and families, and as a consequence had made it easier to be come involved in prostitution. Andrea (aged 27) commented that all she knew about families was 'how to be used and abused' by them and that she had replicated this in her own relationships later in life. Lois (aged 21) said that by the time she was 17 years old, the only thing she had understood about living with others was 'how to be raped and how to be attacked and how to be beaten up, that's all I knew at that time'. But violence, violation and abuse had not only occurred within the women's own families. Three of the ten women who had been placed in local authority care homes when they were younger had been sexually abused by workers employed there.

It was not only being subjected to abuse by others that was deployed to define dependency as intolerable. Interviewees who had lived in local authority care described their carers as 'not wanting to know', as 'not listening' and hence 'not caring'. Ingrid (aged 44) recalled that the carers in the Barnardo's Children Home she had lived in had not told her of the death of her father until the day she was due to go home for a visit. She said:

> I was thinking I was going home that day, you know? They [the carers in the home] didn't tell me that my dad was dead. They didn't bother telling me until the day I was leaving. I'm telling all the other kids, 'I'm going home to me dad'. 'No you're not, your dad's dead' they said. Totally out of the blue. They just didn't care.

Patsy (aged 42) recalled that she had tried telling her carers that her father was sexually abusing her, but 'they didn't want to hear it'. For both Ingrid and Patsy, the insensitivity and unwillingness to listen displayed by the care staff had signified that they did not care about (or for) them.

But such negative constructions of dependency were not necessarily related to the rejection of dependency. This was made clear in the women's discussions of 'freedom' and 'independence'. With the exception of Fiona (aged 41), who described her involvement in prostitution as nothing more and nothing less than a 'career choice', all the other women recalled 'going wild with freedom'. This had typically occurred when they had left their families and become involved in prostitution. They talked as though the restrictions and abuses of dependency had been stripped away and that nothing and no one was going to get in the way of them living their lives for themselves. Barbara (aged 24) summarised this in the following way:

> When I got my freedom, I just went wild! I went mental! Any money I got, I'd bugger off to a club or a pub. I'd make friends and then leave. I kipped on couches or park benches. Got into trouble for

shoplifting. I just went wild with my freedom. Once I finally got out of my family, that was it. Anything and everything went!

In all the narratives, the moment at which the respondents had achieved their freedom from their families was recalled with pride. They saw their 'hard earned independence' as a badge to be worn and shown off. But such independence and freedom had often been achieved at a price – such as being 'on the run', being homeless or being destitute. Any ambivalence shown by the women about the consequences of rejecting dependence on their families or local authority care were quickly erased with the assertion (and conviction) that independence was not only necessary, but something that had to be struggled for.

Similar sentiments were displayed in their discussions of independence from particular male partners. Relationships characterised by dependence on partners were often seen as arenas of (potential) abuse, violence and degradation. Seventeen of the 21 women told of being beaten up, sexually assaulted, humiliated or degraded by their male partners. Four of the interviewees drew direct links between these experiences and the 'ease' of involvement in prostitution. Michelle (aged 33) put it very succinctly when she said:

> But honestly, hustling came easy in the beginning. Because this guy that I was with, this black guy, he was perverted and mean. He used to beat me and used to force me to do things with his dog and all sorts. So I was in a relationship which made it easier for me to sleep with these guys and get paid for it – after all it was easier than doing it at home – it was nothing for me than what I had to go through at home.

As in the discussions of dependency in relation to families, the point at which the women's rejection of dependence on particular men became really obvious was when they spoke of independence:

> I've always been very independent. It probably connects with working because I want my own money. I don't wanna have to rely on anybody else. Never had (Ingrid, aged 44).

> I don't live with him. I don't want to. I like living on me own with the kids. I've had enough. I just want independence, I don't want anyone telling me what to do any more. Been there, done that! No more (Janet, aged 37).

I'm definitely an independent sort of person. I'm on my own, anything I want I have to go out and get it. No one helps me, sort of thing. I rely on myself coz they're ain't no one else you can really rely on (Olivia, aged 28).

Independence from their partners was recounted with pride. The women spoke passionately about their rejection of dependence on particular men and used it as a signifier of competence at survival and providing for their children.

In this context, engagement in prostitution was understood as being a strategy to achieve their ardently desired independence. With no need for qualifications and no need to go through the recruitment procedures of legitimate employment, prostitution provided the means to earn enough money to live independently. Working on a 'cash-in-hand' basis, the informal organisation of prostitution and the fluidity of involvement in prostitution were all depicted as providing a new opportunity to remove themselves from relationships with brutal and violent men, uncaring carers and abusive families.

And yet there was ambiguity and ambivalence. Whilst the women took pride in the degree to which they had become independent, they nonetheless embraced the idea of being dependent on a mythical man within a mythical family. Their aspirations for the future included an ultraconventional nuclear family (cf. Carlen, 1988). They wanted a house or flat and a husband or partner who would support them and their children. They wistfully talked about finding a man who would take care of them. Indeed when asked what would make them give up prostitution, many said that a loving relationship with a man would provide both the structure and impetus for them to leave:

But to come out of this, being by yourself, I think you really need somebody to fall in love with, somebody who understands you and who you can tell your whole life story to and somebody who can take care of you so you don't have to work. Otherwise there's no chance (Sammy, aged 18).

I want a child and a council flat done out nicely, not too posh, but comfortable. I want a man. I just wanna be loved. He can work and then I wouldn't have to see him all the time. That's all I want, nothing extravagant, just a normal life. I could stay at home and he could look after me and the kids (Katrina, aged 20).

I just want someone to look after me to tell you the truth (Olivia, aged 28).

It has been asserted throughout this section that being a woman is a materially risky business. Choices for living exist, but for working-class women with few financial resources and for women involved in prostitution, these choices are made in the context of risk and cost calculation because the social structures of inequality between men and women continue to be real and immediate. Of particular importance in this context, and to the prostitute women in this study, are the ways in which women's economic survival is structured by the social belief that women are ultimately dependent on men. For these 21 prostitute women, however, life with families and life with men was equally (if not more) risky than living independently. Their experience of degradation, violence, abuse and exploitation had enabled them to reject dependency and live independent lives. Prostitution was seen as offering the opportunity to escape from past abuses. And yet ambivalence existed. Dependence on 'good men' within 'good families' was seen by the women as the ultimate goal of their lives.

CIRCUMSCRIBING THE FUTURE: PROSTITUTION AS A THREAT TO SURVIVAL

The social, material and ideological conditions that circumscribed the interviewees' earlier lives by structuring their poverty, their community and social ostracisation and their dependence on men or state welfare benefits led them to see prostitution as a way forward and a realistic (and successful) strategy for achieving independence, financial and housing security and new social networks. But there was a paradox in the interviewees' narratives. For at the same time as describing prostitution as a means to achieve economic and social stability, they also described it as a 'trap' that further circumscribed their lives and brought even greater poverty, community ostracisation, exploitation, abuse, housing difficulties and dependence on men, and thus threatened their social, material and at times physical survival. Gail (aged 28), for example, said that she had become a prostitute to escape a violent partner and continued with it in order to escape ponces and poverty (hence representing prostitution as the means of opening future of possibilities) at the same time as asserting that involvement in prostitution had been the cause of most of the violence and poverty she had suffered (hence representing engagement in prostitution as a cause of reduced possibilities and a threat to survival).

This section examines how prostitution circumscribed the women's options, possibilities and opportunities, and threatened their social and material stability and survival; and how a series of gendered victimisations trapped them in prostitution. The section discusses the institutional practices of prostitution and focuses on prostitution-related poverty, prostitution-related social isolation, prostitution-related housing problems and prostitution-related dependence on men. In each respect, prostitution was understood by the interviewees as an extremely risky business.

Impoverishing Institutional Practices of Prostitution

By differentiating between the act of selling sex and prostitution as the institution that makes that act possible, the impoverishing aspects of prostitution are made visible. Consequently the focus of discussion here will not be whether or not these women made the kind of money that allowed them to sort out their problems, sign off the social security register, obtain housing and leave their male partners, families or local authority care. Instead the focus will be on the institutional practices that circumscribed their options and opportunities for future action and generated a new set of risks to be negotiated in their struggle for material survival. These risks are revealed by examining (1) 'starting up', or the process of becoming a prostitute; (2) 'revolving doors', or the contemporary practice of regulating prostitution by imposing fines on women convicted of prostitution-related offences; (3) the lack of value of undeclared income; and (4) how patterns of 'super-fast' consumption are structured by prostitution.

Starting up: Getting Involved in Prostitution
Becoming a prostitute requires an initial financial investment. As with any new venture, equipment needs to be purchased and a secure working environment has to be found. Because the institution of prostitution is organised informally in that there are few employers, the responsibility of providing these things ultimately falls on the working women. Whilst these 'starting up' expenses differ according to the location in which women work, in all locations there are extra financial burdens on the women.

One of the extra financial burdens (and arguably the smallest) is supplying condoms to the punters. All the interviewees were concerned about their sexual health and insisted that their punters use condoms. This was hardly surprising given that half of the interviewees in this study had been contacted through a sexual health outreach worker, although recent literature does support the view that non-drug-injecting prostitutes are assiduous in their use of condoms with punters (see Scambler *et al.*, 1990; McKeganey and Barnard, 1996).

The sexual health outreach service (SHOS) supplies prostitute women with condoms, femidoms, dental dams and other forms of sexual health protection and birth control. But because of the budget restrictions imposed on the SHOS by the health authority, the interviewees received only a limited supply. Any extra condoms and so on they might need they had to purchase themselves.

Those interviewees who worked from the streets tended to be extremely wary about carrying more than two condoms because of their belief that, if they were arrested, the possession of more than two condoms would be used as proof that they were soliciting. Those women who worked in saunas and brothels (which potentially reduced the risk of arrest) had to pay the management or owners a fee each week for tea, coffee, towels, condoms and so on. Purchasing condoms and other items to ensure sexual health may not have cost the street-working women a large amount of money relative to their incomes, but it did constitute a regular expense and an expense that has become increasingly important. With the increase in general awareness about sexually transmitted diseases, particularly in the context of the moral panic surrounding the spread of HIV/AIDS, prostitutes in Britain and abroad have been vilified as reservoirs of sexual disease (McKeganey and Barnard, 1996). In this context the possession of condoms has a significance beyond their practical use in that they signify 'cleanliness' and 'health'. Hence many of the women spoke of 'clean' prostitutes and 'dirty' prostitutes – the difference being whether or not a woman 'did business' with or without condoms.

Three of the interviewees had incurred multiple debts in the process of starting up. Gail (aged 28), after 'doing a runner' because she had refused to be dependent on a man and had been refused a loan by the social services, had decided to start work as a prostitute. She vividly recounted the period after her decision to become a prostitute, but before she had actually started working:

> So anyway, I got my flat and this flat cost me – the guy was quite reasonable, he said forty pounds a week and some of the flats in the area I worked were about sixty pounds a day! So, this guy said forty

pounds a week and I thought, 'Great, it's a lot of money, but I'll be all right because I will make money.' Of course, I had to buy a bed and that was another forty pounds and, um, I live near there so it wasn't too bad, but we used to get a taxi home every night, so that was another expense. And the childminder was another expense and then came the big night. Get ready, I put my glad rags on and my heels on and off I went.... Anyway, I got down there and I couldn't go through with it. I just stood there for two whole weeks.... But I run into debt. I owed the baby-sitter an astronomical amount. I owed money on the flat, the bed and taxis. And, of course, every time I seen a vice car, I'd be throwing away the condoms. So I've never got no condoms – I'm not using them, not taking any money off them.... So the pressure was really on – the bills were building up and I was robbing the housekeeping money coz I had to pay for the taxis, condoms, tissues and whatever.

Patsy (aged 42) remembered that when she had returned to work after a two-year break she had bought clothes, wigs and a mobile phone, and had placed an advertisement in the local paper. But she had not had a punter for the first three weeks. Thus by the time she did start to work she had accrued debts from living for three weeks without an income and the cost of setting up work as a prostitute. Sammy (aged 18) spoke about the money she had had to give to the sauna owners for being able to work there:

Some saunas they charge you 10 pounds for cleaning, 10 pounds for Makro, 10 pounds for this and 10 pounds for that. You know what I mean? You end up paying more to go to work than you end up earning.

Although these experiences were similar to those many people have when starting a new job or changing their working environment (such as the need to purchase new or different types of clothing, the cost of transport and perhaps relocation expenses), for the interviewees they were more difficult because their lives were generally circumscribed by the material effects of poverty. Their housing difficulties and the financial burden of being a single mother and living on social security benefits meant that the interviewees had no financial resources to fall back on. At various points in the interviews all the women, spoke of prostitution as a means of escaping escalating debt or the constraints of living in poverty. But an extra financial burden had been placed on them simply through the process of becoming involved in prostitution. But the burden had not stopped at that point – continued involvement in prostitution, particularly from the streets, had brought with it its own unique financial problems and risks.

Revolving Doors: Fining Women for Prostitution-Related Offences
All but two of the interviewees had been convicted of a prostitution-related offence – typically, loitering or soliciting. In most cases these convictions had been punished with fines (Table 4.4), which are a source of impoverishment among prostitutes. The fining of prostitutes became sentencing orthodoxy in 1983 as part of the decarceration movement in the punishment of prostitutes. Thereafter there was a concomitant increase in the number of convictions for soliciting and the level of fines meted out. This had the contradictory outcome that *more*, not fewer, women were sent to prison, but for non-payment of fines rather than prostitution-related offences (Matthews, 1986, p. 191).

Few of the interviewees could remember precisely how many times they had been arrested or the exact amount of the fines they either still had to pay or had paid in the course of their involvement in prostitution. However my own observations in court and comments by the women suggest that fines tend to be in the region of £50–100 per charge and that women often have three or more charges against them each time they go to court.

The practice of fining women varies according to where their work is conducted (see Matthews, 1986; McLeod, 1981, 1982; Sumner, 1981). It is accepted that in both the letter and the exercise of the laws on prostitution, women working from the streets are more heavily regulated than women working from locations such as saunas, brothels or home (see Chapter 1). This was certainly borne out by the interviewees. The two women who had never been convicted, Sophie (aged 28) and Fiona (aged 41), had avoided working from the streets because they knew that if they did there was a greater chance of being arrested and fined than if they worked from home or saunas. However the other 19 women risked street work because there was a higher turnover of punters on the streets than in any other venue. Arrest and conviction was a regular occurrence, so much so that the women accepted it as an integral part of street work (cf. Dunhill, 1989):

> I think the police are fair. If they think that they can let you off coz you were nicked last night, they will. But the only time you'll get nicked regular is if it's the head saying, 'We need convictions, make

Table 4.4   Arrest and punishment for prostitution-related offences

Name (age)	Reasons for arrest	Punishment
Andrea (27)	Loitering/soliciting*	Fines and three terms of imprisonment for fine defaulting
Anna (36)	Loitering/soliciting	Fines and one term of imprisonment for fine defaulting
Barbara (24)	Loitering/soliciting	Fines and three terms of imprisonment for fine defaulting
Christina (23)	Loitering/soliciting	Fines and three terms of imprisonment for fine defaulting
Diane (37)	Loitering/soliciting	Fines, probation order for two years and imprisonment (pre-1983)**
Gail (28)	Brothel keeping	Two years' probation
Georgie (35)	Loitering/soliciting, brothel keeping	Fines
Helena (35)	Loitering/soliciting	Fines
Ingrid (44)	Loitering/soliciting	Fines and imprisonment (pre-1983)
Janet (37)	Loitering/soliciting, brothel keeping	Fines and one term of imprisonment (pre-1983)
Jasmine (30)	Loitering/soliciting	Fines
Katrina (20)	Loitering/soliciting	Fines
Lois (21)	Loitering/soliciting	Fines
Margie (32)	Loitering/soliciting	Fines
Michelle (33)	Loitering/soliciting	Fines and one term of imprisonment for fine defaulting
Olivia (28)	Loitering/soliciting	Fines
Patsy (42)	Loitering/soliciting, brothel keeping	A year's probation and several terms of imprisonment (pre-1983)
Ruthie (25)	Loitering/soliciting	Fines
Sammy (18)	Loitering/soliciting	Caution

* In recounting their involvement with the criminal justice system, the women did not distinguish between their arrests for loitering and soliciting.
** Prior to 1983, imprisonment was an accepted punishment for prostitution-related offences.

up the things. Get out and nick everyone that's moving'. Or if there's a purge on, you've got no chance. You don't even get a warning.... When there was a purge on, I can remember coming out the cafe years ago ... I come out the cafe ... I walked up the road and straightaway – nicked! I come out the police station, I walked half way back up the road to go home and I got nicked again by the same police and there wasn't a thing I could do about it! (Andrea, aged 27).

Some nights they'd have a purge on. Some days they'd leave us alone. Sometimes they used to say, 'If you give us the reg. of a couple of punters like, we'll give you a run for a week'. They wouldn't nick you for a week. So you had that time to make up your money and pay your fines (Barbara, aged 24).

When I was working on the beat it was worse [that is, being arrested]. I was getting nicked every night. Every single night – sometimes twice! (Christina, aged 23).

That fining prostitutes for prostitution-related offences is particularly ironic is especially clear in relation to the general material circumstances of the interviewees – many of them did not have the financial resources to pay their fines so prostitution had become a trap:

The system grinds you down. Because you're doing it [engaging in prostitution], you get arrested, you go to court, you get a fine. You gotta carry on doing it to pay the fine.... You get stuck in the system. You go to work, you make your money, you get arrested, you get fined, you have to go back to work to pay the fine, then you get another fine. It's just a vicious circle that you get stuck in for years (Andrea, aged 27).

I got done once for three charges on the same day – five hundred pounds! I mean, I owed six grand once, four grand and I got fourteen days in prison – which was good. Some people get six months for that amount. The one, he said, 'How much benefit do you collect?' I said 'Fifty four pounds a fortnight'. They said, 'We order you to pay fifty pound a week off your fine'. I said, 'Well how am I supposed to do that?' They said, 'Well you're earning a living aren't you?' So it's all right to work if you have to pay your fines (Christina, aged 23).

They let my fines build up to over one thousand seven hundred or something and they give me six weeks in nick coz I told them to f**k off – that I weren't gonna pay it. So you got no chance. 'You can whistle for it – coz I'm only gonna go back out there and work to pay the fine anyway'. 'Well', they said, 'you can't do that'. I said, 'Well how am I supposed to pay the fine. I ain't getting benefits for the fine! F**k off like'. I got done for contempt of court and six weeks for non-payment of fines (Barbara, aged 24).

Not having the money to pay the fines and wishing to avoid imprisonment left many women with few options but to carry on with their work
in prostitution. This was so clearly the case that it prompted one court
clerk to comment:

> What we have here is a revolving door policy. The women come in
> and we tell them that soliciting is not okay by giving them a fine. But
> then we know, and they know, that the only way they're going to pay it
> is by going back out on the streets. And we wonder why they do that.

Hence the practice of fining women whose involvement in prostitution
is a result of their experience of poverty acts to further that poverty. It
was a risk that many of the interviewees had been aware of prior to
their engagement in prostitution, but a risk they had chosen to take
because of the short-term economic benefits of working. As is evident
from the above extracts, the practice of fining makes involvement in
prostitution a threat to economic survival and a strategy for economic
stability that costs more than it benefits the individuals concerned.

'Money has no Value'

The above discussion does not mean to imply that sufficient money cannot be earned by engaging in prostitution. But for those with a good
income, because the money has been earned through involvement in a
quasi-legal and certainly socially stigmatised institution, the purposes
to which that money can be put are limited. That is to say, earnings
from prostitution are not the same as income from legitimate employment. The specific differences between money obtained through prostitution and money obtained through licit work inhere in (1) what can be
done with the money and (2) how the institution of prostitution impacts
upon the value of money and encourages super-fast consumption.

Money from prostitution clearly has a use value in terms of consumption and spending power. The source of money is irrelevant to the value
of a pound in terms of what it can buy. But the source is very relevant in
terms of spending power beyond the direct exchange of money for particular consumer items. Money obtained from legitimate work ('income') has borrowing value in that it can be tied to mortgage borrowing
and hire purchase, to obtain credit cards, overdrafts and so on, and thus
provides individuals with flexibility in their personal finances.

The interviewees spoke at length about the difficulty of establishing
long-term economic stability with money that was undeclared, unofficial
income. Fifteen of the 21 women did not have bank accounts and could

not envisage a time when they would. Michelle (aged 33) commented: 'Even though you have a fairly good life, you're not able to get credit cards, or bank accounts where you can go to the bank and say, "Well, I wouldn't mind getting a little house somewhere".'

Ingrid (aged 44), who had been involved in prostitution for the longest, discussed in detail the problems she had had in trying to secure private rented accommodation because she could not supply an employment reference (even though she could afford the rent on the flat). Consequently she had decided to redecorate and refurbish her housing association flat, but had discovered that she had no access to hire purchase because, again, she had no employer and no official income. Most of the other interviewees feared that banks, hire-purchase companies and landlords might ask them about the source of their income, and as a consequence they had chosen not to use their money to borrow money. This meant that the women had no financial flexibility and effectively lived 'cash-in-hand'.

Another problem the interviewees discussed was their exclusion from 'deferred benefits', which are accorded to individuals who have a legitimate, declarable income. Sammy (aged 18) said that legitimate employees contributed to their state pensions through their weekly pay, but unless she regularly contributed to a private pension fund (a financial commitment she perceived to be beyond her means) she would never receive a pension. She also refused to claim social security benefits as she was concerned about the regulatory practices to which she would be subjected (especially the regulations governing availability to work). Sophie (aged 28), who had been ill for a month prior to the interview, talked about how legitimate employees are able to claim sick pay when ill and therefore still have an income when they need to take time off work. Most of the other women commented that they were not in a position to take time off to have a holiday, or even be ill, because they would have no income if they did.

Many of these problems are experienced by other cash-in-hand and self-employed workers, but the ways in which involvement in prostitution encouraged super-fast spending made the small risks of earning undeclared income much more pressing. It was demonstrated earlier that the women perceived that money obtained from prostitution was 'easy' money – that is, money that is always readily available. It is suggested here that the notion of 'easy money' helps promote super-fast consumption. The women all agreed that, because they could always go out and earn more money, the money they earned had no value. Consequently they thought nothing of spending it:

Hustling money is wasteful money. Easy come, easy go. You don't respect it. Coz it's always been there and it always will (Anna, aged 36).

The money is easy come, easy go. You buy things you don't really need, but you get it and then you gotta pay for it. You want it because you never had it as a kid and you want it when you're older (Ingrid, aged 44).

You know, the money's easy to make and it's just as easy to spend. It's easy come and easy go (Georgie, aged 35).

The money's so easy it's almost like being a millionaire – you don't have to worry coz you can always get more tomorrow (Sophie, aged 28).

The effect of the notion of 'easy come, easy go' was, simply, that the women rarely had savings to fall back on. When this is coupled with the lack of deferred benefits and undeclared income's lack of borrowing value, discussed above, it can be seen that earning money through prostitution poses a specific risk. Namely, as the women commented, the very fact that reasonable amounts of money could be earned and that the money was spent quickly acted to impoverish the women in the long term. As Diane (aged 37) poignantly remarked: 'I've sold my body for half my life and what have I got to show for it? Nothing. I'm worse off now than I was before'. Thus on the women's own admission, the notion that money from prostitution is 'easy money' is a myth that hides the fact that engagement in prostitution serves to increase poverty.

Taken together, the extra financial burdens of engaging in prostitution, the practice of imposing fines for prostitution-related offences and the 'easy money' myth pose real risks for women involved in prostitution. The interviewees spoke of prostitution as a financial trap that creates further problems and risks, rather than as a means of securing economic and social survival and stability. Certainly the reality of the impoverishing aspects of prostitution stand in direct contradiction to the representation of prostitution as offering protection against poverty. Prostitution was recognised by the interviewees as being a very risky business. Moreover, because of the general socio-structural constraints on their lives, they did not have the resources to cover or successfully counter those risks. In short, in terms of income and money, involvement in prostitution was described as extremely costly.

Prostitution-Related Housing Difficulties

Involvement in prostitution can be linked to prior housing difficulties inasmuch as it is seen as a strategy to obtain secure housing. But involvement in prostitution also creates its own specific types of housing problem. Amongst these are 'tied housing', prostitution-related eviction and a life that is spent 'on the move'.

Nine of the interviewees had had experience of what is referred to hereafter as 'tied housing' – accommodation that is integral to the individual's involvement in prostitution. Tied housing is a complex arrangement, but it usually consists of housing provided by a ponce, who acts as a landlord. It is also a problem that dramatically threatens women's survival, increases their dependence on particular men, increases their risk of victimisation (that is, exploitation and/or physical abuse) and limits their chance of turning to a 'conventional' life (that is non-involvement in prostitution).

Tied housing is a practice that is strategically used by ponces to secure two different ends: (1) to control women's participation in prostitution; and (2) to exploit the economic rewards of women's work in prostitution.

The story of Barbara (aged 24) most clearly demonstrates how tied housing can be used by ponces to control prostitutes' lives. Barbara said that she had been kidnapped from the streets by three men at gunpoint. They had then beaten and raped her and forced her to work as a prostitute. The men

> took my keys off me and kept me in their house. There was no chance of doing a runner because they'd got more of their mates. . . . There must have been sixteen of us girls there. [JP: So they kept you there?] Well, yea. But no, they had a house where his girlfriend was. It was a three-bedroom house. They took us there later. We could leave only if we was working and then there'd be someone watching us. But the house was bad!

Barbara's experience shows how housing can be used to coerce women into prostitution, and into continuing to engage in prostitution. Barbara's ponce effectively controlled her and the others by keeping them locked up.

Janet and Lois recalled similar events:

> [JP: How did you start working?] When I was thirteen, me and me friend come out of Ireland [that is, ran away from Ireland] and used

to shoplift and whatever. I used to hang around up town with gay people and whatever – I mix with everyone.... I met a fella – a black fella and I went to live with him. He put me on the game that week. [JP: How did that happen?] I was living with him...all these men turned up at the flat and I hadn't got a clue what to do...I had no where else to go (Janet, aged 37).

When he [Lois' sister's boyfriend] put me on the game, he took me to this house where this guy was based down in Greenvale. Like where he runs from. [JP: Then what happened?] They both took me out in the car, showed me around [pause]. They took me back to the guy's house and told me that the next morning I was to go and get my stuff from my sister's, my clothes and that and I would go with this guy and work. Well, he took my clothes and everything from me and I stayed in that house and that was that. I was working. He made sure I never had anything and didn't go anywhere (Lois, aged 21).

The ponces who had put Janet and Lois on the game had strategically used housing to heighten the women's insecurity. Janet, who had been just 13 years old when she ran away from her parents, had been given accommodation by a man but only in return for becoming a prostitute. Similarly Lois, having run away from several types of accommodation, had eventually been taken to a 'secure' place. Her possessions had been confiscated and she had nowhere else to go – she had been 'put on the game'.

Lois recalled a series of events, later in her life, that demonstrate how tied housing is used by ponces to exploit women's earnings from prostitution. Lois had done a runner from the tied housing where she had been living and had turned to an ex-boyfriend:

Then, like, I seen this ex-boyfriend and he knew what had been happening [that she was involved in prostitution and that her accommodation was tied]. And he said, 'You can leave. I can get you a flat to use. Suit yourself.' Which he done. But he used the nice way of being a ponce – it was the same as what I left. [JP: What do you mean?] Well, it was his friend's flat and he wasn't using it. So my ex-boyfriend and the guy with the flat started saying, 'Oh, you've gotta pay rent and you want your own flat which means you gotta give us money' and I went along with it. In the meantime, I got no where to live but this guy's flat. Well, I was handing all me money over to this guy who was telling me he was going to get me my own flat.

Michelle (aged 33) had had a comparable experience. After serving a prison sentence for fine default (a fine resulting from prostitution-related offences), her ex-husband had kicked her out of their house but kept all her possessions:

> So I went to the Blues [illicit parties] and met this dreadlocks guy. This black guy who was saying to me, 'Oh I love you – just give me one hundred and fifty pounds a week and I'll sort you a flat'. I said, 'Yea'. He was a nice guy because I dropped it to eighty pounds and then the next week to twenty pounds. But of course, I lost the flat then. Then I started working Birchfield in a house and I could stay there – it was meant to be forty pounds [rent] a day.... Well, he [the landlord] saw how good I was doing and the one night he says he wants more for rent – he wants half my earnings every day!

After three weeks Michelle had done a runner, leaving all her possessions. She had then approached a local church organisation, which had arranged hostel accommodation for her. She had stayed in that accommodation for six months until MidCity Housing department gave her a 'hard to let' property.

There are many issues that can be untangled from these stories about tied housing. Tied housing demonstrates how women's accommodation is mediated by and through their relationships with particular men. Although this constrains the lives of most working-class women, it has different consequences for different groups of women – particularly women who have few financial resources and are socially marginalised by their involvement in prostitution. Tied housing also had a direct influence on the interviewees' perception of the opening and closing of future options and opportunities. When reflecting on her experiences of tied housing, Michelle (aged 33) commented:

> I suppose [pause], I worked all over and in loads of places. The trouble starts when you live where you work. You got no chance of leaving without being homeless. You give up your independence, because when you work as well as live somewhere – if you work, its easy for you to *say,* 'I wanna stop, I'm leaving', but when you live there what you gonna do? Pack up everything and go? You just cannot do that all the time – so you're bound to stay where you are and carry on working.

In other words, on one level tied housing literally locked women into prostitution by creating a situation in which the perceived risks of staying

(control and exploitation by ponces) were measured against the perceived risks of leaving (doing a runner and facing potential homelessness and the violent retaliation of ponces). And the risks of leaving
were often believed to be greater.

Tied housing was not the only prostitution-related housing difficulty
experienced by the interviewees. Stories of prostitution-related evictions were typical. (The 1996 Housing Act introduced 'probationary
tenancies' in local authority accommodation, so it is possible that this
type of housing difficulty has become much more pronounced than it
was when my fieldwork was conducted in 1994.) Three of the 18 women
who had experienced housing difficulties had been evicted because of
their involvement in prostitution. Anna (aged 36) told of her neighbours' concerted effort to get her evicted because they had objected
to her taking punters home. Eventually the housing association had
evicted her, but relocated her the same day in another flat, which
Anna recalled as 'being a nightmare' in that it had rats, damp and 'all
sorts of problems'. Anna had been explicitly told that she would not be
offered any other house or flat, and that if she rejected this one she
would be making herself intentionally homeless and would therefore
exclude herself from any help they could offer. Similarly Andrea (aged
27) recounted being evicted because her neighbours had continuously
complained to the local housing authority about her involvement in
prostitution. That these women had worked from their homes in order
to avoid the risk of punter violence and police arrest associated with
street work makes these stories all the more poignant.

Ingrid (aged 44), after doing a runner because she could no longer
take the beatings she was getting from her ponce, had gone to the
council:

> I played on the kids and I got me first little council flat – oh it was
> brilliant! I had me own front door! I thought it was great. Got it all
> done up before I moved in. Decorated it. Carpet – the lot! I was there
> for three years, but the neighbours got me out. I was taking punters
> there, wasn't I? And that little clique up there [the neighbours] didn't
> like that. They hated me. Mind you any white girls that lived on that
> road that was seeing black men they got out.

Afterwards Ingrid had found temporary housing association accommodation, only to be faced with eviction a year later. This last eviction
had resulted in Ingrid being blacklisted by both the housing authority
and the local housing associations. In Ingrid's case, however, it was not

just prostitution but also her involvement with black men that had resulted in her housing difficulties.

Eviction and subsequent homelessness lead to the third prostitution-related housing difficulty: being 'on the move' (although this is not restricted to women who are involved in prostitution). Many of the interviewees, outwith the ideology of the family, judged and found wanting by public housing organisations, often locked into tied housing and/or undergoing physical and sexual abuse at the hands of their male partners or families, recounted periods of their lives when they had been on the move and said that this was part of life as a prostitute. Indeed a type of survivalism accompanies most women's involvement in prostitution, particularly in relation to housing (see Carlen, 1996). Olivia and Ruthie described their time on the move:

> Frannie [Olivia's daughter] was living in Hightown with me mum and I was sending money down there. And like I was living with this guy in Greenvale – he'd let me stay there and whatever. But I couldn't get it together for a while. I just, dunno, couldn't get it together. I'd be working but not doing something constructive. That was it. I was just waiting for a house.... So I was living with this guy, I had nowhere. Then the council gave me this place, but I still couldn't get it together and I moved in with these other people. [JP: Why?] I dunno, I just couldn't get it together. It was all part of working, you move on. [JP: So you were homeless?] No, I've always had a house but I haven't always lived in it – I just moved around. It's just part of the life. But when they [the social services] took Frannie that made me get my house together. That gave me the push. I had to get a base for her (Olivia, aged 28).

> I had a council house, but I moved from there.... Then I lived here, there and everywhere – I just couldn't settle. But I stopped when I moved in with Alvin – it's a housing association house – but I just couldn't take the lifestyle anymore. I didn't want to move around anymore, I just wanted to stop with the kids and Alvin and I've lived there ever since (Ruthie, aged 25).

Such moving around had directly affected the women's perception of future possibilities. The women had continued to move around until something else happened. For Olivia the 'something else' had been the social services taking her daughter into local authority care. For Ruthie it had been moving in with a man with whom she wanted to stay.

A final note is required on the question of the interviewees' housing problems, both prior to and during their involvement in prostitution. The three types of housing difficulty experienced by the women (doing a runner, economic difficulties and prostitution-related difficulties) were not mutually exclusive. Some women experienced all three, others experienced only one or two whilst three women experienced none. In an attempt to negotiate and survive one type of difficulty, the women had often found themselves with another. For instance many of the interviewees who had run away from violent partners had ended up in tied housing in order to avoid homelessness. They might subsequently have escaped from the tied housing and presented themselves as homeless to the local authority, but found themselves unable to maintain the housing provided by the authority (because, for instance, of the breakdown of a particular relationship), and so would spend a period of time 'on the move', and so on. The women's involvement in prostitution often went hand in hand with their housing difficulties inasmuch as struggling to survive one type of housing difficulty often meant entering, returning to or continuing to work in prostitution, which of course perpetuated the risk of housing insecurity, poverty, exploitation and abuse.

Exemplified in the issue of housing difficulties is the extent to which the women's material existence was characterised by a dynamic of risk. Underpinning the moments at which women chose to leave their partners, were divorced by them, chose to do a runner, accepted tied housing or brought punters back to their flat for business was a calculation of risk. Depending on the degree to which the women's housing security and insecurity was mediated by and through their relationships with men, they either faced a threat in their present housing arrangement (violence, exploitation, control) or they faced the uncertainty of economic instability and homelessness.

The discussion of housing difficulties also illustrates the degree to which engagement in prostitution represents a trap that is difficult to escape and a strategy that comes with a high price. Their experience of tied housing, prostitution-related evictions and being on the move meant that the interviewees portrayed prostitution as a trap that circumscribed their future possibilities and threatened their economic survival.

The Institutional Practice of Poncing

Earlier it was stated that the interviewees had originally seen prostitution as a way of escaping from particular men and living independent lives. But by their own accounts, engagement in prostitution had in fact prevented them from living independent lives because of the practice of poncing. Studies of prostitution (for example Barry, 1979; Hoigard and Finstad, 1992; Faugier and Sargeant, 1997) have tended to equate the individuals who practise poncing with the practice itself. Analysis of the phenomenon has been limited to examining the 'quality' and 'type' of relationship that exists between the women and their ponces (see Phoenix, 1998). Hence Barry (1979) has provided a detailed, if cynical, description of the strategies by which ponces give the impression that they care for and love the women they want to ponce. Hoigard and Finstad (1992, pp. 166–9) portray the relationship between ponces and prostitutes as compassionate, loving and 'real relationships'. However, by distinguishing between the institutional practices of prostitution and the individuals who are located within the institution of prostitution, it is possible to examine the practice of poncing separately from the quality of the relationship that exists between prostitutes and ponces. That is to say, the effects of poncing are brought into relief when poncing is treated as an institutional practice, and not merely the individual actions of particular men.

The practice of poncing, as defined by the interviewees, is the financial exploitation of women who engage in prostitution. It is an ever present risk for them, and it disrupts and fractures their material and social options. It would be difficult to overstate the connection between the practice of poncing and engagement in prostitution. All but two of the interviewees had at some point been ponced, and six of the 16 currently working women were still being ponced.

The significance of poncing, like the significance of housing difficulties, inheres not necessarily in the practice itself (although in its more extreme and violent manifestations the practice is significant), but in its consequences. Poncing can fracture women's lives in three interlinked ways: (1) by dramatically increasing their poverty; (2) by cutting them off from other social networks (both within prostitution and outside), thus isolating them from the support or practical help of friends and family; and (3) by crushing their belief in their ability to resist poncing. Nineteen of the interviewees said they had been ponced, often for a considerable time and by different ponces, but the experiences they recalled most vividly were those that had had the most profound consequences.

Lois and Ruthie angrily described their lack of money when being ponced:

> I never seen a penny of the money I earned. I was only given two pound fifty a day. He even took my social money off me as

well.... Two pound fifty and it's hard when you're out there from 10.00 in the morning till any time up to about 9.00 at night. You've got two pound fifty and you've gotta decide which is more important, cigarettes, condoms or food (Lois, aged 21).

When I started working every penny went to him. Every penny! I was given a fiver, like, for a packet of Durex and 20 fags or something. Sometimes he bought things for me from the money he had off me – I was thinking, 'Oh, all these nice new clothes'. But he was spending MY money on clothes to make me look nicer. When I look back now, I think I was f**king stupid (Ruthie, aged 25).

Margie (aged 32) recalled that, after being ponced for ten years by the same man, it was not only her earnings from prostitution that had been taken from her, but any legitimate work earnings as well: 'I didn't see [any of] it! Not even me wages. None at all. Everything, he took everything. I got really browned off – I had nothing.' Gail and Patsy spoke of the 'knock-on' problems of being ponced:

I got this house from the Council and while I was in this house, every one pence we had, everything, Shiner [her ponce] took. So like, things like rent and rates, water rates all that kind of stuff never ever got paid. When he left [he was sent to prison] and I stopped working I wanted to get rehoused, but I was in arrears with never paying rent and stuff. So I had to work to pay that debt (Gail, aged 28).

I mean I was in debt! I was working out how to pay my rent, how to pay my mum back, how to buy my food. I was [pause] you don't get no money for bills in this game unless it's essential! And you gotta plead with him – even for your fines – nothing ever gets paid (Patsy, aged 42).

In these cases, poncing had had the effect of increasing the interviewees' poverty. All their income – whether from their work as prostitutes, social security or legitimate work – had been taken by their ponces. They had been left with a subsistence 'allowance' to get them through each day. This had often meant not having the money to pay their bills, maintain a reasonable standard of living or buy consumer durables such as washing machines, clothes, cars and so on. In short, the economic consequences of being ponced had been rapidly accumulating debts and a life lived in destitution.

Poncing also had the effect of cutting the women off from wider social networks such as families, friends or even other prostitute women.

Gail (aged 28) described how, when being ponced, her days had been spent in her house; that Shiner would not let her go out unless she was working and would not let her associate with other prostitutes, except for the other women he was poncing. Anna (aged 36) recollected similar circumstances when she was being ponced by the man she had eventually murdered. He would let her speak only to her children and himself, and he had cut her off from her two sisters and her friends. Margie (aged 32) commented that her ponce would not allow her to speak to any other women 'on the beat', much less have regular punters:

> I haven't ever mixed with any other working girls. I'm not allowed to. He says, 'You're not out there to mix with none of those girls'. He doesn't even like it if I have the same punter more than twice – just in case I do a runner with him.

Such tales were standard. Cut off from other social networks, the women were unable to receive the type of support that family and friends could offer (for example financial support, emotional support and/or practical help), and consequently they 'had no one to turn to' and 'no one to help' (Sammy, aged 18).

The interviewees' tales of social isolation because of their involvement with ponces were intriguing and paradoxical. Gail, Anna and Margie all talked about how poncing had structured and conditioned their isolation. All the interviewees spoke of varying degrees of hostility between themselves and the residents of the areas in which they worked and of the various strategies used by the residents to 'chase them off'. These included individual tactics and the more collective, organised actions of vigilante groups. And yet most also saw their involvement in prostitution as giving them a greater sense of community, breaking down their sense of isolation and providing them with a wider social network.

Another aspect of poncing was the women's belief that there was no effective resistance to this practice, that poncing was inevitable and could not be escaped. All of the women who had been ponced at one point or another spoke of the impossibility of 'just not giving him anymore money'. Too much was at stake. Threatened with violence, controlled through housing and debt, cut off from family and friends, the women believed that there was no way of stopping the practice, no way of effectively resisting being ponced. Eight of the 19 women who had been ponced spoke of their fear that any resistance would result in their being murdered (see Chapter 5 for a deconstruction of the symbolic landscape that enables such a belief).

Perhaps less extreme than living with the fear of murder (but no less circumscribing) was having to endure regular and brutal violence by the ponces. All of the ponced interviewees described episodes in which their ponces had physically attacked them. These events ranged from slaps and punches to extreme violence such as sexual sadism and injuries from gun-shots strangulation and knife attacks. Surprisingly, the women did not seem to view these events as extraordinary (see also Hoigard and Finstad, 1992). Ingrid (aged 44) illustrated the banality and routineness that violence from ponces was accorded when she said:

I lost a kid – well he kicked it out of me. [JP: Really?] Yea. Didn't know I was pregnant. [JP: That must have been hell . . .] Mmm. Well, I dunno. Looking back on it, it's just normal for you. It's just the every-day thing – I mean all the people I mixed with, they lived my sort of life too, so it was the norm.

The anticipation and regularity of violence from ponces contributed to the women's belief that there was no escape from poncing and that any 'misdemeanour' or 'petty resistance' would probably be dealt with by a beating from the ponce. Katrina (aged 20) summarised the interconnection between poverty through poncing, physical violence and the belief that there was no effective resistance:

We're not getting no money out of it. The only way we're going to get money is if we hide it. And if we get found out – the beatings! We usually get found out, so we've had it.

So strong was Katrina's conviction of the inevitability of violence that she thought the only way she could stop being ponced was to

get him to beat me again. I will go straight to the police and say [pause] I've had enough. I don't want no one poncing me, but I can't think of no other way. You see, there's no chance of doing a runner coz he's got his mates, there's hundreds of them.

Many of the interviewees had tried to escape by 'doing a runner' or going into hiding. But these efforts had often been unsuccessful and the women had eventually been brought back. For example:

I run away not too long ago. I went back to Edinburgh and I made the mistake of telling a friend of mine where I was and he [her ponce] come and kicked off the door and brought me back. And I've only just recovered. My nose was broken and me lips were all split. He still sent me out there to work with black eyes and split lips and a bust nose (Patsy, aged 42).

In short, poncing meant being trapped in prostitution. Caught in the trap of only being able to escape one ponce through the 'protection' of another, the women told desperate tales of being beaten, having all their money taken from them, forced to work until they made more and more money, frightened not only of their individual ponce, but of all his friends and of being sold and traded between different ponces like a chattel. Poncing was represented as an ever-present malignancy and a constant risk within the institution of prostitution. The currently ponced interviewees, when asked if there was anything else they would like to add, all commented to the effect that 'Everybody out there's got one [a ponce]. Not a lot of them will admit it, but they are. They're being ponced. You can't work out there without someone poncing off ya!' (Katrina, aged 20).

In this respect, prostitution did not signify an opening of possibilities and options, but a trap that enclosed the women, forced them 'on to the game', denied them routes out of prostitution, created unconquerable obstacles to leaving prostitution and locked them into relationships and ways of living that they either had not chosen or from which they wished to escape. This trap was constituted by both the reality and the risk of the ponce's physical, often brutal, retaliations and the enforced poverty and dependency that resulted from being ponced.

And yet not all the women had been ponced all the time. Not all viewed poncing as inescapable. Not all recalled such determined futures consequent to being ponced. Some of the respondents (including those whose stories were told above) recollected moments in their lives when poncing had been more 'consensual' (Table 4.5). They spoke of poncing practices that started (and continued) as jointly agreed business arrangements or as intimate relationships. Jasmine (aged 30) said that for two years she had been ponced by a man who would take only a percentage of her earnings in exchange for taking her to work, waiting for her and taking her back home. Olivia (aged 28) spoke of 'turning her boyfriend into a ponce' by giving him an 'allowance' until he got too 'greedy and started taking the piss'. Some aspects of poncing are not easy to explain or understand. Ingrid, when asked how the violent poncing she had been subjected to by one man over a three-year period had ended, commented that 'it just fizzled out'. She

Table 4.5   Type of poncing experienced

Name (age)	Type of poncing
Andrea (27)	Violent[*] and consensual[**]
Anna (36)	Violent
Barbara (24)	Violent and consensual
Christina (23)	Consensual
Diane (37)	Violent and consensual
Gail (28)	Violent and consensual
Georgie (35)	Violent
Ingrid (44)	Violent and consensual
Janet (37)	Violent and consensual
Jasmine (30)	Consensual
Katrina (20)	Violent
Lois (21)	Violent and consensual
Margie (32)	Consensual
Michelle (33)	Violent and consensual
Olivia (28)	Consensual
Patsy (42)	Violent and consensual
Ruthie (25)	Violent and consensual
Sammy (18)	Consensual
Sophie (28)	Consensual

[*] 'Violent' poncing is defined as poncing practices that were not described as consensual, and where the women perceived that they had been coerced through violence and intimidation into being ponced by a particular man.
[**] 'Consensual' poncing is defined as poncing practices that were described by the women as business-like arrangements or intimate relationships and the women perceived that they had the choice of whether or not to be ponced.

had 'just stopped giving him money'. When the two women who had never been ponced were asked how they had managed to avoid it, they both replied that it was not for the lack of men trying. They had just said no. The women's tales of resistance to poncing are very interesting in that they are so contradictory. At least ten of the interviewees who talked about 'just saying no' also talked about how there was no effective resistance to poncing. (The subject of ponces and poncing is returned to in Chapter 5.)

In summary, when the women talked about poncing they depicted prostitution as a trap that could not be escaped, a trap that comprised dependence on their ponces for housing, paltry daily allowances, enforced isolation from family and friends, and a desperate and heartfelt belief that poncing was inevitable.

Violence within Prostitution

Continuously interwoven into the accounts of the interviewees were tales of violence. Violence by ponces, however, was only one aspect of the violence the women discussed when talking about prostitution as a trap. All the interviewees had experienced violence at the hands punters, and these were not simply one-off or freak episodes – the women had been attacked repeatedly. Whilst rape was the most typical experience (sadly, only two women had not been raped by punters and six women had been raped several times), other attacks included being mugged, beaten up, pushed out of moving cars, kidnapped, slashed with knifes and strangled. For instance Ruthie (aged 25) had been raped by four separate punters and mugged three times. She had also been kidnapped for four days by a punter and in that time had been repeatedly raped, beaten with a kettle flex and stabbed.

Surprisingly, when questioned about these events, the women responded with comments such as 'It's all part of the job' (Ingrid, aged 44) and 'we know the dangers – we walk into it' (Anna, aged 36). These comments indicate that, on one level, the women accepted that violence from punters was integral to prostitution – particularly when working from the streets (this belief is deconstructed in Chapter 5). In fact it was this aspect of street work that had informed the decision by Fiona (aged 41), Sophie (aged 28), Michelle (aged 33), Georgie (aged 35) and Christina (aged 23) to work only from saunas or their own homes. They explained that they felt they could better protect themselves in the enclosed and regulated environments of saunas and homes.

But violence was not limited to ponces and punters. The women shared the streets with petty criminals who posed a threat of violence. Andrea (aged 27) described how the streets were populated with crackheads who hung around waiting to mug prostitutes, and according to Patsy (aged 42), 'We're easy targets for nutters. We got more money on us than most people wandering around and there's them that know that.' And of course most of the respondents, when discussing their fear of being murdered, talked about 'psychos' who posed as punters but who really just wanted to kill someone.

The interviewees had also suffered violence at the hands of the police. Helena (aged 35) described the regularity with which certain 'beat' officers (as opposed to vice officers) picked up particular women, including herself, and demanded sex. Katrina (aged 20) recalled being arrested by a vice officer and raped in his car. Katrina had been pregnant at the time and the rape had been so brutal that she had miscarried in the officer's car and had to be hospitalised. She had reported the incident and the officer had been convicted, but Katrina was still waiting for compensation from the Criminal Injuries Compensation Board.

Potential violence from the police was a particular problem for the interviewees because the police were the only people present late at night who could (or would) provide a modicum of protection against the 'nutters' and street criminals. But the interviewees also recognised that there was always the risk that the police too might attack them.

These stories of violence clearly demonstrate the riskiness of prostitution. They also show the paradox of the women's narratives in that while they realised that they were far more victimised than women not involved in prostitution, seven of the 21 women commented that they would never really leave prostitution – or rather that prostitution would never leave them because the repeated violence to which they had been subjected had fundamentally altered how they perceived themselves and the world around them (see also Hoigard and Finstad, 1992). In this respect prostitution constituted a trap that had shattered their emotional wellbeing and threatened their survival.

SUMMARY

Risk pervades the life of most women in late-twentieth-century Britain. For the poor and working-class women in this study, however, the manner in which they had negotiated the risks they had encountered in their struggle to survive had led to their turning away from conventional patterns of living towards involvement in prostitution. In this context, though, their talk about involvement in prostitution has been shown to be paradoxical and marked by profound contradictions. So much so that the interviewees' narratives appear to make little sense in that involvement in prostitution signifies both an opening up of opportunities and a successful survival strategy, *and* circumscription of opportunities as a result of being trapped in a series of victimising situations. But because the interviewees felt that there were no alternatives to their current lives, they had to live within the paradoxes inherent in prostitution.

Hence in outlining and analysing the context in which the interviewees' involvement in prostitution had taken place, the paradox of the women's narratives became visible. Accordingly, questions need to be asked about the processes by which the contradictory tales of involvement in prostitution can be rendered meaningful. This is the subject of Chapter 5.

5 Men, Money, Violence and Identity

The previous chapter explored the social and material context in which the interviewees lived. However they explained their involvement in prostitution in such a manner that there appeared to be no justification for remaining in prostitution. For example the women claimed that they were involved in prostitution to get money, and yet they also claimed that involvement in prostitution had led to poverty. They asserted that becoming a prostitute had helped them to gain independence from their families, boyfriends, partners and/or local authority care and to escape from violent and abusive partners or families, and yet they also asserted that becoming a prostitute had made them dependent on violent and abusive men for money and housing. The women declared that they could remedy their housing difficulties via prostitution, and yet they also declared that involvement in prostitution had created housing difficulties. In short, the interviewees said that involvement in prostitution was a means by which they could live the lives they wanted and survive the social and economic difficulties they encountered, and yet they also said that involvement in prostitution had jeopardised their social and economic survival, and at times their very lives. Deployment of such conflicting representations of life as a prostitute meant that the interviewees' tales were highly paradoxical.

This chapter explores the paradox of these women's stories, focusing on how the women rendered their narratives coherent and plausible via the construction of a 'prostitute identity'. Risk remains a predominant theme in this chapter, although not in the sense of the social, structural and material uncertainties experienced by the 21 prostitute women in their struggle to survive. Rather, risk is applied in this chapter to individuals, events or activities that are constituted by and inscribed with specific meanings that enabled the interviewees to redefine the paradoxes of involvement in prostitution. Such discursively constituted risks merge with the issue of identity, for when assessing who poses a specific threat or danger, who provides safety or security and who can or cannot be relied upon as an ally, individuals imagine themselves in relation to other individuals. In short they continuously redefine the boundaries, differences and similarities between themselves and others (see also Habermas, 1987, pp. 296–7).

It is therefore argued in this chapter that involvement in prostitution comes to make sense because the contradictions of involvement in prostitution and the paradox of their explanations are accommodated (that is, the narratives become plausible and coherent) within the construction of a very distinct identity – a prostitute identity. Such an identity was neither authored nor authorised by the women. It was made possible by a symbolic landscape underpinning the women's narratives that comprised contextually specific but shifting sets of meanings of men, money and violence. So in examining the discursive strategies that enabled these women's stories to make sense, this chapter firstly examines the necessary conditions for the construction of the prostitute identity – or the objectification of these women's sexual relationships, which was itself conditioned by the ways in which involvement in prostitution removed the boundaries between the women's work lives, private lives, intimate relationships and family relationships. The chapter then moves on to explore three contradictory (and contingent) elements of the interviewees' prostitute identity (prostitutes as workers/ prostitutes as commodified bodies, prostitutes as business women/prostitutes as loving partners, and prostitutes as victims/prostitutes as survivors) and the three meanings of men, money and violence that make such identifications possible (men as income, men as an expense and men as risk).

Thus Chapter 5 charts the complexities and nuances of meanings that underpin the experiences of the 21 prostitute women who were interviewed for this study. By examining the contradictory and diverse ways in which they identified and located themselves, this chapter demonstrates how it was possible for the interviewees to make subjective sense of their involvement in prostitution by recounting stories that at first hearing appeared too contradictory to make any sense at all.

THE OBJECTIFICATION OF SEXUAL RELATIONSHIPS

The fundamental element of the prostitute identities constructed by the interviewees was objectification of the sexual relationships that had resulted from the coalescence of all aspects of their lives. For these women, the consequence of engaging in prostitution was that the structure, order and (to some extent) segregation of their everyday activities and relationships had broken down. Their everyday lives were not organised by boundaries between work, intimate relationships, family relationships, experiences of and in a particular community and so on.

Rather, all these aspects of their lives had coalesced and were bound up with their work in prostitution.

The blending of the interviewees' personal lives with the institution of prostitution provided the social conditions in which all their sexual relationships had become objectified and transformed into objects of knowledge with specific meanings. Of course such a process of objectification (whereby differentiations are made between the individual and others) is part of the construction of any social identity – be this a prostitute identity or otherwise. But the difference between the prostitute identity discussed here and any other identity is that it was specifically the interviewees' *sexual* relationships that were objectified. Thus the women thought of themselves not simply in relation to generalised others, but in relation to the actual and imaginary men around them.

Hence the disintegration of the 'traditional' separation of everyday life into home, work, community, intimate relationships, family and so on created the conditions in which all the interviewees' relationships with the men around them became objectified and provided the necessary conditions for the construction of their prostitute identity.

'I'VE GOT SOMETHING TO SELL AND THERE'S ALWAYS MEN WHO'LL PAY FOR IT'

One contradictory aspect of the prostitute identity constructed by the interviewees was that they saw themselves as both 'workers' and 'commodified bodies'. This was a result of conflating the meaning of men and money, whereby men were a source of income that could only be tapped by selling sex to them.

Prostitutes as Workers

The prostitutes-as-workers identification emanated from the ways in which the respondents talked about themselves in relation to a universalised, imaginary notion of punters. Within this identification, prostitute women were portrayed as rational economic agents pursuing monetary goals, or more specifically, workers doing a job and getting paid for it. The prostitutes-as-workers identification was contextualised by and within the women's experience of poverty. However it was also decontextualised in that the women distanced their engagement in prostitution from its wider social setting and effects, and thus represented it as nothing more and nothing less than a simple economic activity.

The prostitutes-as-workers identification was made explicit in the women's challenge of two notions: that they were involved in anything that was illicit, criminal or illegitimate; and that prostitutes sell sex. As well as talking about themselves as workers in general, the women particularly saw themselves as workers who provided a valuable personal and social service. This nuance arose from and in relation to a generalised notion of punters as 'normal', 'natural men'.

A euphemistic phrase that most of the women used to describe both their involvement in prostitution and the prostitute–punter exchange was 'just making money' – a description that was commonly employed by them to challenge the legally constituted construction of prostitutes as criminals. Andrea (aged 27), who was very angry about the criminalisation of prostitution, remarked: 'I can't see the sense in making it illegal, because it's some man willing to pay his money and it's my body. I'm not hurting anyone taking his money. I'm just making my money'. Similarly Ingrid (aged 44), having been imprisoned four times for prostitution-related offences, commented: 'We shouldn't have to go to prison for selling what's ours and just making a bit of money!'

Clearly, 'making money' is one of the elements in a common-sense understanding of work, but for these women (whose social and material existence was marked by the risk of *profound* poverty) 'just making money' was also seen as an urgent task. For, implicit in the interviewees' discussions about making money was the belief that more legitimate ways of earning money were (at least perceptually) closed to them.

Other examples of the interviewees' view of themselves as workers emerged in general talk about what involvement in prostitution meant to them. They discussed such involvement as though it was simply and merely a 'job':

> I'm doing a job, I was doing a job. Like any other person who goes out in the morning, goes to work, gets paid for it and goes home. That's what I do (Lois, aged 21).

> You do it because you need the money for yourself. It's a job and it should be recognised as a job (Sammy, aged 18).

> You're selling a skill. It's a job – that's what you class it as – a job (Christine, aged 23).

This is further illustrated by the interviewees' descriptions of the punter–prostitute exchange. All but Michelle (aged 33) challenged the notion that, for prostitutes, the punter–prostitute exchange has anything to do with sex. Instead they asserted that the exchange is 'only work' and therefore not sex (cf. McKeganey and Barnard, 1996, p. 33).

> You don't have sex with punters! F**k no! That's not sex, you don't even think of it as sex. That's money. It's a job (Janet, aged 37).

> It's not sex, it's work! (Jasmine, aged 30).

> At the end of the day, you're getting money from a punter. It's not sex, it's money – it's *work*! (Ruthie, aged 25).

> You don't think about it, you think of it as work . . . because you think of it as a job, it's just like doing paper work (Andrea, aged 27).

It was only by denuding their involvement in prostitution of its institutional setting that the interviewees could make these statement because such decontextualisation permitted them to reduce their involvement in prostitution to (merely and only) a series of individual, economic exchanges between themselves and individual punters. This in turn allowed them symbolically to transform their prostitution-related activities into 'just making money' and 'work', and hence identify themselves as workers.

However, as stated above, the prostitutes-as-workers identification had a more specific aspect because the interviewees also saw themselves as workers who were providing a valuable social and personal service. Manifest in 15 of the 21 narratives was the construction of a generalised, imaginary punter as a normal, natural man who was only 'doing what men do'. Interestingly this was conditioned by a redefinition of the exchange between themselves and their punters as a *sexual* exchange. The women deployed discourses that ascribed to prostitution a wider social role and function with manifest benefits at both the individual and social levels (see Davis, 1937, for a good example of these discourses). The women claimed that prostitutes save marriages and relationships because men were understood by them to be driven by a biological imperative – the *need* to have sex. The availability of prostitutes, according to the interviewees, means that men's conventional (and more unconventional) sexual desires can be fulfilled without it being a threat to their marriages:

> I think we provide a service – we do. We save marriages you know. Some men love their wives, but they come to us because they want things, like beatings, that their wives won't do (Janet, aged 37).

The women claimed that by doing the work that they do, they remove the necessity of men becoming involved with someone other than their wives or girlfriends just for sex, and thus prostitutes help to save relationships by permitting men 'to have their cake and eat it too':

> We save men from having affairs or splitting up their marriages because their wives might not give them sex (Margie, aged 32).

> Punters aren't doing anything wrong. They're just doing what's natural. How do you know that their wives aren't sick and she says, 'You'll have to go elsewhere' and they don't wanna get involved with anyone else? (Sammy, aged 18).

At the social level, the same 15 interviewees asserted that because men's sexual desires are accommodated by prostitution, prostitution 'contains' the social problems that the women believed would ensue if men's sexual desires were not satisfied. By utilising discourses in which men's sexuality is constituted as a dangerous impulse (see also Wilson, 1980, pp. 159–60; Davis, 1937, pp. 747–9) and that prostitution provides a catharsis for men's sexuality (Malamuth and Donnerstein, 1984; Yaffe and Nelson, 1982), the women frequently drew direct connections between men's easy access to anonymous sex through prostitution and the reduced incidence of rape:

> My doctor is always saying, 'Ingrid, I have a lot of respect for people like you, because it is the likes of you lot that stop the likes of my daughter getting raped'. You see, they [the punters] come to us and so they don't need to rape (Ingrid, aged 44).

> I think that by doing this, it's gonna stop more rapes and all that (Anna, aged 36).

> It's people like me that keep rapes down. If some bloke needed it and there weren't no prostitutes he might go and rape someone for it (Katrina, aged 20).

So by locating themselves within a social context in which the risk of poverty was imminent, yet denuding their involvement in prostitution of any institutional setting whilst simultaneously invoking a generalised notion of punters as 'normal', 'natural' men, the interviewees were able to construct a prostitute identity in which prostitutes are workers who provide a valuable service that is both sex and not sex. Such an identity allowed the women to speak of their engagement in prostitution as though it was a feasible strategy for economic and material survival.

Prostitutes as Commodified Bodies

The second element of the interviewees' prostitute identity was 'prostitutes as commodified bodies'. This identification was explicit in 16 of the 21 narratives and the remaining five alluded to it. The prostitutes-as-commodified-bodies identification was made possible by the way that these women located themselves within the everyday realities of engagement in prostitution. It allowed them to place themselves in relation to the particularity of the prostitute–punter exchange (in street work in particular the turnover of punters is high, regulars are relatively rare and very little time is spent with each punter) and the specific practices of poncing. But there were subtle and contradictory aspects of this identification. Defining their bodies – especially their vaginas – as objects of temporary exchange (that is, 'rentable'), the 16 women talked about having: (1) ownership and control of the object for rent in relation to an understanding of their bodies as both peculiar to and distinct from their selves; (2) ownership but no control when their bodies were continuously rented in relation to a symbolic subsumption of their selves to their bodies; and (3) no ownership and no control as slaves to their 'ponces as owners'. Each of these variations is described in turn below.

One of the more striking and saddening features of the interviewees' narratives was the overwhelming unhappiness, dismay and regret that came across in their talk about what it meant to be engaged in prostitution. Many of these emotions were expressed very clearly in their comments about being 'fed up with being mauled'. It is undeniable that such statements demonstrate the adverse emotional consequences of involvement in prostitution, and this has been the focus of much feminist-oriented research on women in the sex industry (for example Hoigard and Finstad, 1992; Barry, 1979, 1995; MacKinnon, 1987, pp. 127–215; Dworkin, 1979). It is not my intention here to discuss the psychological damage that involvement in prostitution undoubtedly inflicts. Rather I just wish to stress that when the interviewees expressed their sadness and dismay, they often also depicted themselves as commodified bodies and 'rentable vaginas':

> It bothered me in the beginning that all I was, was a piece of meat someone was f∗∗king (Katrina, aged 20).

It's not easy to go out and do a client and then do another one and keep that up. You have to keep up the smiling and the chat. You turn yourself into something to sell (Janet, aged 37).

Expression of the prostitutes-as-commodified-bodies identification occurred in relation to a contextualised construction of punters. Here punters are any (anonymous) men who are interested only in gratifying their own sexual desires and are willing to pay money to do so. Such an understanding is in direct contrast to the prostitutes-as-workers identity, where the women located themselves in relation to a generalised, imaginary and decontextualised notion of punters. Contextualising their understanding of punters within the everyday realities of the institution of prostitution enabled a portrayal of the prostitute–punter exchange as devoid of any meaning or interpersonal and social interaction beyond the satisfaction of immediate sexual wants and the exchange of money. In short, the prostitutes-as-commodified-bodies identification was contextualised within a specific definition of what the women believed they were selling to their punters. Instead of selling skill or expertise (as in the case of the providers of specialist services such as bondage and discipline) or time or companionship (as in the case of high-class call girls and mistresses) these women saw themselves as providers of rentable vaginas. Lois (aged 21), who had become involved in prostitution when she was 17 years old, concisely and poignantly described this:

It hit me when I was 19 that I was actually a prostitute. I didn't really think about it before – it was just work. But then it hit me. I was actually selling myself. I was just a hole. I was nothing more than a body men paid to f**k. I was a prostitute (Lois, aged 21).

The first aspect of the prostitutes-as-commodified-bodies identification is that 15 of the women also talked about themselves as though they owned and controlled the object that was for rent. This occurred in relation to a symbolic body–self split, and the interviewees made frequent remarks about 'not being there' in the punter–prostitute exchange:

They aren't allowed to touch me – I can't stand that! [JP: Why?] Because you have to cut yourself off. When he touches you, you just feel like a piece of meat. You see, it's not *me* he's having sex with, it's just my body (Olivia, aged 28).

It's much easier these days. I just shut my eyes and think of something else – switch off. I've learned how to block it – it's not me that's there, it's my body only (Katrina, aged 20).

[When] you're constantly having sex with different guys every night – up to six or even eight – and getting paid for it, you have to switch off and mentally say 'It's not me' and 'It's my body he's paying for' (Helena, aged 35).

These are interesting remarks. Similar statements about prostitutes dissociating themselves from their bodies have been used to explore the psychological damage experienced by prostitutes as a result of their work (see Hoigard and Finstad, 1992, pp. 63–74, 106–16). Other researchers have made sense of similar statements in terms of the strategies that prostitutes deploy to distance themselves (indeed their assumed 'authentic selves') from the socially stigmatising label of prostitute and thus refuse to accept the socially condemned personal characteristics associated with that label (see McKeganey and Barnard, 1996, pp. 82–98). But I argue that it is by constructing their bodies as distinct and separate from their 'selves' that the women were able to see themselves as owning (that is, ultimately being in control of the disposal of) their 'rentable vaginas'. Consider the following extracts:

The way I see it, there's me and my body and my body's just there to be sold (Ingrid, aged 44).

When I'm here, I'm me. But when I'm out there, I'm not there. I'm something else. I'm just a prostitute – I'm something I can sell (Patsy, aged 42).

The second contradictory aspect of the prostitutes-as-commodified-bodies identification which appeared in eight of the interviewees' narratives, was their talk of having ownership but not control of their bodies. Interestingly, rather than involving the separation of self from body, these eight women saw their selves as having been *subsumed* by their continuously rented vaginas, and because of this, their punters had control over them:

In the end, you hate yourself for selling your body. They [the punters] do what they want to you. Your body's an object and you've got no control over it (Lois, aged 21).

You end up *becoming* the hustler. You do. You find that you're constantly working. And you don't really switch your brain off. You think
of yourself as just a body all the time.... But you end up losing yourself to your body and having no control over it anymore (Georgie,
aged 37).

The third and final contradiction in the prostitutes-as-commodified-
bodies identification emerged during discussions on poncing practices,
when four of the interviewees placed themselves in relation to the
notion of 'ponces as owners'. There seemed to be acceptance of one of
the more 'feudal' poncing practices – the selling of women by their
ponces to other ponces. Barbara (aged 24), Lois (aged 21), Gail (aged
28) and Patsy (aged 42) had all been sold in this manner either when
their earnings from prostitution had diminished or when tension between the women in the ponce-provided accommodation had reached
such a level that the ponces had felt obliged to intervene. For example
Patsy described an episode when, a few years previously, there had
been a sharp increase in the number of very young girls working in her
neighbourhood. As a result Patsy (aged 42) 'couldn't make money – all
the punters wanted those young girls'. Her ponce had therefore sold
her to another ponce for £120 Similarly Barbara, Gail and Lois had
been sold by their ponces in response to the constant fighting and arguments that were taking place in the over crowded flats in which the
ponces kept 'their women'.

This practice of selling women does not necessarily demonstrate the
women's perception of having no ownership or control over their commodified bodies. But their reactions to and remarks about being sold
do. When questioned about the practice Barbara simply remarked:
'Yea. I was sold. Oh yea that was rife down there'. Gail and Patsy also
treated the practice of being sold as banal. Each of the women were
asked whether the fear of violence by their ponces had contributed to
their acceptance of being sold, but they both asserted that this had not
been the case. Being sold was seen, by these women as a standard poncing practice and they were aggrieved not by the fact that they had been
sold, but by how little they had been sold for! The amount obtained represented to the women a symbolic measure of the worth of their commodified bodies. Lois remarked: 'Can you believe it? Kevin sold me to
Steve for just fifty pounds! Fifty pounds!! I was worth more than that!'

Thus by contextualising their understanding of punters and poncing
practices within the institutional location they inhabited they were able
to place themselves in relation to anonymous punters and 'ponces as

owners'. Consequently the interviewees variously discussed themselves as though they were commodified bodies (that is, 'rentable vaginas') as something that they owned and controlled, owned but did not control, or neither owned nor controlled. Such a symbolic landscape enabled them to tell stories in which their engagement in prostitution represented (1) an effective and efficient use of their own economic resources and (2) something they had no control over because they had no sense of self (as it was subordinate to their bodies) and had therefore lost control, and because they were slaves in relation to their ponces (who had control of their commodified bodies).

MEN AS INCOME: THE CONFLATION OF MEN AND MONEY

The prostitutes-as-workers and prostitutes-as-commodified-bodies identifications were made possible by a metonymic movement in the women's narratives of the meaning of men and money. Men were constituted as both income (that is, sources of money) and income that can only be generated by exchanging sex for money. The women's narratives revealed that certain types of men (sugar daddies and good punters) were seen as particularly good sources of income.

The everyday realities of lives that had been fractured by poverty and the impoverishing effects of engagement in prostitution provided the material context in which these women constituted men as money. This existence, where the option to earn a legitimately income was actually or perceptually foreclosed, created a real and urgent need for money – as in income.

The construction of men as sources of income was one of the primary myths behind the interviewees' involvement in prostitution. This idea was mythical (cf. Walkowitz, 1982) because the construction of men as income was an understanding of particular men that (1) was generalised and applied to all men and (2) contained a specific message for these women – that men will pay money for sex. This message was encapsulated in the women's often repeated claims that 'all men are punters':

Working has f**ked up my head because to me a man, all men, are just punters. A man, to me, is a punter and not someone to have a relationship with or anything else. They're just punters (Ingrid, aged 44).

> In the beginning you see the differences between punters and other men. In the end they're all punters (Gail, aged 28).

> All men are punters to me. I can't help but look at a man and say, 'Punter' or, 'He's paying for that'.... I'd honestly say that you cannot tell me that any man, even down to my father, has not paid for a girl. Yup, every man is a punter (Sophie, aged 28).

Underpinning the notion that 'all men are punters' (that is, all men will pay money for sex) was the construction of a normal man who is only doing what is innate and comes naturally. Such a construction was enabled by (1) the interviewees' acceptance of particular discourses of masculinity and (2) their belief that men, as a group, have easier access to and more money than women.

In all the narratives there was noticeable acceptance of discourses in which male sexuality is constituted as a difficult to control, physical impulse (cf. Ellis, 1936; Wilson, 1980; see also Hall, 1994 for a deconstruction of this discourses). The women portrayed male sexuality as biologically driven, an aggressive need, 'instrumental' rather than 'expressive'. Such a universalised and essentialised depiction of male sexuality permitted the women to encode all ordinary 'normal' men as though they are 'always on the prowl' or 'always looking for the latest shag'. Witness Gail's remarks: 'As far as I'm concerned, I couldn't do it if it wasn't bought, you know? And if it's not needed then why are we able to sell it?'

In addition, this encoding of male sexuality allowed the women to characterise the punter–prostitute relationship as nothing more and nothing less than a routine economic exchange in which a normal (that is, ordinary, typical and not deviant or unusual) man buys an outlet for his physical needs (see Faugier and Sargeant, 1997, pp. 128, 130). Witness the women's euphemistic description of the sex for which their punters paid as 'relief' or 'satisfaction', and the manner in which they discussed whether or not their punters were being unfaithful to their partners:

> Men who come to me are generally faithful to their wives. They don't see coming to me as being unfaithful. To be honest, I don't either. It's non-committal and he's just getting a little extra relief that he probably needs (Sophie, aged 28).

> Some men feel guilty when they come to us, but I say 'You can go home thinking that there's no feelings between us, you may never see

me again and that's it. You got out your frustration. You got relief and I got paid' (Ruthie, aged 25).

According to the interviewees, then, the sex that punters buy is simply physical satisfaction, purely instrumental, devoid of any meaning and just a natural function undertaken by normal men.

Earlier it was stated that the notion that 'all men are punters' was informed by the women's belief that men have easier access to and more money than women. Interspersed throughout most of the women's narratives were observations of men's relative economic privilege which, these women suggested, was a result of men having fewer impediments to work. So, for example, those interviewees who were also single mothers remarked that it is easier for men to go out to work because they do not have to look after children. Moreover they believed that men's easier access to money applied equally to legitimate and illegitimate ways of earning money:

> Men can do things that women can't. They can make money more easily and get jobs more quickly. If they're not working they can do things like burglary and drug selling and get away with it whereas women can't do it so easily (Olivia, aged 28).

The belief that men have fewer obstacles to surmount in order to obtain an income formed the basis of the interviewees' claim that men have more money than women. Combined with a biologically essentialised construction of male sexuality, this belief also provided the requisite ideological conditions in which the women inscribed all normal men as punters (that is, willing and able to pay for sex).

The set of significations in which men represented income was contextualised by the women's risk of poverty and in particular by the fact that the risk of poverty generated a pressing need for them to maintain and maximise their income. In this context the income that men provided was not solely defined in terms of its exchange value, it was also defined in terms of its value in providing economic security. The women frequently remarked that 'getting together with a rich man' or working until they 'got a few bob behind them' would allow them to leave prostitution. And given that they were excluded from obtaining an income in its broader sense (credit, loans, borrowing power, earning capacity and so on), it is unsurprising that the income that men were described as providing was translated into an object, the possession of which could ensure the interviewees' economic survival.

The conflation of men and money can be seen most clearly in the women's description of the sugar daddy and the good punter.

The Sugar Daddy

Seventeen of the 21 interviewees mentioned sugar daddies, whom they characterised as the most valued and sought-after clients, particularly for street-working prostitutes. Sugar daddies are regular punters who, in addition to buying sex, give prostitutes extra money. Take for example Christine's sugar daddy. Over the course of a year he had provided Christine with money to rent and refurbish a flat, buy designer clothes and buy a car. When the interviews took place, only three of the women (including Christine) had had sugar daddies at any time during their involvement in prostitution.

Jasmine and Margie described their sugar daddies as follows:

> I've got a sugar daddy. He doesn't go to anyone else and he's very rich. He's a millionaire. Oh, his businesses are worth millions! I've seen his house and it's a six or seven bedroomed house. He's got a Porsche and a Ferrari and mountain bikes and he's only thirty-four. Every time I see him, he gives me a hundred pounds. If I phone him and say I need money, he'll give me the money I need (Jasmine, aged 30).

> One punter – I call him my sugar daddy – he gives me loads of money. I got three or four hundred [pounds] off him once. I dropped him for about six months because Krypton [her ponce] didn't like it. But he come back and being as he was willing to come up with money, I had him back. Sometimes, I don't do business with him, but he still makes up me money to keep Krypton off my back. He has even paid my bills off. . . . If I say I've got to pay this bill or that, he'll go through hell and high water to pay them (Margie, aged 32).

There are two interesting features to note in the above notions of a sugar daddy. First, a man becomes a sugar daddy when a prostitute woman believes she can easily tap into his economic and financial resources. Jasmine, obviously impressed by her sugar daddy's wealth, claimed she only needed to phone him to obtain money from him. Similarly Margie explained that her sugar daddy did not have much money, but that whatever he could raise he would give it to her. That the figure of the sugar daddy exemplifies the 'men as income' articulation of meanings becomes clear in the women's definition of a sugar daddy. Barbara (aged 24) defined a sugar daddy as 'a well loaded punter – a big fat unending wallet'. In other words a sugar daddy is his money.

Irrespective of whether or not any individual woman had a sugar daddy, or how rich he actually was, this type of punter occupied a pivotal position in the interviewees' symbolic landscape and constituted one of the central myths of prostitution in their narratives. For the significance of a sugar daddy was not that he was seen by the women as a regular punter upon whom they could 'rely', but rather that, with respect to the women's material circumstances, the sugar daddy was viewed as a source of not just one-off sums of money, but a supply that was large and regular enough for the women to support themselves. In short, the significance of a sugar daddy was that if a woman had one, she could be 'kept' by him.

It is tempting to compare the relationship between a sugar daddy and prostitute with the relationship between an economically stable man and his financially dependent partner, lover or even mistress. In each case the woman's economic survival is bought within a sexual relationship at the price of being dependent on a particular man. But the interviewees did not perceive the sugar daddy as a boyfriend, husband, lover or partner. First and foremost the sugar daddy was a punter. Therefore the women had no emotional ties with their sugar daddies. The relationship was not marked by exclusivity, there were no bonds of loyalty or commitment and there were no other hallmarks of an intimate relationship. Thus the relationship between a sugar daddy and a prostitute was seen as radically and qualitatively different from that between an economically dependent wife, lover or mistress and her partner.

The second interesting feature of the women's talk about sugar daddies is that as the figure of a sugar daddy was contextualised within the women's experience of poverty and poncing, he became a particularly ironic construction of men. Any economic security that a sugar daddy might have provided was, more often than not, taken by the women's ponces. Many of the women who did not have sugar daddies talked about women they knew who did, and whose ponces had not only told them how much to get from their sugar daddies, but had taken the money as well. Margie (aged 32) indicated this in the extract above when she said that her sugar daddy 'makes up me money to keep Krypton [her ponce] off my back'. Thus although the imaginary sugar daddy is a mythical figure who supposedly provides access to a (perceptually) unlimited pool of cash, in reality the sugar daddy primarily protects women from their ponces.

The Good Punter

References to good punters, 'a better class of punters' and so on were
scattered throughout the interviewees' narratives. This categorisation is
rather loose, but basically, good punters were seen by the women as 'respectable' men. Occasionally good punters were described as regulars,
in that they were repeat customers, and a type of camaraderie had
developed between them and the women. Alternatively good punters
were described as men who made limited sexual demands but paid well;
that is, compared with the 'average' punter, good punters appeared to
have more money and were willing and able to pay larger amounts of
money for the same sexual services. So the defining characteristic of a
good punter is not the quality of the relationship or the type of sexual
encounter that occurs between him and the prostitute – it is his money:

> I only work days because you get a better class of punter in the day.
> [JP: What do you mean?] You get all the reps and people just passing
> through. These punters spend more money and don't take so much
> time. They're good clients (Diane, aged 37).

> I think the businessmen are good punters. They only ever want
> straight relief and they pay the best money (Lois, aged 21).

> You get better punters in the saunas. [JP: Why?] They pay more and
> it's easier work – they're all shopkeepers and businessmen (Sammy,
> aged 18).

The significance of the good punter not only inheres in how much money
he pays. The good punter, like the sugar daddy, is a symbolic figure. He
is the 'ideal' punter and acts as a yardstick against which to measure
other punters. And as a symbolic figure he has an 'added value' because
he signifies successful economic survival through prostitution. Helena
(aged 35) remarked that most of her punters were good punters and,
more importantly, that the good punters she had were also regulars.
When asked why this was significant, Helena explained that it proved
she could make her money.

Implicit in the notion of the good punter is a particular notion of 'cli-
entage'. Eight of the interviewees claimed that good punters only go to
and with 'good' and 'successful' prostitutes. Indeed it became clear as
the fieldwork progressed that a damning indictment and proof of a
prostitute's inadequacy is the revelation that her claims about having
good punters are false. Thus when Helena discussed her good punters,

she frequently remarked that her claims could be verified by any of her friends and that having so many good punters made other women jealous of her.

Yet the reality of involvement in prostitution for these women whose material existence was disrupted by poverty and the specific institutional practices of prostitution (especially poncing), was that any material benefits that accrued from having good punters were often offset by financial exploitation by ponces, the fines they incurred and the prostitution-related housing difficulties they experienced. Thus the good punter, like the sugar daddy, is both a myth – insofar as he is a symbolic figure that enables women to 'measure' their other punters and gain an identity of themselves as successful, good prostitutes – and a reality – insofar as he provides women with protection against their ponces and poverty.

'THERE'S ALWAYS A PRICE TO PAY'

Two further contingent elements of the interviewees' prostitute identity were 'prostitutes as businesswomen' and 'prostitutes as loving partners'. These identifications were made possible by a symbolic landscape in which involvement with men was constituted as requiring some form of payment.

Prostitutes as Businesswomen

The prostitutes-as-businesswomen identification was one whereby 17 of the interviewees located themselves as rational economic agents actively engaged in weighing up the costs and benefits of particular courses of action in relation to strategies for maximising their profits whilst simultaneously minimising their risks. Such an identification may at first appear analogous to the prostitutes-as-workers identification, but it is quite distinct; for the prostitutes-as-workers identification occurred in relation to the women's experience of poverty and the (perceived) impossibility of legitimate work. In contrast their identification as *businesswomen* occurred in relation to the specific hazards of working (primarily) from the streets, that is, violence, robbery, abuse and assault. Moreover, whilst a decontextualised and generalised notion of punters as 'normal' men provided the requisite ideological conditions for the prostitutes-as-workers identification; it was, specifically, a contextualised understanding of their involvement in prostitution (particularly in relation to notions of 'working the right way') that provided the conditions for the businesswomen identification.

The 17 interviewees spoke about what engagement in prostitution meant to them via descriptions of 'being in business' and of 'doing what's necessary' in order to maximise their actual and potential earnings and minimise their risks (especially risks that result in a drain on their 'profits' and in violence and abuse). In their narratives, the women talked about themselves as 'being smart' and able to identify and weigh up the costs and benefits of involvement with ponces, police, partners and punters, and of engaging in prostitution from the streets, saunas or their own homes. For example Helena (aged 35) described volunteering to get arrested:

> When they're doing a big swoop and arresting everyone in vans, they start by buzzing you in a car. You want to get them to pick you up in the car instead of the van – in the van they drive around for about an hour before they actually take you into the station and they pick up all the girls. If you get arrested in the van you're usually locked up for three or four hours while they do all the girls, charge them and that. But if you get them in the car – you're first in. You're in and you're out. ... So while they're picking up all the other girls, it gives you free reign to work the streets. So, me, I'm not a mug. I've worked it out, and if you're going to work, you have to be smart. I am – I volunteer to get arrested.

Barbara (aged 24) also spoke of 'doing the smart thing' and working from the streets rather than saunas:

> I can honestly say that I work the streets because I'm doing the smart thing. I reckon that it's a better deal to work the streets. [JP: Why?] Because if you're in a sauna, you're in a room and you can't run. If you get a bad punter and he's bashing your head up against the wall, you can't run. You can't do nothing. If you're on the street, you can fight, you can kick, you can run. You got all that street to run through. For all its grief and trouble, I'm being smart by working the street – I can make my money and protect myself better.

But of vital importance to any discussion of the prostitute-as-businesswoman identification is awareness that this identification is constructed and expressed very differently according to whether or not a woman is currently being ponced. The interviewees' notions of 'being smart' and 'doing what's necessary' were contextualised within a set of constructed priorities regarding the risk of financial exploitation that they believed to be inherent in involvement with partners or ponces and/or the dangers of violence accompanying street work especially. This can be seen in the interviewees' differing notions of 'the right way to work' (see Mc-Keganey and Barnard, 1996, pp. 27–9, for a discussion of prostitutes' notions of 'professionalism').

'GET RID OF YOUR MAN': BUSINESSWOMEN, WORKING THE 'RIGHT WAY' AND BEING INDEPENDENT

Eleven of 17 women in whose narratives the businesswoman identification was manifest were not being ponced at the time of interviews. Their businesswoman identification relates to their belief that working independently was 'the right way to work' and to the manner in which they differentiated themselves from other prostitutes and other women not involved in prostitution. There was a consensus among this particular group of women that there were two fundamental 'rules' for working: (1) do not have any personal and intimate relationships with men whilst working, and (2) do not be 'naive' or 'innocent' about men as partners.

Working 'the right way' for these women meant working independently, and their willingness to do so signified their businesslike approach to work:

I would say, I am a prostitute who has found a way through all of it and I'm doing it the right way now. I do it for meself. Before, I'd take the money and give it to some man, thinking I was loving him and he was loving me. F**k that! If you're going to make a go of this you got to work independently (Michelle, aged 33).

The only way I work now is the right way – independently. I work for myself. This is a business and I won't have any man dragging down what I earn! I will not! (Jasmine, aged 30).

About two years ago, I thought to myself that the proper way to work is without an old man altogether. So I said to myself, if I work from now on, I work for myself and by myself. It will be on my on terms. You gotta be serious about this business, otherwise you won't have anything to show for it (Ingrid, aged 44).

I'm the kind of person who goes out and I might do three hundred pounds, but I still go out and work the next day. I bank my money – I don't give it to no man. You've got to, haven't you? Because the way I look at it, it's time I got serious. I've got to plan my money for the future (Diane, aged 37).

These women also discussed the necessity of not being 'naive' or 'innocent' about men as partners:

I reckon if you work, you gotta stop being naive. You have to see men for what they are. [JP: Do you mean punters?] No. I mean men. You have to be professional about how you see all men. They'll live off you if they can (Olivia, aged 28).

When I was younger, I lived with men that took advantage – I think that's what it was – I didn't see it coming. But once it happened again and again, I'd seen I'd been taken for a right c**t. You put it down to experience and say, 'No more'. You can't be innocent about men and you have to run your life like a business (Georgie, aged 35).

Drawing comparisons with their previous experiences of working whilst being ponced, nine of the 11 women implied that, unlike before, they now knew the rules and worked in the most efficient way possible so as to maximise their profits and minimise their costs by taking action to limit the risk of the financial exploitation that they believed was caused by involvement with men.

There are other indications of the prostitutes-as-businesswomen identification. Those women who were not being ponced at the time of the interviews all spoke of the necessity to pay for protection, and their willingness to do so demonstrated their businesslike approach to their lives as prostitutes. Gail (aged 28) said that when she did the 'odd few punters – for a big bill on something' she paid a man to mind her. She commented: 'I'm not stupid. It may mean I have to do an extra punter to pay Gripper, but it's worth it and it's the smart way.' Similarly Fiona (aged 41) discussed her willingness to give the police information in order to pay for their protection. Fiona had never been ponced during her involvement in prostitution and at the time was running her own sauna:

They can just come in here and raid me any time. Or if I need to get rid of a girl's ponce or we have a bad punter, I want them to come right away. So when they said that they just wanted information about paedophiles, I decided to give them what they wanted. I ring them up every now and then and give them a little snippet of information. Well, what else can I do? I've gone this far. I've got me own business. I just look at it as paying for the police's help.

The identification of themselves as businesswomen is further manifest in the way that they differentiated between themselves, other prostitutes and other women not engaged in prostitution. The distinction that these women drew emanated from their own businesslike approach to sex with men. Other women (both prostitutes and those not involved in prostitution) were putting themselves at risk of abuse, exploitation and poverty: they were seen as 'stupid', 'not working the right way' and 'not making their money':

> I said to this friend of mine, 'Lorraine, if you're gonna do it, then you might as well do it right, otherwise you're on a slippery slope. Get rid of your man and think about how much you can make'. I said 'Get your business head on!' (Sophie, aged 28).

> I have this friend. She goes out on a Friday for the sole purpose of finding a man to f**k him – anyone! I think, 'Well, I wouldn't do that!' Coz half these straight women, they give it away – a few drinks and they're in the sack! F**king no – I'm sorry. It will cost you more than that for me. But I'm in business for myself and they're not (Ingrid, aged 44).

> This is business. I'm not doing the same sort of thing at the local pub for free [laughter]. That's what I think sometimes, 'Oh look at her. A different man every bloody week! She might as well charge' (Christine, aged 23).

'YOU GOTTA HAVE SOME MAN TO WATCH YOU': BUSINESSWOMEN, WORKING THE 'RIGHT WAY' AND PONCING

Six women who were being ponced when they were interviewed described in great detail their belief that reducing the risk of the violence inherent in street work was of primary importance to any 'smart' prostitute or businesswoman. For these women, the prostitutes-as-businesswomen identification was contextualised by the everyday realities of street prostitution, especially the ever-present risk of punter violence, harassment from potential ponces, hassle from street vigilante organisations and robbery or assault from other people inhabiting the streets from which the women worked.

In direct contrast with the previous 11 respondents, these six women used their willingness to be involved with ponces to signify that they were working 'the right way'. Hence Anna and Sammy remarked:

> The street's a dangerous place. If you're gonna be smart you have to have a man to protect ya and make sure no one kidnaps you or drives off with you. So what, if you have to give him some money? (Anna, aged 36).

> It's the done thing where I work. Every working girl has an old man – she needs one if she's going to do it properly. Ya need someone to watch out for ya coz there are too many creeps out there (Sammy, aged 18).

For this group of women the financial exploitation resulting from involvement with ponces was symbolically transformed into a signifier of their success as businesswomen:

> I have worked with a ponce for most of the time I've worked. There is girls that work without ponces. But the majority of them that don't – it's because they're that heavy on drugs that a ponce wouldn't touch them, because they wouldn't be getting anything if they did! (Andrea, aged 27).

> You want your ponce to look good, man. You want them to dress good, get nice cars and wicked gold. You give them your money so they can look good. I look at it as good advertising, you know what I mean? [JP: Not really.] Well, it's like this, if I were some stupid crackhead or something, I couldn't be earning the money I earn to make my man look good (Katrina, aged 20).

So by locating themselves within the context of the risks accompanying involvement in prostitution, and by constructing a landscape in which (for 11 of the interviewees) the risk of financial exploitation and violence from ponces and partners was prioritised, and (for six of the interviewees) the risk of violence and intimidation from street work was prioritised, a discursive space was opened in which these women were able to locate themselves as businesswomen making rational economic decisions and choices. As a consequence they were able to narrate stories in which their engagement in prostitution represented the end result of a series of economic calculations in their endeavour to secure economic and social stability.

PROSTITUTES AS LOVING PARTNERS

Nine of the 21 interviewees exhibited a prostitutes-as-loving-partners identification – in which they were located as loving women making choices based on the love they felt for the men they were involved with. In contrast to the prostitutes-as-workers, prostitutes-as-commodified-bodies and prostitutes-as-businesswomen identifications, the prostitutes-as-loving-partners identification was contextualised by and constructed within the specific relationships the respondents had with those men who financially exploited them. Paradoxically, although this identification emerged in the context of prostitution-related intimate relationships, it was constructed through decontextualising such relationships. In other words the women were able to locate themselves as loving partners when they symbolically transformed their relationship with ponces (and other men who financially exploited them) into intimate, passionate and romantic relationships that had nothing to do with prostitution. And so a notion of 'not ponces but boyfriends' gained these women their identity as loving women.

Drawing on discourses in which intimate and romantic love, as experienced by women, is constituted as a sublimation of women's desires (Person, 1988) and a concomitant centralising of men's desires (Sayers, 1986), these women talked about their willingness to sacrifice everything for their partners regardless of how they were treated by them. So, for example, when the women who had experienced violent poncing were asked why they did not report their ponces to the police for assault, the common response was 'because I love him' (cf. Wilson, 1983, p. 92). Andrea (aged 27) recounted her experiences with Cain – a man who had violently ponced her for five years, forced her to work seven nights a week and allowed her to keep the money she earned from only one of those seven nights. Reflecting on this time in her life, Andrea commented:

> I don't suppose he really was a ponce. . . . I think he's the only person I ever really loved. Even now I sometimes get upset over it, coz I did love him. I was willing to give him everything I'd got – body, soul, EVERYTHING!

Ruthie (aged 25) described her relationship with her previous ponce in similar terms:

> To tell you the truth, I was that besotted with him that I'd give him everything. I'd give him the f**king world. I'd give him all my money and he'd beat me up. But I carried on giving him my money. You do, don't you, when you love some one?

The prostitutes-as-loving-partners identification was also enabled by a blurring of the line between the symbolic meanings of love and money, so that giving money to a particular man signified loving him. The comments made by Ingrid (aged 44) on a poncing relationship that had lasted for nine years illustrate this:

> He used to kill me. I mean, I stayed for nine years and he was always beating on me, took all my money, but I stuck it out. [JP: Why?] You do, don't you? I think it's because you wanna be loved. [JP: What do you mean?] Well, it's hard to put. Cutter made me feel good. I loved him and so I gave him my money.

Hence giving their ponces the money they earned and not reporting them to the police signalled the women's love for their 'not ponces but boyfriends' and consequently their loving-partner identification:

> I stayed with him but I had a right dog's life. [JP: Why?] He was a very bad alcoholic and was a very bad heroin addict and I used to get battered. I worked because of him – I was keeping his drink habit and his cars and you know [pause]. I worked harder for him than anyone else I've been with. I was under more pressure, then, than all the fifteen years I've worked. I had to earn one hundred and fifty pounds EVERY DAY for his habit. But I loved him, so I did it (Andrea, aged 27).

> You meet someone and they're the type of people that you like.... You know, they talk very, very nice to you and make you feel special. Then before you know it, you fall for them, you work for them and you give them all your money because you've fallen for them (Georgie, aged 35).

But the symbolic conflation of love and money did not occur only in relation to intimate relationships. It also occurred when the interviewees discussed their children:

Put it this way – I get more of a buzz to go out of the house and I look like a tramp and me kids look immaculate. I just love buying them clothes and making them look nice. I like to see them have everything (Andrea, aged 27).

I could never walk around in fifty and sixty pound trainers. But my kids do now. I think nothing of going out and buying, like, thirty pound boots for them just to knock about in, and things like that. Some people say to me, 'You're stupid, because your kids will grow up to always want it'. But, don't get me wrong, I don't do it all the time. But, when I do, I like to buy the best for them. I love them and want them to have the best things (Barbara, aged 24).

Recalling an episode when the Social Services had investigated a neighbour's allegations that she had been physically and mentally abusing her children, Ruthie recounted that the social worker had decided that the allegations were unfounded:

Well, she did turn around to me and say, 'At the end of the day, I don't care what you do for a living. I can see that you've got your house clean and that the baby's bedroom is clean'. [JP: Are you still angry about this?] No, because at the end of the day, I mean, what can they have me for? Being a prostitute? I don't think so. Besides, it is clear I love my kids because of all the things I buy for them. I mean, they have more toys than any other kids I know (Ruthie, aged 25).

Thus for Barbara, Andrea and Ruthie spending money on their children was not only to do with maintaining their children, but was also used to emphasise and prove how much they cared for their children and the importance of their relationship with them.

Hence the women gained their identity as loving women by decontextualising their prostitution-specific relationships with ponces and by symbolically transforming these relationships into intimate ones that had nothing whatsoever to do with prostitution. Furthermore it was this identification that enabled them to constitute their engagement in prostitution as a trap threatening their survival. By depicting themselves as 'caught' and 'compelled' by their love for men who were financially exploitative and violent, the women identified themselves *not* as rational economic agents, but as simply loving their men by giving them their hard-earned money and not resisting their poncing practices.

MEN AS EXPENSE

The prostitutes-as-businesswomen and prostitutes-as-loving-partners identifications were underpinned and made possible by a men-as-expense symbolic landscape. In this articulation of significations, men were defined in relation to money. However, unlike the men-as-income set of meanings, here men were defined as an expense because involvement with them was seen as requiring payment in the form of opportunity costs (payments made for the purpose of achieving something) or hidden costs (payments that are unknown at the time of calculation).

The men-as-expense set of significations was decontextualised. It was a mythical construction of involvement with men in general rather than involvement with men in the context of engagement in prostitution. For Jasmine, Katrina and Sophie involvement with any man was seen as incurring costs – regardless of who he was, the type of relationship they had with him and whether or not the relationship was influenced or conditioned by their engagement in prostitution:

> You know, a lot of women break their hearts over men, but not me. I'm not like that. I do not want another man in my life! Not at all! As far as I am concerned, if you get involved with any of them, in any way – I mean not just your old man ... it costs you in the end (Jasmine, aged 30).

> If you get involved with a man – *any man* – there's always a price to pay. There's always responsibility to give him money or something. You never can get away with it for free (Sophie, aged 28).

> I'm always wary of my friends – my men friends, like. If they make a comment, I always take it the wrong way. Say, like they say, 'Oh I'm broke'. I think, 'Oh no! Don't look at me'. I just think that they all want money (Katrina, aged 20).

Yet the construction of involvement with men as expensive *was* contextualised in that it occurred in relation to (1) the women's perceptions (and experiences) of poverty and violence, and (2) specific prostitution-related relationships with punters, partners, police and ponces. The contextualising of the men-as-expense articulation of meanings can be seen in the women's differentiation between the different types of payment that involvement with men incurred.

Opportunity Costs

Involvement with boyfriends, policemen and ponces was portrayed by most of the interviewees as incurring 'opportunity costs', or a form of expense or payment that was paid in order that the women could obtain something – typically 'sanctuary' from prostitution or protection from prostitution-related violence.

Most of the respondents spoke about boyfriends who had provided or were providing them with 'sanctuary' from their engagement in prostitution by financially supporting them. The women described such involvement as costing them their independence:

> The guy I'm with now didn't even know I worked till just recently. He's trying to get me to give it up – that's why I work day time. He hates me working, and he says it's dangerous and everything. But before I give up, I just want a few bob behind me and my flat sorted out. I want my own things and a little pot of my own money, before I live off him (Janet, aged 37).

> Me and Tim are going out, but he doesn't touch me money. He hates me working, coz of all the crackheads and crazies. I mean, he wants me to give up. He wants to look after me and give me a flat. But I don't want that. I want to look after myself, and I like my flat and my own money. I don't want to give up my independence (Helena, aged 35).

These women went on to say that their unwillingness to pay the opportunity cost of giving up their financial independence would probably result in these relationships breaking up.

Patsy (aged 42) and Georgie (aged 35) had previously sought 'sanctuary' from prostitution through and because of their involvement with particular men. Patsy had returned to her home town when she married a man who said he would take her away from 'all the hassle' and support her. But the marriage had broken up because Patsy did not like 'being the normal housewife, waiting for him to give me my housekeeping and sh∗t'. Georgie's description of her current relationship was similar. Her boyfriend (now ex-husband) had intervened between her and her violent, brutal and often sexually sadistic ponce and had helped her to escape. Twelve years later the marriage was not working – Georgie wanted to be her own woman again and have her own money.

Involvement with policemen was also considered by many of the interviewees as an opportunity cost. The women understood such involvement as providing them with protection against prostitution-related violence, and in particular against violence from ponces. Patsy (aged 42) indicated this in her description of 'working' Green Road in Birchfield:

> The conditions aren't too bad. I think the main factor about working on the street is, if you stay out past, say 1.00 a.m. – I mean from, say, 5.30 p.m. till about 1.00 a.m., you can't move through police. Police are everywhere, man! So, if you get into trouble, if you get a funny punter, or trouble with a ponce, at least you can flag down a police-man or vice [sqad officer], or ring them up...after 1.00 a.m., you hardly see any police. And that's when most of the attacks happen, because there's no police around.

This is an interesting statement given that the police, in their law-enforcement capacity, threatened the women's economic survival through constant arrest. Not all of the women felt the same about the police (see also McKeganey and Barnard, 1996, pp. 19,74; English Collective of Prostitutes, 1997, pp. 85–6). Rather than seeing them as 'pro-tectors', five of the interviewees saw the police as a problem because they believed that punters were inhibited by a visible police presence in the red light areas. But most of the interviewees implied that police-men, as *men* who are not intimidated or frightened by ponces, were able to offer them protection from ponces. When asked about their strategies for leaving ponces, seven remarked that policemen were the only people who could really help. Lois and Sammy recalled that after a number of attempts to leave their ponces, they had eventually enlisted the aid of policemen:

> I like the vice cops, because one day I thought, 'I can't go on any longer'. I mean he [her ponce] was beating me and I was starving! I tried going to me friend's and me dad's, but he would always come and get me.... So one day, like I got arrested earlier in the after-noon, and I said to the policemen, 'Arrest me again later'. So they come back around 9.00 p.m. But, you see, they weren't really arrest-ing me, they were just making out, because he [her ponce] was there on the corner. They took me down to the station and I just told them what was happening – that I'd gotta get out. And like, they took me to a safe place – this hostel – and I managed to get out. I think the vice cops are the only ones who can really help you (Lois, aged 21).

There were these two policemen – really nice guys. When they arrested me, like the one guy gave me twenty pounds to help me on my way, like. I mean, he took it out of his own pocket! And they took me to my sister's. They even got me a few bits and bobs, like flannels and towels – just to help me on my way, and get away from Smasher. I didn't know anyone else who would stand up to Smasher (Sammy, aged 18).

The interviewees claimed that when policemen provided protection, they often asked the women to make statements and press charges against their ponces. Sometimes they also asked for information about other illegal activities in the red light areas. For example Margie (aged 32) said that after seeking the protection of a particular policeman when she had been threatened by her violent ponce, the policeman had said that he wanted information about the ponce's drug dealing activities before he would help.

It is important, however, to emphasise that the women did not see the policemen's requests for information, nor their requests for the women to press charges against their ponces, as opportunity costs of being involved with policemen (although these requests were considered in the women's calculations about the overall costs of involvement with the police). Instead the cost was seen in terms of being 'indebted' to particular policemen. Thus the interviewees described becoming designated individuals to whom particular policemen went for information whenever they deemed it necessary. When the women were asked to elaborate on this, or if they could provide any examples, only Christine (aged 23) felt able to do so. She recalled that after she had asked a policeman for his help in dealing with a violent ponce, the policeman had 'kept coming round and asking questions'. Christine said that he had done this because he knew her by name and thought they 'were friends'. Christine believed that his constant badgering of her was a result of her 'indebtedness' to him. She said, 'he was on my back all the time', and that when she had stopped giving him information he had 'made it harder for me on purpose', he 'nicked me *all* the time man – sometimes three times a night'. Her concluding remarks on this episode are illustrative:

You have to be careful when you ask for their help. The police can make your life hell and treat you like sh*t, if you don't give them what they want. They may help you in the beginning, but it will cost you in the end.

Interestingly, involvement with ponces was seen by many of the interviewees as incurring opportunity costs. In common with the women's construction of involvement with the police, involvement with ponces was understood by them as providing protection against violence, but protection specifically from punters and/or other men trying to ponce them. The interviewees talked about the necessity of making calculations about the type and quality of protection that the ponces could offer them in exchange for the financial exploitation they would have to endure:

> I'm not so frightened of him now [her previous ponce]. I got this new ponce to stand up for me, and he has told him to f**k off and leave me alone. I have to pay him though (Diane, aged 37).

> After Dagger got arrested for poncing me, I paid Germaine. Germaine was somebody that was friends with Dagger, but I paid him to watch us girls while we was out, for a little extra protection like (Gail, aged 28).

The construction of involvement with ponces as generating costs is most clearly illustrated in the interviewees' discussion of 'bad' ponces – that is, men who have a reputation for being 'nutters', 'psychos', 'hard cases' or not ordinary, normal men. During these discussions the women emphasised that the opportunity costs of being involved with ponces were extremely high. In addition to subjecting themselves to financial exploitation, the women also ran the risk of violence and abuse from ponces. However, they constituted such opportunity costs as worthwhile because they believed that the protection these men offered was the best available:

> The only time he's liable to protect you is if another man is trying to ponce you. . . . You can say, 'Well, leave me alone coz I'm with him'. Like one night at two in the morning, I nearly got robbed by a punter. But because of who I was with – the guy had been in a prison cell with my old man and knew what he was like – he said, 'No problem. On your way' (Andrea, aged 27).

> There's a thing around here. Once they know who you're working for and what status he's got in Greenvale – like who's the baddest, who's the hardest, who's got the gun and who hasn't [pause]. You only have to mention 'X' [her ponce], and that was that. People would leave you alone. The other ponces and other girls would just leave you be.

They wouldn't meddle. We had a whole street to ourselves. [JP: Why?] He's notorious! He's psychotic! He's one very sick, twisted individual. People are afraid of him (Barbara, aged 24).

Involvement with 'bad' ponces also permitted the women to gain an image of themselves as 'bad' prostitutes who had 'street credibility' and 'kudos':

Red is the guy that I was with when I was young. He was a big, bad ponce with a big, bad car, and it was the in thing to be seen with somebody that had got a bad name. It meant you were bad (Andrea, aged 27).

[JP: Why did you have a ponce then?] It was like – I dunno. It's just unwritten rules, I suppose. Girls like to brag, 'Oh, I'm with so and so', and everyone knows who he is. Whereas, if you're with a man no one knows, people are just gonna go, 'So what'. I suppose it's kudos, street cred. People go, 'Oh I'm not gonna mess with her' (Anna aged 36).

My pimp's a BIG man in Greenvale. He has loads of girls and he's dangerous, man. It's good I'm with him (Katrina, aged 20).

Involvement with 'big, bad ponces' as a signification of 'street credibility' prompted Olivia to comment that she no longer associated with other women working from the street because she was fed up with their bragging. She said: 'They're always on about their men. How hard he is. How many women he's got – it's just bollocks!'

The irony of these relationships is that, although the women saw their ponces as a form of opportunity cost in that they were supposed to protect them from punter violence and other ponces, in reality these ponces provided little protection and in fact exposed the women to further violence (and certainly further financial exploitation). For example Sammy (aged 18) remarked that even though she had a ponce, he was never there when she was 'doing the business with punters' and so could not intervene in the case of trouble. Gail (aged 28) remarked that Germaine never really protected her (or the others he was paid to protect) from her ex-ponce, Dagger. In fact Germaine had told Dagger where Gail was hiding. Consequently Gail was beaten up by both Germaine (in an attempt to get more money from her) and Dagger (in an attempt to intimidate her into withdrawing her charges of poncing). Katrina (aged 20) discussed the brutal violence that her ponce regularly inflicted on her. Hence although the women saw involvement with these men as an opportunity cost incurred in their endeavour to protect themselves against prostitution-related violence, such protection was seldom forthcoming.

Hidden Costs

Nineteen of the women considered that intimate relationships and involvement with partners incurred 'hidden costs'. To be more precise, involvement with men as partners was seen as having a cost attached that was unknown at the time the relationship began, but became apparent as the relationship progressed and/or broke down. This cost was sometimes forced engagement in prostitution and/or financial exploitation.

In terms of women not wanting to lose their men, two of the 21 respondents talked about their intimate relationships incurring the hidden cost of *entrance into* prostitution. This cost was hidden because it only emerged after their relationships were established. So Margie said that she had become involved with a man who had 'asked her to do him a favour' and become a prostitute so that she could earn the money for him to buy a new car. Reflecting on this and why she had eventually agreed, Margie (aged 32) commented: 'He was a lot stronger in character than me, and to be totally truthful, out of anybody I'd ever seen, he was the only person I really did love and find attractive and fancy. I did it because I wanted to be with him.' In similar fashion, Ruthie (aged 25) concisely summarised her entrance into prostitution as resulting from having 'the knickers charmed off' her. She had met a man who later convinced her that he needed money:

> I started going out with this guy. I fell for him. . . . But I suppose, I fell for the wrong one. He put me on the game. [JP: What do you mean?] Well, he charmed the knickers off me. He kept saying it was real easy, and how I would really help him out, coz he needed money for this, that and the other. I really liked him, and the time we spent together. I wanted to stay with him and thought, 'It would be no big deal to help him out for a while'.

Both Ruthie and Margie characterised their initial involvement in prostitution and their subsequent financial exploitation as the hidden cost of 'keeping' their relationships. For 17 other interviewees the cost of their relationships was their *continued engagement in prostitution*. According to Anna (aged 36): 'There's a lot of pressure. You have to do it, coz you need the money yourself. Then you get mixed up with someone, and you have to do it again to help him, to keep a hold of him, and because you love him.'

It is tempting to treat the interviewees' thoughts about the hidden costs of intimate relationships as though they had somehow 'misrecognised' the practices of financial exploitation inherent in their relationships. In other words, it is tempting to reconstruct their narratives and characterise these men simply as ponces and not boyfriends. However the interviewees did not see these men as ponces – they saw them as their partners.

> A ponce is somebody that beats up a girl and says, 'Get on the corner and make the money'. But I suppose, that's not true. You meet a man.... You're working, and first of all you give them a tenner or whatever coz they're skint. And then you think, 'Oh I love you', and you give fifty or a hundred pounds. And eventually... you're having to raise a certain amount and you're keeping, maybe, five or ten pounds for yourself (Andrea, aged 27).

The following extract provides an indication of how the symbolic transformation of poncing occurred:

> Roger – I classed him as my boyfriend. I mean he had all his clothes at mine, and he had a jewellery shop, so he was doing his own thing. But he still used to have a hundred pounds off me a day, like. But I had strong feelings for him, although they weren't good enough, really. Coz no matter how hard I worked, or how much money I gave him, he still left me (Christine, aged 23).

Fiona (aged 42), who had never been ponced at any time during her involvement in prostitution, reflected on why some women 'allowed' themselves to be ponced:

> One girl came in here, and she was really nice. She was 18, got a little baby, and she was convinced that her guy loved her. And it came out that this fella had got five girls working for him. She couldn't understand, 'Oh yea, I bought his whatever, his clothes' and I says, 'Yea, but you're giving him your money that you've earned'. She says, 'No I'm not. I'm helping him out! I love him!'

These extracts indicate that, within the context of an intimate relationship, the interviewees reconstructed the practice of financial exploitation

and deployed it to signify the value that they placed on their relationships.

Hence what is suggested by the women's talk about their intimate
relationships with men is that in the context of involvement in the bread
and butter end of prostitution, where financial exploitation by men is
prevalent, the demarcation of a relationship with a particular man as a
'poncing relationship' (that is, characterised by abuse, control and
exploitation) or an 'intimate relationship' occurs at a symbolic level,
and is not delineated solely in terms of the *practice* of financial exploitation. As this section has sought to illustrate, there exists a nexus of
meaning wherein involvement with men is understood as incurring hidden costs. Consequently the practice of giving money to partners (or
even becoming engaged in prostitution to begin with) is not seen as
unusual or atypical. It is merely part of prostitute women's intimate
relationships.

In a similar fashion to the way that 'keeping a man' was understood
to incur hidden costs, 12 of the interviewees understood 'leaving men'
as incurring the hidden cost of returning to prostitution. When discussing leaving the men with whom they had had intimate relationships,
the respondents talked primarily of the economic difficulties they
had experienced. This is common to all women, whether or not they
are engaged in prostitution, as structural inequalities between men
and women continue to condition women's economic relationships
with men.

Diane (aged 37) described the time when she left the father of her
two children. She said that after a four-year break from prostitution
she had had no intention of returning, but shortly after she left him it
had become clear that she would either have to go back to him in order
to escape the poverty she had been plunged into, or go back to prostitution. Speaking of that time she declared: 'I suppose it was the price
I had to pay to get rid of him. There's always a price, isn't there?
You just don't know it at the time'. Patsy and Georgie made similar
comments:

I suppose if I never got with him, I wouldn't be back here on the
streets. I didn't think that, when I tried to leave him, I'd have to
return (Patsy, aged 42).

What could I do? I had two children, nowhere to go and no money of
my own. Sometimes, I think, I bought myself out of that marriage by
selling myself on the streets (Georgie, aged 35).

It must be emphasised that the women's discussion of the difficult economic choices they had had to make after leaving their straight partners does not suggest that they saw separation from their partners as incurring the hidden cost of engagement in prostitution. Rather it was the causal connections the interviewees drew between their relationship break-ups and their engagement in prostitution that suggests this. So Diane, Patsy and Georgie talked about their return to prostitution as though it was the direct result of leaving their partners. Indeed as, Jasmine (aged 30) succinctly put it: 'If I never left him, I wouldn't be working now'. Such an understanding was made possible by the simultaneous encoding of 'men as expense' and 'men as income'; for implicit in the women's talk about the hidden cost of leaving their partners was a construction of intimate relationships with men outside prostitution as an economic relationship in which men provide women with income, economic security and stability.

'YOU CAN'T TRUST MEN'

The two final contingent elements of the interviewees' prostitute identity were 'prostitutes as victims' and 'prostitutes as survivors'. These identifications emerged from an articulation of the meanings of men and money whereby men were understood as being 'risky' and money was understood as the object conditioning women's vulnerability to men's 'riskiness'.

Prostitutes as Victims

In all of the interviewees' narratives (with the exception of that of Fiona, aged 41, and regardless of their specific prostitution-related experiences) there was a manifest prostitutes-as-victims identification. Drawing on a discourse of victimhood whereby victims are constituted as 'blameless' and 'not responsible' for the fate that befalls them (cf. Walklate, 1989), these prostitute women were located as individuals who were unable to control the events in their lives relative to those who injured, hurt or mistreated them in order to control them. In this respect the construction of certain key others as having the ability to determine the course of the interviewees' lives and against which, the women believed, there was no effective resistance was of significance. In some instances the prostitutes-as-victim identity was constructed in relation to people and events in the women's past (that is, prior to their engagement in prostitution), whereas in other instances it was constructed in relation to people and events in their present lives in prostitution.

Of the 21 interviewees, nine had been physically or sexually abused or emotionally neglected when they were children. All drew direct links between such instances of abuse and their lives as prostitutes. They described their experiences of abuse or neglect as not merely (and only) instances of victimisation (that is, having injuries inflicted on them) that had had profound psychological effects, but these experiences were also seen as dramatically affecting their future lives by turning them into victims. For example Lois (aged 21) recounted that by the time she had become engaged in prostitution she had already been beaten by her mother and father, sexually abused by her cousin and raped by her brother-in-law:

> I didn't have a clue then. All I knew was how to be raped, and how to be attacked, and how to be beaten up, and that's all I knew. So when he put me on the game, I was too down in the dumps to do anything. All I knew was abuse.

Ruthie (aged 25) expressed similar thoughts:

> There was one time that my uncle (he used to look after us) did do something. He did try to play about with all us kids. Do you know what I mean? And, anyway, they do say, don't they, that a lot of prostitutes have got abuse in their pasts. . . . It's funny isn't it, because it's only when you're older that you realise what he did to you was much more than just played about. He made me what I am today. So I suppose, that it weren't surprising I ended up a prostitute.

Diane (aged 37) talked much more generally about her past experiences of abuse and neglect:

> [JP: Sounds like it's been a struggle for you.] I brought it all on myself. Got involved with the wrong people – people who hurt me and just did what they wanted to do with me. I suppose, I'm just a born victim otherwise I wouldn't be here now.

Those interviewees who saw themselves as victims in relation to events and people in their *present* lives did so because of their belief that their ponces and/or boyfriends were able to determine everything about their lives. That their identities were constructed in such a manner was illustrated by the ways in which the women implicitly situated themselves as passive agents who quiescently accepted the injurious actions of others, where events 'just happened' and there was nothing they could do to alter the course of their lives.

> Minnie said to me, 'Oh he's mad, he's gonna kill you' [Christine had had a particularly heated argument with her ponce/boyfriend]. And he come back and kicked in the door. He was going mad. And then he went and took Minnie home. He came back about 1.00 a.m.... He was being all friendly, and all of a sudden, he just clicked and battered me. My nose was all cracked and bleeding and I had two black eyes. I left for a few days, and he took me telly, me jewellery, the video. [JP: Why?] Thought he owned it. Suppose I left him and so all my assets were his (Christine, aged 23).

> At that point I'd had enough. I went to him and he said 'You're going back on the streets'. I said, 'No'. He said, 'You will if I tell you to. If I want, you know, you gotta go'. I said, 'Well I'll report you'. And that was that. That was the final straw. He just started slapping, slap, slap, slap on me head and me earrings shot out. He stormed off and I went back to the streets to get his money (Margie, aged 32).

> I ain't got no personal life. My life is *completely* ruled by Fabulous (Katrina, aged 21).

Even when the interviewees were asked directly about their relationships with brutal ponces, they continued to describe such relationships as 'just happening' and spoke about them as though they were unable to change the nature of or end those relationships:

> At the end of the day, we're all gonna get thrown away with nothing. We're gonna be disrespected. Nobody's gonna want us. But, we got no choice. He's ruining our lives (Katrina, aged 21).

> When I had a ponce – I had no choice about what I did, I was completely controlled by him. [JP: Did you report him to the police?] No. [JP: Why not?] I couldn't. I was completely controlled by him (Anna, aged 36).

Most of the women who had been ponced at some point or other discussed their reasons for not resisting their ponces or not reporting them to the police:

[JP: Why didn't you just stop giving him the money and stop seeing him?] Coz he'd kill me. He'd beat the hell out of me. I know that. You just know it at the back of your mind. It's easier to just do what he wants (Margie, aged 32).

He put me on the game. [JP: Why didn't you say no?] Well, it's not just him. He's got a BIG family. When I say big – you mess with one, and you mess with a lot of them. I'd have ended up dead, and I'm not into that! (Katrina, aged 21).

[JP: Why didn't you go to the police about him?] Coz I've felt his punches. Anyway, it doesn't matter if I did, coz wherever I go he'd hunt me down (Sammy, aged 18).

If you haven't got their money – the money they want – you've had it. You could end up dead (Patsy, aged 42).

Clearly, one of the reasons for the women's passive acceptance of being controlled by their ponces/boyfriends was fear of reprisal. Indeed of the 21 interviewees, 14 expressed their fear of being murdered by their ponces:

I did as I was told. You know what I mean? Otherwise you're dead. When they've got a gun pointed to your head, you do as you're told (Barbara, aged 23).

I said to my barrister [after being charged with running a brothel], 'You know, my life won't be worth living. There's not a corner big enough in this whole world for me to hide if I go and point the finger at anyone of them in there. I could end up dead' (Gail, aged 28).

Every time I came back without the money he'd asked for, I'd be shitting myself. Coz you never know whether they're gonna kill you or not (Janet, aged 37).

It is not surprising that the women feared reprisal from their ponces/boyfriends given that they could recount numerous episodes of brutality, violence and sexual assault. However, in addition to describing some of the realities of their everyday lives with violent men, in their statements they constituted themselves as victims in that resistance to their violent ponces/boyfriends was seen as futile because these men controlled their lives to such an extent that they could determine whether the women lived or died.

The prostitutes-as-victims identification also emerged in relation to boyfriends who were not financially exploitative. This is illustrated by the following comments from Olivia (aged 28), who had never been ponced by the man of whom she spoke. He had 'pinched' their daughter and Social Services had intervened, where upon he had claimed that she was an unfit mother on the grounds that she was a prostitute, that she took drugs and that she had left her daughter alone for long periods of time.

> But I weren't doing that! I mean I was working, but she was looked after really well. [JP: Did you tell Social Services that?] No way. I just started drinking and going off my head. Threw myself into work, got a job in a sauna. You know that type of thing. I was too scared to write a statement and sign it, coz I was scared of him. I used to have these welfare meetings, and all that, and I wouldn't open my mouth and say what I wanted, coz he was sitting there. I was too scared.

Sophie (aged 28) made the following comments about a violent boyfriend she had been involved with just prior to her engagement in prostitution:

> I had no control over my life. I was absolutely petrified of him. You would sit down and watch telly and the next minute, you know, you'd just feel a whack. Half the time you ignore it and you'd think to yourself that didn't really happen.... A lot of people were really shocked that I'd put up with it. But in the end, I thought. 'Well, this is it. I'm going to die because of him'. So when my boss suggested that I start doing B&D [bondage and discipline], I was that much of a victim that I never said no.

The interviewees also saw themselves as victims in relation to 'uncaring' statutory agencies (agencies such as the court welfare teams, the probation service, social services and so on who 'do not listen' and do not appreciate what is 'really happening' and therefore leave the women to their fate). This is most clearly depicted in the remarks made by Gail (aged 28) about when she had been taken into custody and charged with running a brothel – her five children had been placed in local authority care:

> I sat there watching them take my children away and I thought, 'I'm the victim here'. I mean all I could think was that it was Dagger who

forced me on the streets, Dagger that brought all those girls to my house, and Dagger that made me keep my kids in the back room. [JP: Did you tell them that?] No. What was the point? The social workers didn't want to know. The police couldn't care less. I think if they cared, I wouldn't have been in that situation to begin with (Gail, aged 28).

Andrea (aged 27) made similar remarks about her experience in the Magistrates' Court:

But in court, I say to them, 'The reason I do this is because I got no money off the social. I'm a single parent. What the f**k do you expect me to do!' But they don't listen. They just tell me to pay another fine, and guess where I gotta get that money from!

The police too were seen by the women as 'uncaring'. This was illustrated in discussions about why they did not report any of the violence they experienced from punters, ponces, partners, police officers, vigilantes and other street criminals:

What're the police going to do? The police don't do shit! At the end of the day, they don't care. You're the sh*t beneath their shoes (Barbara, aged 24).

The police aren't bothered, because our words don't stick in court. We're just prostitutes and we're lying. We've got sour grapes for whatever reason. That's what I honestly think, and that's why I don't ever report funny punters or the old men I've been with. Even when somebody's murdered, they don't follow it up as much as they should do. A couple of days they're buzzing around, and then it's back to normal (Andrea, aged 27).

A profound irony is that the prostitutes-as-victims identification occurred in a context in which the women's status as a 'legitimate' victim (the defining yardstick of a legitimate victim is that she is seen to be 'innocent' and not involved in her victimisation – see especially Walklate, 1989) was often denied by the agencies that the women approached for aid (see also Dunhill, 1989, p. 206; McLeod, 1982). For example it was explained to me during informal discussions with the sexual health outreach worker that, although it was not 'official policy', none of the battered women's refuges in MidCity would accommodate women whom they suspected were prostitutes. Referral by the sexual health outreach service was taken as evidence of a woman's prostitute status. The refuges' administrators and management committees claimed that prostitutes would endanger the other residents of the refuges because, they said, prostitutes would bring punters back to the refuges or give the secret addresses of the refuges to their ponces.[1] The sexual health outreach worker was asked if she had ever heard of prostitutes endangering other residents. She replied: 'No. The problem is that they think that working women are not "innocent" enough. They think that they [the women] put themselves at risk, and so they should protect themselves.'

The interviewees were aware of the context in which their status as victims was often denied by official agencies (and with that any help that such agencies could offer). They spoke about 'giving the courts some soppy story' that enabled the courts to reinterpret the women's engagement in prostitution in such a fashion as to make them less culpable for what had happened to them. Typically this included encouraging the women to recount stories in which they would describe themselves as engaging in prostitution because of the need to provide for their children (thereby demonstrating that prostitutes are good mothers and thus 'innocent'). Michelle (aged 33) referred to this process as a 'mickey mouse game':

> Everyone knows that when you go in there, you go and give them some soppy story about how you got three kids at home, and no electric, no gas and they'd just say, 'Well okay then'. You know? In fact, they actually put it in front of you. They ask you if you got problems, like whether you've got kids. You know, it's just a mickey mouse game. I mean, it doesn't help the girls as such...

Ruthie (aged 28) talked about the necessity of having to reconstruct an official version of her engagement in prostitution in order to become what the official agencies saw as a legitimate victim (and thus qualify for aid). She described how 'not wanting to better yourself' disqualified a prostitute woman from being a legitimate victim and thus disqualified her from the help that the probation office, in particular, could offer:

> Probation will help you, I mean they are fairly helpful if you got records, and you've been in trouble, and you want to better yourself. But the catch is, proving to them that you want to better yourself. I mean, if you are a 'fallen woman' and you keep falling, then, they ain't gonna help you. They think it's a waste of their time helping you.

But if you can show them that you had no choice, and that you really wanna stop, then, sometimes they can be quite helpful.

And so the prostitutes-as-victims identification was constituted in relation to the notions of all-powerful and all-controlling boyfriends and/or ponces and uncaring statutory agencies. Moreover it was an identification contextualised by the everyday realities of involvement with violent men, and the processes through which being a prostitute disqualified these interviewees from being officially recognised as victims. The prostitutes-as-victim identification emerged during the interviewees' narratives of engagement in prostitution – they had no choice, and they were held within prostitution by violent and exploitative relationships against which there was no effective resistance. In this symbolic landscape, involvement in prostitution was represented as a trap that was inescapable and a threat to the women's very survival.

Prostitutes as Survivors

The prostitutes-as-survivors identification was evident in 18 of the 21 narratives. It is an identification in which the interviewees can be seen as women who have managed successfully to negotiate the risks and uncertainties posed by the various men involved in the institution of prostitution. Or to be more precise, the prostitutes-as-survivors identity has to do with the manner in which the women can be positioned as individuals battling for control over their own money (that is, relative to ponces) and battling for their own physical well-being (that is, relative to punters). This identification emerged in relation to the prostitutes-as-victims identification and the notion of non-prostitute women as 'weaker', 'not surviving' and 'not strong'.

All but two of these 18 women described themselves as 'lucky' and such talk suggests their survivor identity. Witness Georgie's description of her life when she was being ponced by her last boyfriend: 'Um, I guess, I was one of the lucky ones. I had clothes. I could pay my rent. I wasn't as bad off as some. I suppose I was lucky, and because of that I've survived' (Georgie, aged 35).

In contrast to the prostitutes-as-victims identification, where the notion of an all-powerful, all-controlling boyfriend/ponce was combined with the victim's belief that resistance was futile, these women gained their identity as survivors by representing themselves as winning the 'battle' with their boyfriend/ponces for control of the money that they earned. The following quotes illustrate this point:

I count myself as one of the lucky ones really because I can earn my money, and I got rid of my pimp. It was hard, but I did it, and now I am a survivor (Jasmine, aged 31).

I get treated a lot better than most, as luck would have it. I keep some of my money, but only for the fact that he knows I've been to prison coz I killed someone. He knows what I'm capable of. And he knows I'll always make sure I survive. So he doesn't mess with me too much (Katrina, aged 21).

There's two sort of prostitutes. There's the ones that's out there for themselves, and there's the ones that are working for their guy. I give anyone credit for standing out on the streets, doing it for themselves, taking their money home. But I can't understand anyone that can stand there and then give it all to some man. [JP: But you were in that situation for over two years.] Yea. But, at least I got out of it. I survived. In the end, I'm one of the lucky ones. I was stronger than him (Lois, aged 21).

There are two interesting points to note here. First, the prostitutes-as-survivors identification serves to demonstrate the paradoxical nature of the women's narratives. Both Lois and Katrina were strident when representing their engagement in prostitution as a trap threatening their physical, material and social survival. They both talked about being forced into prostitution through fear of death, about being ponced by men from whom there was no escape and no feasible means of resisting. And yet both women identified themselves as survivors.

Second, although the prostitutes-as-survivors identification would suggest that the women did not see themselves as 'passive agents' whose lives were determined by others (that is, ponces/boyfriends), by describing themselves as 'lucky' the women made it sound as though they were not determining the course of their own lives. Instead they were telling stories in which the 'hand of fate' had intervened.

Further evidence of the women's identity as survivors was provided by their talk of 'gut reactions' about punters. These gut reactions allowed them to protect themselves against the threat of violence and abuse from punters. In this context the women's survivor identification related to the everyday realities of engagement in prostitution from the streets or their own homes. For example Patsy and Michelle made the following remarks:

You learn how to be a survivor. You learn it for safety reasons. You learn that you have to go with your feelings. You can have a conversation with a punter, and you'll get the drift that the punter's not genuine. But now and again, you'll get somebody that asks too many questions. 'Do you do this?' 'Do you do that?' And you start thinking, 'He's asking a helluva lot here' and something inside says, 'Don't go there, don't do that punter'. It's just a gut instinct you get when you learn to be a survivor (Patsy, aged 42).

Ninety nine per cent of the time I'm working I'll have somebody in the house with me ... in the extra room so if I do have to shout out, then I know that person's there. It's a matter of having to these days, if you're gonna survive, and that's what I'm all about, surviving. Or, you don't like the look of a punter, you don't let him in the house. Maybe they talk funny or they ask things. You get a feeling for it (Michelle, aged 33).

Those interviewees who were not currently working as prostitutes identified themselves in the same way and used the same set of representations; but they deployed these representations to stress the necessity of leaving prostitution. The following extract illustrates this most saliently:

The danger's why I gave it up. When I was younger, you never think about surviving. I mean about *being* a survivor. It never enters your head. I mean, you never think about the consequences, and what's gonna happen. But now, especially with these murders that have not long happened, that put the topper on it. Coz I'm older and a lot wiser, and I just think to myself, 'Well, I'm a survivor and my life's worth more than ten, maybe twenty quid. I ain't gonna get murdered for twenty quid'. So, I gave it all up (Andrea, aged 27).

The prostitutes-as-survivors identification was also evident in the distinction the women drew between themselves and non-prostitute women:

I think we're better at surviving than ordinary women. Experience. We've been around and we see. And I think an ordinary woman, they wouldn't tackle a man where we would. If we see a woman in trouble, we would go over and we would tackle them [that is, the men]! But ordinary women would be afraid. We can cope with violent boyfriends better than ordinary women. I ran after my last one with a hatchet knife! I can't see no ordinary woman doing that! We're sur-vivors and they're not (Janet, aged 37).

I think all women have a way of going about things, but I think prosti-tutes are better at surviving, coz we're more honest. We don't say, 'Oh I love you'. The only difference is that the punter's not a stranger for straight women (Gail, aged 28).

Working women are better survivors than straight women. We know a lot more about men than straight women. Well, we would, wouldn't we? We have just loads more knowledge. We know how to get them, how to keep them, and how to get rid of them if we're in trouble. And we know how to survive without them (Sammy, aged 18).

These extracts show that the interviewees saw non-prostitute women as 'weaker', 'not strong' and 'not surviving'. They asserted that non-prosti-tute women (unlike prostitute women) 'don't know what men are really like', 'don't know how to make it for themselves' and 'can't cope'.

And so the prostitutes-as-survivors identification was gained via (1) the women' identification as victims, (2) the notion of all-powerful ponce/boyfriends and 'weaker' non-prostitute women, and (3) the real-ities of everyday, punter-instigated violence conditioned by engagement in prostitution from the streets or from home. Moreover this self-identification enabled the women to recount stories of involvement in prostitution in which the latter was represented as an effective strategy for economic and social survival, even though there might have been risks attached to it. For these women, being a survivor meant having encountered these risks and successfully negotiated them in such a way as to allow continued involvement in prostitution without being entrapped or having their survival seriously threatened.

MEN AS RISK: THE DISSOLUTION OF SYMBOLIC BOUNDARIES

The prostitutes-as-victims and prostitutes-as-survivors identifications were made possible by a symbolic landscape in which men were consti-tuted as 'dangerous' (that is, individuals who posed specific threats to the women's social, material and physical safety and security) and 'sus-pect' (that is, individuals who could not be trusted), and in which money was believed to be the object conditioning these women's vulnerability to 'risky men'.

The notion of men as 'risk' was decontextualised and mythologised in that it was applied to all men, irrespective of whether or not they were involved with the women or with the institution of prostitution, and contained a specific message:

> Men – bastards! The bloody lot of them. You can't trust them. They just use and abuse women. You can't tell me there's a man out there who hasn't, or won't one day (Ingrid, aged 44).

> There's a lot of people I don't trust, but I especially don't trust men. You never know what they're going to do to you (Georgie, aged 35).

> Men are all the same. They'll twist your brains, they'll want to control you. They'll take your money. I ain't met one yet who isn't like that – right down to my father and brothers (Christine, aged 23).

The message that emanates from statements such as these is that women cannot be certain about men: all men are risky, untrustworthy and likely to cause harm to women.

But such a symbolic landscape was also contextualised by an understanding of men that was expressed in relation to the specific institutional practices of financial exploitation, violence and policing, as well as in relation to ponces, partners and punters, and as such this symbolic landscape was highly differentiated in that particular types of men were constituted as presenting specific types of risk. This symbolic landscape was also constructed in relation to the everyday realities of engagement in the institution of prostitution, where working in particular ways increases the risk of exploitation, violence and venereal disease (see McKeganey and Barnard, 1996, pp. 58–69; Ward and Day, 1997, pp. 141–7 for discussions on women's understanding of venereal diseases).

The notion that specific types of men pose particular types of risk was a very important part of the women's symbolic landscape. For in this symbolic landscape the conventional distinctions between 'normal' and 'abnormal' men and ponces and boyfriends were dissolved. Consequently it brought uncertainty in the interviewees' lives. That is to say, the ways in which they constituted men as risky resulted in their never being sure whether the men they were with were dangerous men, predatory men, suspect men or perhaps not risky at all. The following sections trace the ways in which men were seen as risky.

Men as 'Dangerous'

The construction of men as dangerous was illustrated in the women's talk about 'ponces' and 'black men'. These men were seen as dangerous in that they posed specific threats to the women's material and social security in terms of violence and financial exploitation. Indeed ponces and black men were talked about by nearly all of the interviewees as though they were predators, preying on the women in order to achieve their own financial security and using tactics such as violence to achieve their ends.

Before examining the interviewees' thoughts on ponces, it is important to note that in the women's narratives the term 'ponce' signified two things. First, the term was used to describe men whose relationship with prostitutes was one of financial exploitation. The second use of the term was more to do with imagery in that it was used to signify the dangers of engagement in prostitution. Ponces occupied a pivotal position in the respondents' symbolic landscape for the image of the ponce contained all the assumed, actual and experienced threats to the women's survival. Moreover ponces were seen as distinct and separate from boyfriends. They were discussed as though they were sadistic and violent men who would kidnap and entrap women, take all their money and treat (and trade) them like chattels, and from whom there was no sanctuary, no escape and no evasion:

> A ponce makes a girl stand out there, and if she hasn't raised the money he wants, he beats her up and sends her back. They don't live with the girls, and they've got about eight or nine girls all over the streets and one's for his petrol, and the other's for his food and the other's for his clothes and that's the way it goes (Helena, aged 35).

> A ponce is someone that beats up a woman and takes every penny she earns – her and a half a dozen others. That's how he gets his money (Janet, aged 37).

This construction of ponces was made possible by the women's deployment of particular discourses of masculine criminality and masculine violence. Of relevance is the interviewees' deployment of discourses that constituted criminal men in terms of being 'tough' and 'alien', which conjoined in the expression 'bad' (cf. Katz, 1988, pp. 80–113). These discourses positioned ponces (whom the women understood to be criminal) as 'not only not here for others, but native to some morally alien world' (ibid., p. 113). In short, when describing ponces the women drew on constructions of criminal men that portrayed the latter as 'outsiders' to 'ordinary' morality who were interested only in what they could get for themselves; thereby the women constructed a symbolic boundary between ponces and partners. Consider the following extracts:

> Ponces don't give a sh∗t about you. They only care about what they can get for themselves and how much money you'll earn them (Sammy, aged 18).

> Ponces are not like other men. They ain't got no heart. They only ever want money. Like once, there was this young girl, she had a ponce, and he used to beat her up all the time, man! There was one time she hurt her leg really, really badly and we told him to take her to the hospital. He wouldn't. He shoved her back on the street, and she fell, running for a punter, and she couldn't get up. Her leg was that bad. All he could say was, 'Oh leave her! She's gotta earn money'. Now that's a ponce, a big, bad man who doesn't give a sh∗t (Helena, aged 35).

In addition to drawing on discourses of masculine criminality, the women also drew on discourses that essentialised male violence in order to construct an image of the ponce. These discourses portray men as always and already (at least potentially) violent, and construct violence itself as masculine (cf. Segal, 1996; Kersten, 1996). The deployment of both discourses permitted the women to talk about ponces as always posing the danger of financial exploitation and violence:

> What you gotta understand is that he was a *ponce*. I mean, if I didn't make enough, he'd send me back out. He was the proper order ponce. He wanted – I got. And if I didn't, he'd kill me (Ingrid, aged 44).

> After I killed my ponce, I realised that it weren't really his fault that he was like that. [JP: Like what?] Well, beating up on me, raping me, making me have sex with dogs and sh∗t, taking all my money. Some men are just like that. I think it's in their nature. The one thing I've learned through all this is that you gotta steer clear of ponces. It's just too dangerous to get involved with them (Anna, aged 36).

Related to the women's inscription of ponces as essentially dangerous men was their construction of black men as essentially dangerous.

Indeed one of the more striking features of the women's narratives was the way in which they spoke about black men. The women (20 of whom were white and one of whom was of mixed parentage) talked about 'strict rules' for 'not going with black punters', about how 'all the black men want is to ponce white women' and so on. But at the same time most of the women had black boyfriends and they talked about how 'attractive' and exciting black men were.

Within the articulation of meanings where men were described as risky was a set of racist representations in which black (that is, Afro-Caribbean) men were held to be (1) dangerous, in that they were believed to threaten the women's material, social and physical security and safety, and (2) predators because they were seen by the women as individuals who secured their own economic survival by exploiting prostitutes. The following extracts indicate this:

> Black men are like leeches on you. They will take your money and leave you for dead. Like leeches, they need to be burned off (Janet, aged 37).

> There's not many black girls that hustle. They have more f**king sense than us white girls, haven't they? They don't let their men use and abuse them, so instead their men use and abuse us by taking our money, by beating us and raping us (Ingrid, aged 44).

> You have to be strong down here. You have to know who's gonna take advantage of you. You have to watch the black men. Me, if they pull up, I just run away. They're dangerous, and I'm not gonna mess with them! (Diane, aged 37).

> It's scary here. There's the black men – the ponces and the drug men. And that ain't no stereotype. The thing is that all those black men do it and you hear about it everyday. [JP: What do they do?] It's like there's four or five of them in the car and they'd all be there smoking drugs, whatever and loud music. It gets really frightening. If they do drag you in their car, rest assured that they was all gonna have a dabble. You'd be raped by all of them, and probably ponced (Gail, aged 28).

Talking about black men in such a way was made possible by (1) a contextualisation of the women's experience of prostitution-related exploitation and violence in terms of the demographic distribution of MidCity, and (2) the interviewees' deployment of discourses of racial differentiation. To say that the women's portrayal of black men as posing particular risks was contextualised in terms of their engagement in prostitution *within* MidCity requires elaboration. Chapter 1 outlined the socio-demographic context of the areas in which the women worked and lived (Birchfield and Greenvale), thereby demonstrating that Mid-City is a large English city with a very diverse ethnic population. Both Birchfield and Greenvale have a strong representation of the main minority ethnic groups, and a three times greater than city-average representation of Afro-Caribbean people. Thus the women worked and lived in predominantly Afro-Caribbean areas, and hence had extensive contact, in both their working and private lives, with Afro-Caribbean men. That black men *per se* came to occupy a pivotal position in the women's symbolic landscape is therefore not surprising. But it is extremely important to separate analytically the reality of the women's extensive contact with Afro-Caribbean men (which provides the social context in which these women saw black men as posing particular types of risk) and the ways in which black men were constructed as imaginary figures. More precisely, asserting that the women constructed black men as predators and dangerous is not the same as asserting that Afro-Caribbean men *were* the women's predators or that the Afro-Caribbean men known by the women were more dangerous than other men.

Drawing on discourses of racial differentiation enabled the interviewees to construct the image of dangerous black men. The women consistently referred to black men as 'them', 'not like us', 'different' and so on. In this respect black men were encoded as 'other' (cf. Anthias and Yuval-Davies, 1992). But more than this, the women drew on specific early modern discourses of racial differentiation (see Fryer, 1984; Gilroy, 1987; Walvin, 1994), in which black men's 'otherness' was both sexualised and essentialised in that black men were represented as 'ignoble' (and hence 'savage', 'predatory' and 'dangerous'), sexually threatening and dominant 'others' (see Hall and Gieben, 1992, pp. 297–303). This characterisation, combined with the actual knowledge gained by engaging in prostitution in Birchfield and Greenvale in MidCity, provided the requisite ideological background to enable the respondents to talk about all black men *as though* they were, by virtue of their ethnicity, always and already risky, dangerous and ponces.

This is most conspicuous in the conflation of black men and ponces in nearly three quarters of the women's narratives. This conflation became apparent as the fieldwork progressed and prompted me to ask the respondents about the possibility of white ponces. The standard response was laughter. Only Ruthie (aged 25) took the question seriously: 'There are some, but they aren't big ponces. They're just little sh∗t-head creeps that get a hold of young girls that don't know any better. They're nothing.' The metonymic movement between black men and ponces was so complete that many of the women referred to being ponced by simply stating that they were involved with black men. Christine and Patsy provided succinct examples of this:

> I never earned much money then. I was with black men (Patsy, aged 42).

> A lot of girls have been forced into working, especially the ones that started at 13, 14 or 15 years old. They had bad family lives and were in and out of homes. They run away from homes, and before you know it they're with some black man. They've got no chance then (Christine, aged 23).

But it was not only by conflating the meanings of black men and ponces that the women constructed black men as dangerous. This image was also evident in most of the interviewees' talk about black men as punters who might, in all probability, murder, rape, kidnap, rob or seriously sexually assault prostitute women:

> I used to work in London. [JP: Did you like it there?] No, I didn't work regularly. I really didn't like it. It was too dangerous. Too many black punters and if you don't watch them, or let them know someone is watching you, you're liable to get kidnapped and murdered (Anna, aged 27).

> There are many things you don't do if you want to stay alive out here. You stand here and don't go there. Don't talk to black men and especially don't do black men in cars. They'll rape you and rob you (Gail, aged 28).

> You gotta watch black punters, coz they'll rob you. I had one black punter and I don't know, I had a CD player and half an hour it took me to get him out of the flat. I kept saying, 'Come on. I'm gonna phone the police'. Well, he took my CD and I didn't realise till he was gone. But that's the risk you take with black punters (Patsy, aged 42).

> I won't do black guys, but I needed the money this one time and so I thought, 'F**k it. Take the risk coz you'll only get your arse kicked if you go home without the money'. This guy came up and in the end he kidnapped me for four days, raped me that bad that I can't have children no more. Well, that'll teach me for going with a black guy (Ruthie, aged 25).

Interestingly, drawing on early modern discourses of racial differentiation enabled 11 of the women to construct black men as exotic, sexually
competent 'others', as well as dangerous, predatory, sexualised 'others'.
So at the same time as talking about black men as 'risky', the women
also discussed the attractions of 'going with' black men:

> The area I grew up in, there was no black people (well maybe one or
> two black families), and like when I started mixing with black people
> – I'm not blaming it on black people like, it's just that they're into
> prostitution like. Well, I was really interested in the men. I'd never
> had sex with anyone black and well, to be truthful I wanted to know
> if all I heard was true. . . . It was exciting really. But then you get
> caught don't you, you get brought into it by the black men (Christine,
> aged 23).

> Well, I got this girlfriend Kathy, and her and her sister were with
> black guys. And so I thought, 'I'd never been with a black guy before'
> – you know, for sex like. And I was always hearing about how they
> was much better than white guys, so I thought, 'Oh well, it'd be a
> change, let's try it!' So I did, but I fell for the wrong one didn't I?
> I didn't know then that they're all ponces. He took me to London and
> I had to work for him (Ruthie, aged 25).

Earlier it was stated that money was understood by the interviewees as
increasing their vulnerability to dangerous men. Specifically, the women
described themselves as 'easy targets' because they earned money in
the form of cash (which was easily taken from them) and that this was
'easy money' (that is, always readily available). 'We're easy target for
black men and ponces aren't we? [JP: What do you mean?] Well, we've
got all this money that they want. And they know that we can go and get
more tomorrow' (Andrea, aged 27). Therefore money for these women,
represented the 'real' object of 'dangerous men's' desires. They
believed that it was not the prostitutes themselves that dangerous men
(black men/ponces) were interested in, but their money.

MEN AS 'SUSPECT'

Two categories of men were defined by the interviewees as 'suspect
men': boyfriends and 'funny' punters. It is by examining the interviewees' constructions of these 'suspect' men that the dissolution of the

symbolic demarcation between boyfriend and ponce, normal and abnormal men can be traced.

As demonstrated throughout this chapter, the most intricate, subtly nuanced and difficult to disentangle sets of meanings within the women's narratives were those in which the men with whom they had intimate relationships were seen as either ponces or boyfriends. Here, tracing the construction of 'boyfriends as suspect' brings into focus the disappearance of the (conventional) symbolic differentiation between these two categories. Earlier it was shown how financially exploitative relationships were symbolically transformed into intimate relationships, which became instances of the hidden costs of keeping a man. It was also shown how some relationships with men were not intimate relationships at all, but relationships with 'ponces proper'. In each instance a distinction between ponces and boyfriends was maintained, implicitly or explicitly; but in the women's narratives the specifics of what constituted a ponce or boyfriend and where the demarcation line should be drawn were mutable.

What is implicit in the 'boyfriend as suspect' construction is not a new or different symbolic boundary, but rather the removal of the boundary altogether, and simultaneously a subtle reconstitution of the boundary. For boyfriends were suspect because they could not be trusted, and they could not be trusted because they might become ponces. In other words, part of the symbolic landscape of the women's narratives was the construction of all boyfriends as potential ponces. Witness the following comments:

> You gotta watch having boyfriends, coz they'll ponce ya if you're not careful. In the end you think, 'boyfriend, ponce, boyfriend, ponce, what's the difference?' (Barbara, aged 24).

> I didn't mind giving him money. I mean we were together, but then he started expecting it off me. That's when I knew it, that's when I knew he was also my ponce (Christine, aged 23).

> If you had a boyfriend and he found out about you working, he'd start taking your money off you, because they start off very sly without you even realising it (Georgie, aged 35).

Hence in contrast to the essentialised descriptions of imaginary ponces, the interviewees believed that boyfriends had the potential to become ponces because of the women's engagement in prostitution. Many of the women (particularly those who had had extensive experience of being ponced) believed that they turned their boyfriends into ponces by willingly sharing their money with them:

> The father of my second child was good. Oh, I loved him. But I know it sounds crazy, but I turned him into a ponce. [JP: How did that happen?] Coz when I was with him I started spoiling him, coz I had all this money, and we were getting on great and, um, he only had to mention that he wanted this or that and he got it. Coz I had the money, he got it. But then, he got lazy and that's when the beatings started. He'd become a ponce and it was my fault (Ruthie, aged 25).

> Well, to tell you the truth, it was my fault that he turned into my ponce. I'd give him money. I mean, he started to get violent, coz he started to want more and he was spending all my money on drink and drugs. I completely changed him (Michelle, aged 33).

> Everyone's really down on ponces, but you know, all they are is a greedy boyfriend. Women make men into ponces – it's not the opposite way round! You start giving your boyfriend money and eventually, there's never actually any say so, eventually you're having to raise a certain amount and you're keeping less and less for yourself (Andrea, aged 23).

These extracts have two interesting features. First, they are informed by discourses of femininity in which women are placed as ultimately responsible for the ways in which their intimate relationships develop and progress. In this respect the women saw themselves as responsible for the transformation of their intimate relationships into poncing relationships. But this was nonetheless a way of taking charge and not being victims, because, they asserted, any victimisation they had subsequently experienced had been caused by their own active agency.

The second interesting feature is that at the same time as removing the symbolic boundary between ponces and boyfriends, many of the respondents reinstated it. Namely, they asserted that boyfriends became ponces when they 'got greedy'. Put another way, for many of the interviewees the difference between boyfriends and ponces did not inhere in the economic relationship that existed between them and their partners, because they defined all intimate relationships as marked by the exchange of money (and not necessarily an egalitarian sharing of the total economic resources of the couple). Rather the demarcation between ponces and boyfriends depended on whether or not the women believed that their boyfriends were taking more money than they were 'due'. This simultaneous dissolution and reconstruction of the symbolic boundary between boyfriends and ponces is illustrated in Janet's statement:

> I met Freddy and he was all right. Coz, see, I didn't mind giving him my money. He weren't greedy or nothing. He'd take me out to restaurants, he'd bring me out to work and he'd dress me. He always made sure I had a few bob in my pocket. I felt for all that he did, he was due some money. So he was my boyfriend and not my ponce (Janet, aged 37).

Janet deployed a characterisation of Freddy as not being 'greedy' in order to demonstrate that he was her boyfriend and not her ponce (thereby reinstating the symbolic boundary between ponces and boyfriends).

The second category of suspect men were punters. These men were defined as suspect in terms of posing a threat of venereal disease and/or sexual and physical violence. This was contextualised by (1) the everyday reality of the problem of contracting a venereal disease, (2) the progressive medicalisation of prostitutes and prostitution as a problem of sexual health, and (3) the everyday reality that engagement in prostitution in specific settings increases women's risk of suffering violence. The suspect punter category has two separate and distinct components: 'Asian punters' and 'funny punters'. These are dealt with in turn.

All of the interviewees defined Asian punters as suspect solely in terms of the assumed risk they posed of venereal disease. This construction was clearly informed by discourses of racial and ethnic differentiation where Asian punters are presented as 'unclean others':

> If we could have more check-up days [at the genito-urinary clinic], it'd be a lot better, coz if you know that it is only on a Monday, you're in sh.t street. You've gotta make sure that Monday is clear for you. You know what I mean? I mean sometimes you just have to do Paki's for the money, and then you've got to wait all that time to find out what that Paki's given you (Georgie, aged 35).

> Straight women think that prostitutes are dirty.... No! you wash, you bath and use Durex! But you gotta watch the Pakis. They give you the f**king pox. I hate f**king Pakis. They are the best punters coz they're not violent, but they are the dirtiest. They'll always give you something (Ingrid, aged 44).

I quit working in that sauna coz there was Indians in there all the time, and I won't do Indians. [JP: Why?] Coz they're dirty. They'll give you disease (Margie, aged 32).

But it's the Indians I hate most! Oh they're disgusting. I won't do them because everyone says that it's the Indians that give you the pox (Janet, aged 37).

Apart from demonstrating the women's racism towards Asian men, these extracts illustrate the degree to which punters were defined as suspicious in terms of sexual health. Perhaps this is unsurprising given that I had contacted at least half of the interviewees through a sexual health outreach programme and that all were very keen to demonstrate both their knowledge about and their attention to their sexual health. Moreover the progressive medicalisation of the 'problem' constituted by prostitution and prostitutes, in which prostitutes have generally been seen as high-risk groups of individuals in terms of HIV/AIDS, partly underpinned the interviewees' narratives about themselves and their punters. Specifically, by strategically deploying notions of 'sexual cleanliness' the interviewees were able to resist those medicalising discourses.

Earlier in this chapter it was demonstrated that the construction of the prostitute women's identities as workers and commodified bodies was made possible by a notion that all men are punters: a construction constituted within the definition of punters as 'normal men', as 'ordinary' and 'natural' (biologically essentialised) men doing what is innate. The women inhabited a symbolic landscape in which all the men who came to them were 'normal', 'typical' men. But all 21 interviewees contended that some of the punters that came to them were 'funny' or 'odd'. Whilst this categorisation was rather fluid, 'funny punters' were defined in terms of being potentially violent and 'pathological'. In other words the women asserted that some of the men who came to them were 'abnormal'. And so the women occupied a symbolic landscape in which all men were both normal *and* abnormal because all punters were both normal men *and* potentially 'funny' punters. Therefore in examining the category 'funny punter', the dissolution of the distinction between 'normal' and 'abnormal' men, wherein all ordinary men were also defined as abnormal, was manifest. The following extracts illustrate both the definition of funny punters as abnormal, violent men and the dissolution of the boundary between normal and abnormal:

You never know if the punter you pick up is gonna be your last. You just can't tell if they're loopy or nutters. There's always gonna be someone out there (Andrea, aged 27).

I've never had a funny punter – well except for that guy who raped me – because if I don't like the look of them, I don't go with them. But the problem is that looks really tell you sh*t all (Diane, aged 37).

I'm thinking about giving it up soon, because I can't cope with the thought of the weirdoes. I had one once – a real nice guy, or so I thought until he raped me. I learned from that, that you can *never* trust a punter (Jasmine, aged 30).

I've had two funny punters. One was a headmaster. You know, really nice guy, respectable family man. He wanted caning and afterwards he tried to rape me. He said, 'I want sex and I swear to God I'll kick the sh*t out of you unless I get it'. Just goes to show you, you can't tell who's the funny punters (Sophie, aged 28).

The removal of the symbolic distinction between 'normal' and 'abnormal' men demonstrates that the 'normal man' was defined according to everyday, material and social realities that permitted a construction of 'abnormal men' – violent punters who seriously assaulted and sexually abused prostitutes. Similarly the interviewees defined the 'abnormal man' against the backdrop of 'normal men' – that is, run of the mill punters who paid money for sexual services.

The suspect punter, like the sugar daddy and the good punter, was also a mythical figure. By universalising the reality of regular abuse by punters, most of the interviewees depicted the imaginary 'funny punter' in a way that gave expression to their general fear of punter violence. Witness the following:

Where I work is pretty safe, as long as you're not there after twelve. But having said that, you can never tell with punters. There's some that are funny, just waiting to attack girls, cut them up and rape them. There's one girl down the street I work that got picked up by one and was cut really bad and raped for about three hours (Christine, aged 23).

In this job you just gotta reckon that you're gonna get the odd bad punter. You can never tell who he is, but afterwards you have a cry and you're terrified for the week in case you see them again and then you get on with it (Barbara, aged 24).

The biggest thing I'm afraid of is getting a funny punter. I'm very wary and always on my guard. I won't turn my back on any of the punters, because you can't tell if the one you're with is gonna be that funny punter (Sophie, aged 28).

This fear of violence at the hands of punters has a very real basis. As discussed in Chapter 4, all of the interviewees had been seriously assaulted or raped by a punter at least once during their engagement in prostitution. But only three of the women had reported such incidents to the police. Therefore it was unremarkable that the interviewees constructed the mythical 'funny punter' in such a way as to express their fear of punter violence.

SUMMARY

This chapter has traced the constituent elements of the interviewees' prostitute identities, and the symbolic landscape underpinning them, in order to examine the conditions that made it possible for these women to render coherent their paradoxical narratives of engagement in prostitution.

The first two contradictory elements of the prostitute identity were the prostitutes-as-workers and prostitutes-as-commodified-bodies identifications. The identification of these was made possible by a restructuring of the women's understanding of men and money, whereby men came to represent income. Within this symbolic landscape the women were able to construct the punter–prostitute relationship as a routine business exchange (with themselves as either in control of that exchange and thus workers, or the objects of that exchange and thus commodified bodies). The articulation of men as income was contextualised by the women's experience and ever-present risk of poverty and their financial exploitation by ponces.

By deconstructing the prostitutes-as-workers and prostitutes-as-commodified-bodies identifications, and by deconstructing the metonymic movement between men and income, an understanding was generated of the way that, for the interviewees, engagement in prostitution had come to signify both an effective strategy for economic survival and a course of action that entrapped them and threatened their survival. For in a discursive world where the possession of cash signifies security and survival, where normal men are seen as being driven by their inherent sexuality and where there is a belief in men's greater economic privilege, involvement in prostitution is a way in which the income of men can be tapped. Contradictorily, the same symbolic world permitted the women to relate stories in which men as punters (that is, purchasers) and men as ponces (that is, owners) had taken control of their commodified bodies. Hence it was that involvement in prostitution had become a web of economic relationships over which the women believed they had both control via ownership (of the commodity for renting) and absolutely no control and no ownership (as slaves to their ponces).

The second pair of contradictory identifications were 'businesswoman' and 'loving woman'. These identifications were underpinned by a set of meanings in which involvement with men was defined in terms of the costs it incurred. Simultaneous decontextualising and recontextualising of their involvement with men meant that the women did not differentiate between their prostitution-related relationships and other relationships they had had, were having or might have in the future, and that they were able to speak of specific aims that could be achieved through involvement with particular men.

By deconstructing these two identifications and the sets of meanings underpinning them, an understanding was generated of the ways in which involvement with men was economically and strategically 'measured' by the interviewees and also characterised as 'compelling'. Moreover insights were produced into the conditions that made it possible for engagement in prostitution to be discussed as though it was an economically viable option when all the cost calculations had been made, and as though it involved a web of intimate relationships in which the women were caught.

The final two contradictory elements of the prostitute identity were the prostitutes-as-victims and prostitutes-as-survivors identifications. These emerged from a restructuring of the meanings of men and money, where men represented risk and money represented the object that conditioned the women's vulnerability to 'risky' men. Within such a symbolic landscape the interviewees were able to construct their relationships with punters, boyfriend and ponces as (potentially) violent and exploitative, with themselves as either the victims or the survivors of these relationships. In so doing they were also able to remove the conventional symbolic boundaries between ponces and boyfriends, abnormal men and normal men. The articulation of men as risk was contextualised by the reality of these women's increased risk of exploitation and violence compared with non-prostitute women, conditioned by their engagement in prostitution.

By deconstructing the ways in which men had come to represent risk, an understanding was generated of the ways in which engagement in prostitution signified a threat to the interviewees' economic and social survival, if not their very lives. In a discursive world in which the capacity to earn cash from prostitution was understood to condition the prostitutes' vulnerability to violence and exploitation, where normal men and boyfriends were also encoded as abnormal men and ponces, and where there was a belief in the inescapability of victimisation, for these women engagement in prostitution did not represent a strategy for survival, but rather a trap that prevented them from escaping the control of abusive men. Contradictorily, the same symbolic landscape permitted the interviewees to narrate stories in which they had overcome and escaped the violence, control and exploitation inherent in their intimate relationships and involvement in prostitution. Hence involvement in the institution of prostitution had come to signify the interviewees' ability to survive – economically, socially and corporeally.

6 Conclusion

This book has investigated and analysed women's involvement in prostitution, and in particular the social of meanings of prostitution, poverty and violence. Its aim has been to:

- identify and analyse the sense that has been made of women's involvement in prostitution by legal and academic discourse and prostitute women themselves;
- explain the circumstances in which it is possible for prostitute women to resolve the contradictory effects of involvement in prostitution in a subjectively meaningful way and render coherent the contradictions of being both like and unlike other women.

The thesis of this study is that prostitute women are sustained within prostitution because engagement in prostitution comes to make sense. Thus whilst legal and academic discourse has constituted prostitutes as either different from or similar to non-prostitute women, and whilst involvement in prostitution produces contradictory effects, the prostitute women interviewed here were able to make sense of their engagement in prostitution because they lived both within and outwith the fullness of the contradictions of being like and unlike other women. They lived *within* the contradiction insofar as they experienced prostitution contradictorily. It was, for them, both a gendered survival strategy that enabled them to obtain and sustain some degree of social and material security and thus fashion better lives for themselves in the future, and a gendered victimisation that threatened their material and social stability and trapped them within prostitution. They lived *outwith* the contradiction insofar as they believed that their prostitute experiences were merely an accentuation of the paradoxical conflation of men, money and violence that shapes, structures and influences all heterosexual sexual relationships.

The main argument of the theoretical analysis is that the autobiographical narratives of the women interviewed were made plausible and meaningful by the discursive strategies they employed to make sense both of the relationships they had with ponces, partners, punters and the police, and of the material, social and ideological conditions they inhabited. These discursive strategies have been deconstructed, and via this deconstruction the following points have been argued.

First, the meanings that the women ascribed to their involvement in prostitution were paradoxical. They represented their engagement in prostitution as:

- both enhancing and circumscribing the possibility of future economic and social stability;
- both a means of combating their poverty and the source of their poverty;
- both a tactic to provide them with the money to obtain and sustain housing security and a cause of their housing insecurity;
- both a way to escape violent and/or abusive personal relationships and a source of violence and abuse within intimate relationships;
- both a method by which they could achieve financial independence from individual men and a cause of their economic dependency on men;
- both nothing to do with sex and everything to do with sex;
- both an expression of love and the result of their boyfriends' control over them.

Second, the theoretical analysis of the women's narratives suggests that they were able to accommodate the paradoxes of their accounts and deliver meaningful, plausible and coherent reports of their engagement in prostitution by constructing a very specific 'prostitute identity'. This identity is composed of contradictory sub-identities. The women described themselves as:

- both workers (that is, rational economic agents) and commodified bodies (that is, bodies for rent);
- both businesswomen (that is, women who can calculate the costs and benefits of particular courses of action in order to maximise their income and minimise their risks) and loving partners (that is, women who are willing to do anything for the men they love);
- both victims (that is, women who are caught, trapped and dominated by violently abusive men) and survivors (that is, women who successfully negotiate and survive the uncertainties and risks posed by particular men).

Third, the 'prostitute identity' that emerged from the women's narratives was neither authored nor authorised by the interviewees. Rather it was constituted by and within a specific but shifting (and at times contradictory) set of meanings of men and money. Within this symbolic landscape the meanings of men and money were conflated, and consequently men signified both income and expense. Furthermore the symbolic boundary between normal and abnormal men was removed, so that all the men with whom they (or any other women) had (or might have) intimate relationships became both boyfriends and potential ponces, and men in general became both ordinary, normal men (men who are 'just doing what men do') and abnormal, 'odd', 'funny' or 'suspect' men (potentially violent, abusive, exploitative and above all dangerous).

Hence through the dissolution of the conventional symbolic boundaries between men and money, normality and abnormality the women were able to present themselves as both different from and the same as non-prostitute women. For if all men are both normal and abnormal and all partners are both boyfriends and ponces, then all women are just as vulnerable to physical violence and financial exploitation as prostitutes, and are therefore just like them.

In other words the 21 interviewees were able to position themselves as normal women constituted as prostitutes within a very specific constellation of normal (that is, universal) circumstances. They were able to live within and outwith the fullness of the contradiction of being both like and unlike other women. Hence the interviewees believed that although they were like all other women in most respects, they were also unlike them because the experiences they had as a result of being engaged in prostitution allowed them to penetrate the veils of ideology and realise that many dimensions of the sexual relationships between all men and all women are structured and shaped by both financial considerations and men's potential for violence.

DECONSTRUCTION WITH NO END?

It is a shocking indictment of millenium Britain that there are women who lead lives so utterly circumscribed by penury, violence and enforced dependency that opting to sell sexual services in a social context where they are at increased risk of further destitution, exploitation and violence comes to be seen as offering the chance of future stability. Indeed it may seem somewhat surprising, given the poverty and extreme violence that these women encountered and recounted, that in this book I have chosen to focus on the apparently innocuous question of how they accommodate the contradictions in their lives. But such a question was not asked simply in order to reveal these contradictions.

Rather it was asked because these contradictions seemed so extraordinary as to prohibit any sense being made of them at all.

Throughout the book I have tried to avoid characterising prostitutes as somehow different from other social actors because in their narratives the paradoxes are both apparent and accommodated. It is one function of discourse that paradox is resolved into 'a calm unity of coherent thought' (Foucault, 1972, p. 127). Even at a more specific level, these women are not unique because of the particular contradictions they accommodate, for it has been argued that it is not only prostitute women whose strategies for survival (or their relationships with men) both enable survival and threaten it. But, by their own accounts, these women are different because their experience of life as a prostitute has given them a critical knowledge of relations between men and women that is denied to non-prostitute women.

It is hoped that the preceding analysis will go some way towards displacing the 'either/or' analyses and debates that have bedevilled writing and research on prostitution. In particular, by laying bare the social meanings of engagement in prostitution it has been shown that prostitutes are not simply either victims or survivors and are not simply either coerced into or choose to engage in prostitution. Rather they are both victims and survivors and both choose and do not choose to be involved in prostitution. These are important points to make. Political intervention in the form of substantive changes in the law such as the decriminalisation or legalisation of prostitution, or much lower-level intervention such as that seen in the sexual health outreach services, assume (as was shown in Chapter 2) that prostitutes are either one thing or another. They are either a public nuisance or they are not; they are either a threat to sexual health or they are not; they are either forced into prostitution or they are not.

In a time period when it is expected that texts or studies of prostitution end by making suggestions about measures that should be taken to address prostitution, this book breaks with convention. No policy suggestions will be made. There will be no specification of the type of problem prostitution is or what should be done about it. For any successful intervention or policy requires an acutely angled understanding of how individuals live their lives, the pressures and problems they experience and the ways in which they understand what they are doing. It is just such an acutely angled understanding of prostitute-women's lives that this book provides. Indeed, as has been demonstrated throughout, many of the problems identified by campaigning groups are simply not recognised as such by the individuals who are the subjects of such campaigns. Thus, while the English Collective of Prostitutes has continuously campaigned to stop police harassment of prostitute women, many of the women in this study did not see themselves as 'over-policed' and, moreover, commented that highly visible policing of street prostitution provided them with a sense of security and safety. Similarly, many of the women in this study did not see the violence and intimidation they experienced from their partners as violence, coercion or exploitation, and thus did not see themselves as solely victims or coerced into prostitution. Therefore, it is hoped that the following lesson will be learned from this book's deconstruction of the discourses of meaning of a small group of prostitute women: if any social or political intervention into the lives of prostitute women is to be successful, it must be capable of containing and reflecting the contradictory experiences of prostitutes, the paradoxical ways in which they make sense of their lives and the creative strategies they use to give meaning to the way they negotiate social and material conditions not of their own choosing.

Notes

1   Introduction

1. Each gatekeeper identified a group of women who might be willing to be interviewed, approached them and asked whether they would take part in my research. When I was introduced to the women I described the project and asked them to confirm that they did want to take part. It was only then that the interviews were arranged.
2. The names of the women who participated in this study and the name of the city in which they lived and worked have been changed in order to ensure their anonymity.
3. Throughout the book I use the term 'black' to signify Afro-Caribbean as well as Indian, Pakistani and Bangladeshi individuals. Such usage was common among the women interviewed.

2   Prostitutes, Prostitution and the Law

1. The Act stated that 'all light [that is loose] women . . . dicist from thair vices and syne of venerie' and work for 'thair support on pain, else being branded with a hot iron on their cheek and banished from the town' (Mahood, 1990a, p. 20). Interestingly this Act was passed over a century before syphilis was discovered to be associated with sexual intercourse (see Spongberg, 1997).

3   Ways of Talking about Prostitutes and Prostitution

1. The texts that follow are by no means the only ones to employ the pathological explanatory model. Parent-Duchatelet (1836) and Acton (1870) are two early examples. Bell (1994) and Spongberg (1997) present particularly good and detailed analyses of these (and other) pathological (and pathologising) explanations.
2. The difficulties with and limitations of pathological (and positivist) explanations of women's law-breaking in general and their involvement in prostitution in particular have been well rehearsed elsewhere. For particularly good discussions of these limitations see Heidensohn (1985), Carlen et al. (1985) and Smart (1995).
3. In this section only one writer's work is examined. For other examples see Bryan (1967) and Jackman (1967).
4. The women Wilkinson interviewed worked primarily from the streets in many different locations across London. A small number of her sample had experience of working in brothels and from their own homes.

5   Men, Money, Violence and Identity

1.   Blackman (1997, p.) reports that, in order to address employees' and resid-
     ents' concerns about prostitution, the Temporary Accommodation Section
     of the Lambeth Housing Department is to strengthen its monitoring of
     hostels and refuges to ensure that prostitutes do not gain access.

Bibliography

Acton, W. (1870) *Prostitution Considered in its Moral, Social and Sanitary Aspects* (London: Frank Cass).

Anthias, F. and N. Yuval-Davies (1992) *Racialised Boundaries: Race, Nation, Gender, Colour and Class and the Anti-Racist Struggle* (London: Routledge).

Ashford, L. (1995) *Exploring Different Models of Working With Prostitute Women* (Wolverhampton Multi-Agency Prostitution Working Group Report).

Barrett, M. and M. McIntosh (1982) *The Anti-Social Family* (London: Verso).

Barry, K. (1979) *Female Sexual Slavery* (New York: New York University Press).

Barry, K. (1995) *Prostitution of Sexuality* (London: New York University Press).

Barthes, R. (1980) 'An Introduction to the Structural Analysis of Narratives', *New Literary History*, vol. 6, pp. 237–72.

Beccaria, C. (1996) 'On Crimes and Punishment', in J. Muncie, E. McLaughlin and M. Langan (eds), *Criminological Perspectives* (London: Sage).

Beck, U. (1992) *Risk Society: Towards a New Modernity* (London: Sage).

Bell, S. (1994) *Reading, Writing & Rewriting the Prostitute Body* (Bloomington, IA: Indiana University Press).

Benjamin, H. and R. Masters (1964) *Prostitution and Morality: A Definitive Report on the Prostitute in Contemporary Society and an Analysis of the Causes and Effects of the Suppression of Prostitution* (London: Souvenir Press).

Blackman, D. (1997) 'Brothel Claims Lead to Three Suspensions', *Inside Housing*, vol. 11 (April), p. 3.

Bland, L. (1985) 'In the Name of Protection: the Policing of Women in the First World War', in C. Smart and J. Brophy (eds), *Women-in-law* (London: Routledge and Kegan Paul).

Bresler, F. (1988) *Sex and the Law* (London: Frederick Muller).

Bryan, J. (1967) 'Apprenticeships in Prostitution', in J. Gagnon and W. Simon (eds), *Sexual Deviance* (London: Harper and Row).

Campbell, B. (1984) *Wigan Pier Revisited: Poverty and Politics in the 1980's* (London: Virago).

Campbell, C. (1991) 'Prostitution, AIDS, and Preventive Health Behaviour', *Social Science Medicine*, vol. 32, no. 12, pp. 1367–78.

Carlen, P. (1988) *Women, Crime and Poverty* (Milton Keynes: Open University Press).

Carlen, P. (1996) *Jigsaw: A Political Economy of Youth Homelessness* (Buckingham: Open University Press).

Carlen P. and A. Worrall (eds) (1987) *Gender, Crime and Justice* (Milton Keynes: Open University Press).

Carlen, P., J. Hicks, J. O'Dwyer, D. Christina and C. TchiaKovsky (1985) *Criminal Women*, (Cambridge: Polity).

Carrington, K. (1993) *Offending Girls: Sex Youth and Justice* (Sydney: Allen and Unwin).

Cohen, S. (1996) 'The Punitive City', in J. Muncie, E. McLaughlin and M. Langan (eds), *Criminological Perspectives* (London: Sage).

Coleman, L. and S. Watson (1987) *Women Over Sixty: a Study of the Housing, Economic and Social Circumstances of Older Women* (Canberra: Australian Institute of Urban Studies).

Cook, D. (1987) 'Women on Welfare: in Crime or Injustice?', in P. Carlen and A. Worrall (eds), *Gender, Crime and Justice* (Milton Keynes: Open University Press).

Cook, D. (1989) *Rich Law, Poor Law: Differential Response to Tax and Supplementary Benefits Fraud* (Milton Keynes: Open University Press).

Criminal Law Revision Committee (CLRC) (1984) *Sixteenth Report: Prostitution in the Streets* (London: HMSO).

Criminal Law Revision Committee (CLRC) (1985) *Seventeenth Report: Prostitution Off-Street Activities* (London: HMSO).

Daly, M. (1989) *Women and Poverty* (Dublin: Attic Press).

Davidoff, L. and C. Hall (1987) *Family Fortunes: Men and Women of the English Middle Class 1780–1850* (London: Hutchinson).

Davis, K. (1937) 'The Sociology of Prostitution', *American Sociological Review*, vol. 5, no. 2, pp. 749–55.

Dennis, N. and G. Erdos (1992) *Families Without Fatherhood* (London: IEA Health and Welfare Unit).

Denzin, N. (1989) *Interpretive Interactionism* (London: Sage).

Derrida, J. (1972) *Positions* (London: The Athlone Press).

Dibbin, J. (1991) *Wherever I Lay My Hat: Young Women and Homelessness* (London: Shelter).

Dunhill, C. (ed.) (1989) *The Boys in Blue: Women's Challenge to the Police* (London: Virago).

Dworkin, A. (1979) *Pornography: Men Possessing Women* (New York: Perigee Books).

Edwards, S. (1987) 'Prostitutes: Victims of Law, Social Policy and Organised Crime', in P. Carlen and A. Worrall (eds), *Gender, Crime and Justice* (Buckingham: Open University Press).

Edwards, S. (1997) 'The Legal Regulation of Prostitution: A Human Rights Issue', in G. Scambler and A. Scambler (eds), *Rethinking Prostitution* (London: Routledge).

Ellis, H. (1936) *Studies in the Psychology of Sex*, vols 1 and 2 (Philadelphia: F. A. Davies Company).

English Collective of Prostitutes (1997) 'Campaigning for Legal Change', in G. Scambler and A. Scambler (eds), *Rethinking Prostitution* (London: Routledge).

Evans, M. (ed.) (1982) *The Woman Question* (London: Fontana).

Faugier, J. and M. Sargeant (1997) 'Boyfriends, 'Pimps' and Clients', in G. Scambler and A. Scambler (eds), *Rethinking Prostitution* (London: Routledge).

Finnegan, F. (1979) *Poverty and Prostitution: A Study of Victorian Prostitutes in York* (Cambridge: Cambridge University Press).

Fiorenza, E. and A. Carr (1987) *Women, Work and Poverty* (Edinburgh: T & T Clarke).

Foucault, M. (1972) *The Archaeology of Knowledge* (London: Tavistock).

Fryer, P. (1984) *Staying Power: a History of Black People in Britain* (London: Pluto).

Gagnon, J. and W. Simon (eds) (1967) *Sexual Deviance* (London: Harper and Row).

Gilroy, P. (1987) *There Ain't No Black in the Union Jack: the Cultural Politics of Race and Nation* (London: Hutchinson).

Glendinning, C. and J. Millar (eds) (1987) *Women and Poverty in Britain* (London: Harvester Wheatsheaf).

Glendinning, C. and J. Millar (eds) (1992) *Women and Poverty in Britain: the 1990's*, 2nd edn (London: Harvester Wheatsheaf).

Glueck, S. and E. Glueck (1934) *Five Hundred Delinquent Women* (New York: Knopf).

Green, S., D. Goldberg, P. Christie, M. Frischer, A. Thomson, S. Carr and A. Taylor (1993) 'Female Streetworker – Prostitutes in Glasgow: A Descriptive Study of Their Lifestyle', *AIDS Care*, vol. 5, no. 3, pp. 321–35.

Habermas, J. (1987) *Philosophical Discourses of Modernity* (Cambridge: Polity Press).

Hall, L. (1994) 'Deconstructing the Monolithic Phallus', in *The Polity Reader in Gender Studies* (Cambridge: Polity Press).

Hall, S. (1996) 'Presidential Address', British Sociological Association Annual Conference, Reading University, April.

Hall, S. and B. Gieben (1992) *Formations of Modernity* (Oxford: Polity).

Heidensohn, F. (1985) *Women and Crime* (London: Macmillan).

Hoigard, C. and L. Finstad (1992) *Backstreets: Prostitution, Money and Love* (London: Polity).

Hutter, B. and G. Williams (eds) (1981) *Controlling Women: The Normal and the Deviant* (London: Croom Helm).

Jackman, N. (1967) 'The Self-Image of the Prostitute', in J. Gagnon and W. Simon (eds), *Sexual Deviance* (London: Harper and Row).

Jenkins, C. and R. Swirsky (1997) 'Does Constituting Prostitution as Sex-Work Empower Prostituted Women?', paper presented at the British Sociological Association Annual Conference, York University.

Joannou, M. (1995) 'She who would be politically free herself must strike the blow: Suffragette Autobiography and Suffragette Militancy', in J. Swindells (ed.), *The Uses of Autobiography* (London: Taylor and Francis).

Jolly, M. (1995) 'Dear Laughing Motorbyke: Gender and genre in women's letters from the Second World War', in J. Swindells (ed.), *The Uses of Autobiography* (London: Taylor and Francis).

Katz, J. (1988) *The Seductions of Crime: Moral and Sensual Attractions in Doing Evil* (New York: Basic Books).

Kersten, J. (1996) 'Culture, Masculinities and Violence Against Women', *British Journal of Criminology*, vol. 36, no. 3., pp. 381–95.

Kinnell, H. (1989) *Prostitutes, their Clients and Risks of HIV Infection in Birmingham*, Occasional Paper, SAFE Project (South Birmingham Health Authority).

Land, H. (1982) 'The Family Wage', in M. Evans (ed.), *The Woman Question* (London: Fontana).

Langenhove, L. and R. Harre (1993) 'Positioning and Autobiography: Telling Your Life', in N. Couplan and J. Nussbaum (eds), *Discourse and Life Span Identity* (London: Sage).

Lister, R. (1990) *The Exclusive Society: Citizenship and the Poor* (London: Child Poverty Action Group).

Lister, R. (1992) *Women's Economic Dependency and Social Security* (Machester: EOC).

Lombroso, C. (1968) *Crime: Its Causes and Remedies* (New York: Patterson Smith).

Lombroso, C. and G. Ferrero (1895) *The Female Offender: The Normal Woman and the Prostitute* (London: Fisher Unwin).

Lonsdale, S. (1992) 'Patterns in Paid Work', in C. Glendinning and J. Millar (eds), *Women and Poverty in Britain: the 1990's* (London: Harvester Wheatsheaf).

MacDowell, L. and R. Pringle (1992) *Defining Women: Social Institutions and Gender Divisions* (Cambridge: Polity).

MacKinnon, C. (1987) *Feminism Unmodified: Discourses on Life and Law* (Combridge, Mass.: Harvard University Press).

Mahood, L. (1990a) 'The Magdalene's Friend: Prostitution and Social Control in Glasgow, 1869–1890', *Women's Studies International Forum*, vol. 13, nos 1/2, pp. 46–61.

Mahood, L. (1990b) *The Magdalenes: Prostitution in the Nineteenth Century* (London: Routledge).

Malamuth, N. and E. Donnerstein (eds) (1984) *Pornography and Sexual Aggression* (Orlando, FA: Academic Press).

Martin, J. and C. Roberts (1984) *Women and Employment: A Lifetime Perspective* (London: HMSO).

Matthews, R. and J. Young (1986) *Confronting Crime* (London: Sage).

Matthews, R. (1993) *Kerb-Crawling, Prostitution and Multi-Agency Policing* (Police Research Group, Crime Prevention Unit Series, Paper 43).

Matthews, R. (1986) 'Beyond Wolfenden? Prostitution, Politics and the Law', in R. Matthews and J. Young (eds), *Confronting Crime* (London: Sage).

Matza, D. (1964) *Delinquency and Drift* (New York: Wiley).

Matza, D. (1969) *Becoming Deviant* (Englewood Cliffs, NJ: Prentice Hall).

McHugh, P. (1980) *Prostitution and Victorian Social Reform* (London: Croom Helm).

McKeganey, N. and M. Barnard (1996) *Sex Work on the Streets: Prostitutes and their Clients* (Buckingham: Open University Press).

McLeod, E. (1981) 'Man-made Laws for Men? The Street Prostitutes' Campaign Against Control', in B. Hutter and G. Williams (eds), *Controlling Women: The Normal and the Deviant* (London: Croom Helm).

McLeod, E. (1982) *Women Working: Prostitution Now* (London: Croom Helm).

Millar, J. (1997) 'Gender', in A. Walker and C. Walker (eds), *Britain Divided: The Growth of Social Exclusion in the 1980's and 1990's* (London: Child Poverty Action Group).

Morris, A. and L. Gelsthorpe (eds) (1981) *Women and Crime: Cropwood Roundtable Conference* (Cambridge: Cambridge University Press).

Muncie, J., E. McLaughlin and M. Langan (eds) (1996) *Criminological Perspectives: A Reader* (London: Sage).

Murray, C. (1990) *The Emerging British Underclass* (London: IEA Health & Welfare).

Oerton, S. and K. Atkinson (1997) 'Voices From the Valley: Young Single Mothers Talk', British Sociological Association Annual Conference, York University, York.

O'Neill, M. (1997) 'Prostitute Women Now', in G. Scambler and A. Scambler (eds), *Rethinking Prostitution* (London: Routledge).

Overall, C. (1992) 'What's Wrong with Prostitution? Evaluating Sex Work', *Signs: Journal of Women in Culture and Society*, vol. 17, no. 41, pp. 705–24.

Overs , P. (1994) 'Prostitution', *New Internationalist*, no. 252 (Feb.), pp. 114–21.

Pahl, J. (1989) *Money And Marriage* (London: Macmillan).

Parent-Duchatelet, A. (1836) *Policing Prostitution in Nineteenth Century Paris* (Bailliere: Paris).

Pascall, G. (1986) *Social Policy: A Feminist Analysis* (London: Tavistock).

Perkins, R. and G. Bennett (1985) *Being A Prostitute* (Sydney: George Allen and Unwin).

Person, E. (1988) *Dreams and Love and Fateful Encounters: The Power of the Romantic Passion* (New York: W. W. Norton).

Phoenix, J. (1998) 'Prostitutes, Ponces and Poncing: Narratives of Violence', in P. Bagguley and J. Seymour (eds), *Relating Intimacies: Power and Resistance* (London: Macmillan).

Plummer, K. (1995) *Telling Sexual Stories: Power, Change and Social Worlds* (London: Routledge).

Polity (1995) *The Polity Reader in Gender Studies* (London: Polity).

Roberts, N. (1992) *Whores in History* (London: HarperCollins).

Romenesko, K. and E. Miller (1989) 'The Second Step in Double Jeopardy: Appropriating the Labor of Female Street Hustlers', *Crime and Delinquency*, vol. 35, no. 1, pp. 44–59.

Rook, P. and R. Ward (1997) *On Sexual Offences* (London: Sweet and Maxwell).

Room, G. (1989) 'New Poverty in the European Community', *Policy and Politics*, vol. 17, no. 4, pp. 165–76.

Room, G. (ed.) (1995) *Beyond the Threshold: The Measurement and Analysis of Social Exclusion* (Bristol: The Policy Press).

Roos, J. (1994) 'The true life revisited: autobiography and referentiality after the "posts"', *Lives and Works: Auto/biographical Occasions*, vol. 3, nos 1–2, pp. 1–16.

Sampson, E. E. (1989) 'The Deconstruction of the Self', in J. Shotter and K. Gergen (eds), *Texts of Identity* (London: Sage).

Sayers, J. (1986) *Sexual Contradictions: Psychology, Psychoanalysis and Feminism* (London: Tavistock).

Scambler, G., R. Peswani, A. Renton and A. Scambler (1990) 'Women Prostitutes in the AIDS Era', *Sociology of Health and Illness*, vol. 12, no. 3, pp. 260–74.

Scambler, G. and A. Scambler (eds) (1997) *Rethinking Prostitution: Purchasing Sex in the 1990s* (London: Routledge).

Scholes, R. (1989) *Protocols of Reading* (London: Yale University Press).

Scott, H. (1984) *Working your Way to the Bottom: The Feminization of Poverty* (London: Pandora Press).

Segal, L. (1996) 'Explaining Male Violence', in J. Muncie, E. McLaughlin and M. Langan (eds), *Criminological Perspectives: A Reader* (London: Sage).

Sexty, C. (1990) *Women Losing Out: Access to Housing in Britain Today* (London: Shelter).

Shotter, J. and K. Gergen (eds) (1989) *Texts of Identity* (London: Sage).

Sion, A. (1977) *Prostitution and the Law* (London: Faber and Faber).

Skogan, W. (1990) *Disorder and Decline* (New York: Free Press).

Smart, C. (1995) *Law, Crime and Sexuality: Essays in Feminism* (London: Sage).

Smart, C. and J. Brophy (eds) (1985) *Women-in-law: Explorations in Family, Sex and Law* (London: Routledge and Kegan Paul).

Spicker, P. (1993) *Poverty and Social Security: Concepts and Principles* (London: Routledge).

Spongberg, M. (1997) *Feminizing Venereal Disease: The Body of the Prostitute in Nineteenth Century Literature* (London: Macmillan Press).

Sumner, M. (1981) 'Prostitution and the Position of Women: A Case for Decriminalisation', in A. Morris and L. Gelsthorpe (eds), *Women and Crime: Cropwood Roundtable Conference* (Cambridge: Cambridge University Press).

Swindells, J. (ed.) (1995) *The Uses of Autobiography* (London: Taylor and Francis).

Taylor, A. (1991) *Prostitution: What's Love Got To Do With It?* (London: Optima).

Unsworth, J. (1995) 'Why Does an Author Who Apparently Draws So Much on Autobiography Seem Committed to "Alienating" the Reader?', in J. Swindells (ed.), *The Uses of Autobiography* (London: Taylor and Francis).

Walklate, S. (1989) *Victimology* (London: Unwin Hyman).

Walkowitz, J. (1980) *Prostitution and Victorian Society* (Cambridge: Cambridge University Press).

Walkowitz, J. (1982) 'Jack the Ripper and the Myth of Male Violence', *Feminist Studies*, vol. 8, no. 3 (Fall), pp. 543–74.

Walvin, J. (1994) *Black Ivory* (Washington, DC: Howard University Press).

Ward, H. and S. Day (1997) 'Health care and regulation: New Perspectives', in G. Scambler and A. Scambler (eds), *Rethinking Prostitution* (London: Routledge).

Watson, S. and H. Austerberry (1983) *Women on the Margins: a Study of Single Women's Housing Problems* (London: Housing Research Group).

Watson, S. and H. Austerberry (1986) *Housing and Homelessness: A Feminist Perspective* (London: Routledge and Kegan Paul).

Weber, M. (1949) *The Methodology of the Social Sciences* (New York: Free Press).

Weedon, C. (1987) *Feminist Practice and Poststructuralist Theory* (Oxford: Blackwell).

Wilkinson, R. (1955) *Women of the Streets: A Sociological Study of the Common Prostitute* (London: British Social and Biology Council).

Wilson, E. (1980) *Sociobiology* (London: Belknap Press).

Wilson, E. (1983) *What is to be done about violence against women?* (London: Penguin).

Wilson, J. Q. and G. Kelling (1982) 'Broken Windows: The Police and Neighbourhood Safety', *Atlantic Monthly*, March, pp. 29–35.

Wolfenden Committee (1957) *Wolfenden Report on Homosexual Offences and Prostitution* (London: HMSO).

Worrall, A. (1990) *Offending Women: Female Lawbreakers and the Criminal Justice System* (London: Routledge).

Yaffe, M. and E. Nelson (eds) (1982) *The Influence of Pornography on Behaviour* (London: Academic Press).

Index